THE WORLD CUP

THE WORLD CUP

A Definitive History and Guide

Compiled and edited by
SIMON SHIRLEY
and Susannah Wight

JANUS PUBLISHING COMPANY
London, England

First Published in Great Britain 2002 By
Janus Publishing Company Ltd,
76 Great Titchfield Street,
London W1P 7AF

www.januspublishing.co.uk

British Library Cataloguing-in-Publication Data
A catalogue record for this book
is available from the British Library

ISBN 1 85756 542 8

Typeset in 10.5pt ZapfEllipt BT
By Chris Cowlin

Cover Design Chris Cowlin

Printed and bound in Great Britain

CONTENTS

INTRODUCTION

On 8th May 1902 Wilhelm Hirschmann, a Dutchman, wrote down some rules which were approved by some of the local soccer associations. At their business meeting in Paris on 21st May 1904 representatives of seven European countries - France, Belgium, Denmark, Holland, Spain, Sweden and Switzerland - implemented the rules and FIFA, the Federation Internationale de Football Association, was founded. Included in the statutes of what was to become the governing body of world football was a clause to the effect that FIFA would have the exclusive right to organise a world soccer tournament. Membership gradually increased and Germany, Austria, Italy, Hungaryand England joined the federation after the 1905 FIFA Congress in Paris.

On 1st March 1921 Jules Rimet, a 48-year-old French lawyer, succeeded the late Daniel Burley Woolfall as President of FIFA. He was recognised as a fine administrator and held the post for 33 years, during which time FIFA membership rose to 85. Rimet greatly advanced the concept of a World Cup and was assisted by Uruguay's participation in the Olympic Games.

Before the 1930 World Cup, the Olympic Soccer Games were the most important international championships. During the games of 1924, the Uruguayans showed Europe that excellent soccer was being played in South America. They defeated Yugoslavia 7-4, the United States 3-0, France 5-1, Holland 2-1 and Switzerland 3-0 before a crowd of 60,000. In 1928 they repeated their success, beating Argentina in an all-South American final.

On 26th May 1928 the FIFA Congress was held in

Amsterdam and with the active, decisive and convincing participation of Jules Rimet, the following proposal was made: 'The Congress agreed to organise a contest open to all national teams of the affiliated countries. The conditions for such a contest would be studied by a commission selected by Congress'. France's proposal was approved and the first meeting of the commission was held on 8th September 1928 in Zurich, Switzerland. The following resolution was agreed upon: 'Beginning in 1930, FIFA would organise a competition every four years called the World Cup. A trophy, a work of art, would be presented to the winner of the Federation. The competition would be open to all affiliated countries, etc...'

After 25 years and numerous attempts, the World Cup finally became a reality. Five countries aspired to stage the first series: Holland, Italy, Spain, Sweden and Urugary. Meeting at Barcelona in 1929, FIFA chose Uruguay to stage the inaugural event. This was something of a surprise, given that the country was a small republic with a population of just two million. However, they were the reigning Olympic champions and 1930 was the centenary of their independence. They offered to pay all travelling and hotel expenses for the visiting teams and built a new ground for the tournament. The Centenary Stadium. located in central Montevideo, was constructed in only eight months, three of which included the rainy season.

Organising the World Cup in 1930 was a formidable task. The Europeans, in particular, would have to interrupt their domestic competitions and undertake a long and arduous ocean voyage at the time of serious economic crisis and hardship in Europe. Additionally, professional players already existed in some countries and their clubs were concerned about their prolonged absence whilst still paying their salaries.

Jules Rimet's personal intervention ensured that the

tournament was held. He succeeded in persuading Belgium, Romania, Yugoslavia and France to accept the invitation. In the end, four European countries and nine from the Americas completed the picture. The countries from the Americas were Uruguay, Argentina, Paraguay, Brazil, Bolivia, Chile, Peru, Mexico and the United States. Three of the four European teams travelled on the same ship, the *Conte Verde*, leaving France on 21st June 1930. After 14 days at sea, the Belgian, French and Romanian national teams arrived in Montevideo and were welcomed by a very inquisitive crowd. Jules Rimet had also arrived, accompanied by a statue 12 inches high, weighing eight pounds, made of pure gold and sculpted by the Frenchman Abel Lafleur - the trophy.

Four days later, the Yugoslavian national team disembarked from the *Florida*. The assembly was complete and the World Cup was finally about to become a reality.

1930

Uruguay found that hosting the 1930 World Cup was a formidable task. A multiplicity of problems included the refusal of some invited countries to participate, transportation difficulties, a European recession and an uncompleted national stadium.

The four aspirant hosts, Holland, Italy, Spain and Sweden, declined en bloc. Austria, Czechoslovakia, Germany, Hungary, and Switzerland failed to participate owing to economic hardship. The four home countries – England, Northern Ireland, Scotland and Wales – were all ineligible as they had withdrawn from FIFA in 1928 after a disagreement over 'broken-time payments' to amateur players. Only two months before its inception, the World Cup did not have a single European entrant.

The Latin American federations felt understandably hurt and threatened to withdraw from FIFA. Both France and Belgium, under pressure from Jules Rimet, the President of FIFA, and Rodolphe William Seeldrayers, the Vice President, agreed to compete. On 8th June 1930 Crown Prince Carol was elected King of Romania. One of his first actions following his ascendancy to the throne was to grant an amnesty to all suspended Romanian footballers. He proceeded to select the Romanian team and placed pressure on their employers to give them leave for Uruguay. Yugoslavia also agreed to compete, thus making four European entrants.

Many European nations were conspicuous by their absence and the opening World Cup became a tournament dominated by teams from the Americas: Argentina, Brazil, Bolivia, Chile, Mexico, Paraguay, Peru, the United States and the hosts, Uruguay.

Jules Rimet and the Hungarian Maurice Fischer were responsible for establishing the format of the Cup. They decided on a first-round competition of four pools. There would be three pools comprising of three countries and one pool comprising of four countries. Each country played the other pool members and the winner of each pool would contest the semi-finals. The semi-final winners would play the final game for the title. The four pools were:

Pool 1: Argentina, France, Chile and Mexico.
Pool 2: Brazil, Yugoslavia and Bolivia.
Pool 3: Uruguay, Romania and Peru.
Pool 4: United States, Paraguay and Belgium.

Four countries were chosen as seeds; Argentina in Pool 1, Brazil in Pool 2, Uruguay in Pool 3 and the United States in Pool 4. The United States were seeded as they were considered to have a strong team with naturalised American Scottish players including Alec Wood, James Gallacher, James Brown and Bart McGhee.

On 13th July 1930, a Sunday afternoon, France met Mexico in Pocitos, Montevideo, in the very first World Cup match, watched by a crowd of 1,000. Although the French goalkeeper Alex Thepot had to retire after only ten minutes of the Pool 1 encounter after being kicked on the jaw, France won comfortably 4-1. Lucien Laurent enjoyed the honour of scoring the first World Cup goal, with a powerful shot after 19 minutes. Further goals by Langiller and Maschinot established a 3-0 lead by half-time. Carreno scored for Mexico before Maschinot netted his second with only three minutes remaining. (Alex Villaplane, the captain of France, was subsequently executed in 1944 for collaborating with the Nazis.)

Two days later, France were involved in one of the most controversial ties of the tournament against Argentina. A growing bitterness was already surfacing between Argentina and Uruguay, as Argentinian supporters arrived for the

French match in ten boats and were searched for weapons both at the docks and before entering the ground. A highly absorbing contest was settled nine minutes from time when Monti scored for Argentina. But with six minutes remaining, and France reduced to ten players, Marcel Langiller raced the length of the field. As the Uruguayan crowd, supporting the French team, anticipated an equaliser, the Brazilian referee Almeida Rego suddenly whistled to end the game. The field was invaded, the French players assailed the referee and the linesman finally convinced the match official that he had erred. Mounted guards escorted jubilant Argentinian fans off the park and the game resumed. However, the remaining minutes were an anti-climax as France had lost their momentum. At the end of the game there was a further pitch invasion, with Uruguayan spectators triumphantly carrying French players shoulder high. Argentina's delegation threatened to return home. This proved to be the beginning of a fierce rivalry between Uruguay and Argentina.

Chile started their campaign with a resounding victory over Mexico at Central Park, Montevideo. A crowd of only 500, most of whom were Chileans who had crossed the Andes, watched their side dominate the match. Subiabre (2) and Vidal were the scorers in a 3-0 triumph.

Chile then eliminated France, when Subiabre scored the only goal in the 64th minute with a header.

Argentina faced Mexico without their captain, Ferreyra, who had to return to his country to sit a university examination. He was replaced as captain by Adolfo Zumelzu.

Argentina started at lightning speed. Two goals from centre-forward Stabile and one from Zumelzu gave Argentina a 3-0 lead within the first 12 minutes. Manuel Rosas of Mexico scored the first World Cup penalty before half-time. Within ten minutes of the second half Argentina had established a 5-1 lead with two goals by Varallo. Felipe Rosas, Manuel's brother, scored and Lopez gave Mexico a modicum of hope before Stabile became the first player to amass three goals, ten minutes from time.

The final group one match between Argentina and Chile would determine who would progress to the semi-finals. Ferreyra returned to the Argentina attack, having completed his finals. Stabile was rapidly establishing a reputation for prolific goalscoring. He netted twice in the 12th and 14th minutes before Subiabre of Chile quickly reduced the arrears only two minutes later. Shortly before half time Luisito Monti, a belligerent, combative figure, kicked at Torres of Chile. The police had to intervene to stop fighting between players in the ensuing fracas. Chile stretched the Argentinian defence during the second half but Evaristo ensured Argentina reached the semi-final with a decisive third goal in the 51st minute.

Yugoslavia ensured their semi-final place by winning with consummate ease against Bolivia in Central Park, Montevideo. Although goalless for an hour, Bolivia capitulated in the final 30 minutes. Beck opened the scoring and within five minutes Marianovic had doubled their lead. Further goals by Beck and Vujadinovic secured a 4-0 win.

Brazil and Bolivia met at the Centenary Stadium in a meaningless match. Moderato and Preguinho each scored twice as Brazil regained their pride with a 4-0 victory.

Romania met Peru on Bastille Day, a public holiday in Uruguay. This, to some extent, accounted for an embarrassingly sparse crowd of 300. Adalbert Steiner of Romania suffered a broken leg in an ill-tempered game. Peru's captain, Mario De Las Casas, gained notoriety by becoming the first player to be sent off. Alberto Warken, the Chilean match official, dismissed the player for violent conduct.

Romania scored with a goal by Desu after only one minute. Souza equalised during the second half but two goals in the last 14 minutes by Stanciu and Kovacs completed a 3-1 win for the Europeans.

Uruguay played their first game in the Centenary Stadium on 18th July, which was National Day. The nucleus of the side was based on a half back line of Jose Andrade, Lorenzo Fernandez and Alvaro Gestido, known as 'La costilla metallica' – 'the

4

iron curtain'. The 100,000 capacity was reduced for the inaugural match as work on the stadium was uncompleted. Peru, following their disappointing performance against Romania, were expected to succumb easily to Uruguay. However, the anticipated deluge instead became an arduous and laboured victory. Peru's right-winger, Lavalle, was a constant source of menace, easily breaking the Uruguayan defence. Castro, who had lost the lower part of one arm, scored the only goal after an hour. The host nation had been extremely fortunate to survive.

Uruguay, without a coach, took cognisance of their weaknesses against Romania and used player power to implement radical changes. Mascheroni replaced Tejera in defence and Pablo Dorado, Hector Scarone and Peregrino Anselmo were introduced to the forward line.

The revamped side routed Romania with four first-half goals. Dorado opened the scoring after only seven minutes. Further goals by Scarone, Anselmo and Cea followed, as the South Americans gave an exquisite exhibition of football during the first 45 minutes.

The United States were nicknamed 'The Shot Putters' by the French because of their muscular build. In their Pool 4 match with Belgium, they swept past their opponents displaying a British style of play. This was perhaps not surprising given the number of British professionals in the United States soccer league who held 'green cards'. The North Americans adopted an unusual strategy, playing with only three forwards. However, the tactics were very effective, with two goals by McGhee and one by Patenaude completing a 3-0 win.

Paraguay were less diffident in meeting the United States. They had achieved an excellent 3-0 win over Uruguay in the previous year's South American Cup. In front of a crowd of only 800 in Montevideo, the United States adopted a short-passing game which outmanoeuvred the South Americans. Patenaude scored after only ten minutes. Five minutes later Gonsalves claimed the unfortunate distinction of being the first player in the World Cup to score an own goal. A second goal by Patenaude in the second half produced an impressive 3-0 victory and justified the United States' seeding.

The final match in Pool 4 between Paraguay and Belgium was of no consequence. Paraguay scored the only goal through Pena five minutes from half-time. It was the first occasion during which Paraguay had triumphed over a European opponent. However, the South Americans, perhaps overburdened by optimism, exited a disappointed side.

The first semi-final paired Argentina with the United States. Two years earlier, Argentina had crushed the United States 11-2 during the Olympic competition in Amsterdam. It was perhaps surprising, therefore, that the United States were favourites. Jack Coll, the United States manager, foolishly declared before the game that he was concerned only about the Final.

The United States started ominously, with their centre half, Tracey, breaking his leg after only ten minutes. Their goalkeeper, Douglas, was severely handicapped by an injury and left half Auld received a facial wound. Monti scored after twenty minutes to give the highly physical and combative Argentinians the lead. In the second half the United States were overrun by a rampant Argentina, who scored three goals in a seven-minute period. Stabile and Peucelle each scored twice and Scopelli also netted. Brown scored a late consolation goal as his side were crushed 6-1.

The most memorable moment of the match occurred when the United States trainer, an excitable man, rushed onto the pitch to protest against a decision and started to harangue the referee. As his diatribe continued, he threw down his box of medicaments. This was a mistake, as he accidentally smashed a bottle of chloroform and was engulfed by its soporific vapours. He had to be carried off the field as he approached unconsciousness.

A capacity crowd of 93,000 watched in anticipation of Uruguay advancing to a meeting with Argentina and the opportunity to become the first holders of the World Cup.

Yugoslavia were the strongest of the European participants and shocked the hosts when Seculic scored after only four minutes. But goals by Cea, who appeared to be offside, and Anselmo, had established a lead for the hosts after only 20 minutes. Yugoslavia then had a goal disallowed before Anselmo scored with a controversial goal. The ball appeared to go out of play before being netted. In the second half Yugoslavia were overwhelmed. Iriarte scored on the hour and two further goals by Cea completed a 6-1 win, thereby producing identical semi-final scorelines.

The first World Cup Final thus became a re-run of the 1928 Olympic final, with the champions Uruguay facing their neighbours and arch rivals, Argentina. Thousands of Argentinians crossed the River Plate to support their team. On the day of the Final supporters began to fill the stadium in the early hours of the morning. Some 93,000 fans managed to get in; a multitude had to stay outside. The rivalry between the two countries was such that, after heated discussions, the halves of the final were played with different balls, one manufactured in each country.

Uruguay left out an unfit Anselmo and replaced him with Castro at centre forward. Pablo Dorado gave the home side a 12th minute lead when he shot through the legs of goalkeeper Botasso. Within eight minutes Argentina were level when outside right Peucelle received a pass from Ballesteros and scored with a powerful shot. Stabile then gave Argentina a half-time lead with a disputed goal, his eighth of the competition. He appeared to be offside on receiving the ball, but the Belgian referee, Jean Langenus, remained unmoved. After the interval Uruguay's territorial domination and technical superiority translated into goals. Pedro Cea scored an opportunist equaliser after 57 minutes. The storm of sound from the stands, and the sheer will to win, led to a brilliant third goal when Iriarte scored from 25 yards. Receiving a pass from Mascheroni, he was being policed by Evaristo. However, the winger suddenly unleashed a thunderous shot. Argentina pressed forward and Stabile struck the bar. In the dying seconds Castro headed home a Dorado cross to ensure victory.

All through the night church bells rang, car horns blared, and ships' sirens wailed down at the waterfront. The following day was declared a national holiday. In Buenos Aires the defeated Argentinians raged; mobs took to the streets, even stoning the Uruguayan consulate, and diplomatic relations between the two countries were broken off.

Results: Uruguay 1930

Pool 1

France	4	Mexico	1
Argentina	1	France	0
Chile	3	Mexico	0
Chile	1	France	0
Argentina	6	Mexico	3
Argentina	3	Chile	1

	P	W	D	L	F	A	Pts
Argentina	3	3	0	0	10	4	6
Chile	3	2	0	1	5	3	4
France	3	1	0	2	4	3	2
Mexico	3	0	0	3	4	13	0

Pool 2

Yugoslavia	2	Brazil	1
Yugoslavia	4	Bolivia	0
Brazil	4	Bolivia	0

	P	W	D	L	F	A	Pts
Yugoslavia	2	2	0	0	6	1	4
Brazil	2	1	0	1	5	2	2
Bolivia	2	0	0	2	0	8	0

Pool 3

Romania	3	Peru	1
Uruguay	1	Peru	0
Uruguay	4	Romania	0

	P	W	D	L	Goals F	A	Pts
Uruguay	2	2	0	0	5	0	4
Romania	2	1	0	1	3	5	2
Peru	2	0	0	2	1	4	0

Pool 4

United States	3	Belgium	0
United States	3	Paraguay	0
Paraguay	1	Belgium	0

	P	W	D	L	Goals F	A	Pts
United States	2	2	0	0	6	0	4
Paraguay	2	1	0	1	1	3	2
Belgium	2	0	0	2	0	4	0

Semi-finals

Argentina	6	United States	1
Uruguay	6	Yugoslavia	1

Final:

Uruguay	4	Argentina	2

Uruguay: Ballesteros, Nasazzi, Mascheroni, Andrade, Fernandez, Gestido, Dorado, Scarone, Castro, Cea, Iriarte.

Argentina: Botasso, Della Torre, Paternoster, Evaristo, J., Monti, Suarez, Peucelle, Varallo, Stabile, Ferreyra, Evaristo, M.

Scorers: Dorado, Cea, Iriarte, Castro for Uruguay.
            Peucelle, Stabile for Argentina.

1934

The 1934 World Cup reverberated to the hideous strains of a growing, pervasive Fascist ideology which would seriously threaten to undermine world stability and the democratic order in years to come.

This tournament clearly demonstrated that sport could be highly politically charged, long before the Right hypocritically condemned the anti-apartheid movement for 'politicising' sport.

Unsuccessful in their bid to host the inaugural event, Italy petitioned to stage the World Cup before the 1930 tournament had concluded.

Benito Mussolini was in power, Fascism was spreading like a virulent cancer and Il Duce was determined to win the Cup and thus achieve an important propaganda coup. General Giorgio Vaccaro was instructed by Mussolini to obtain the rights to the Cup at any cost. However, he only succeeded in 1932 after FIFA had convened eight meetings.

Even before Italy had won the right to host the tournament, General Vaccaro had chosen the manager, former journalist Vittorio Pozzo, to organise a plan that would enable Italy to triumph.

Mussolini taught the team to perform a Fascist salute before each game. The Italian crowds were embarrassingly jingoistic and embraced a style of nationalism better suited to a Nazi rally.

Uruguay, the holders, felt slighted by the apathy surrounding their own series. They had domestic concerns and refused to enter. They are, as yet, the only reigning champions who have failed to defend their title. Although their absence was regrettable, they were no longer the powerful force they had been in the World Cup of 1930. Uruguayan soccer was in a state of crisis afflicted by players' strikes.

Thirty-two countries originally entered a considerably expanded format and were geographically grouped in 12 sections of a qualifying tournament. Peru, Chile and Turkey did not confirm their registration and so 29 initial entrants were reduced to a more manageable 16 after the qualifying stage. Even Italy had to compete, and the organising committee were hugely relieved when they triumphed 4-0 against Greece.

The 16 finalists were paired in a straight knock-out round, eight seeded against weaker opposition in eight different venues. The pool system which operated in Uruguay was dispensed with. Although a high level of excitement was generated by straight elimination ties, a justifiable criticism was that half of the field were reduced to one game only. Defeating Cuba on three occasions enabled Mexico to play off against the United States in Rome. But the long journey was unrewarding as they lost the eliminator 4-2 and so did not participate in a single match in the finals.

Twelve of the 16 finalists were from Europe: Austria, Belgium, Czechoslovakia, France, Germany, Holland, Hungary, Italy, Romania, Spain, Sweden and Switzerland; one from Africa: Egypt, one from North America: United States of America and only two from South America: Brazil and Argentina.

Italy were the favourites, largely because the Austrian 'Wunderteam' managed by Hugo Meisl was considered to have peaked. However, they had comfortably defeated Italy 4-2 in Turin only two months prior to the start of the World Cup. Vittorio Pozzo, the astute Italian manager, had fashioned a highly talented side which married strength with impressive team work. He had been enormously influenced by Manchester United's style of play and particularly admired Herbert

Chapman, who had enjoyed major success as manager of Huddersfield and Arsenal. Spain were also an extremely strong side and would pose a very real threat to the hosts.

The first round ties were:

Italy v United States
Czechoslovakia v Romania
Germany v Belgium
Austria v France
Spain v Brazil
Switzerland v Holland
Sweden v Argentina
Hungary v Egypt

Both South American countries proceeded to be eliminated after the 8,000-mile trip. Argentina deliberately left their star players at home in order to avoid 'defections'. Several of their highly gifted 1930 squad had been signed by wealthy Italian clubs and one, Monti, was actually in the Italian squad of 1934. Without a single member of the 1930 side, Argentina, not surprisingly, lost 3-2 to Sweden.

In Genoa, Brazil were swiftly eliminated by Spain 3-1, with all the goals scored in the opening half. The Brazilian cause was handicapped by a missed penalty.

The United States were deeply embarrassed as they capitulated to Italy 7-1. Schiavio and Orsi shared five goals in the rout. The United States fielded only two of the players who had valiantly reached the semi-final of 1930.

Only European countries advanced to the next round, with Egypt, despite a gallant effort in Naples, losing 4-2 to Hungary.

Czechoslovakia struggled against Romania, conceding an early goal. They toiled to a 2-1 win largely earned by excellent goalkeeping from the highly adept Planicka.

Switzerland defeated Holland 3-2 with two goals from Kilholz, one of which was bizarrely deflected, and one from Abbegglen III.

Germany were trailing Belgium 2-1 at half-time but won in dramatic fashion with a deluge of goals after the interval.

Conen scored three and Kobierski two as the Germans achieved a spectacular 5-2 victory.

Austria beat France, as expected, but only 3-2 after extra time, following a highly dubious goal.

The countries qualifying for the quarter-finals were Germany, Sweden, Czechoslovakia, Switzerland, Austria, Hungary, Italy and Spain, and produced the following matches:

Germany v Sweden
Austria v Hungary
Czechoslovakia v Switzerland
Italy v Spain

In Florence, Italy and Spain produced two hours of thoroughly absorbing football in a searing heat. Italy adopted a brutal approach, with the downright violent Luigi Monti intent on inflicting as much physical damage to the Spanish side as possible. Spain led with a goal by Regueiro in the first half which was miskicked but deceived Combi in goal. Ferrari equalised following a free kick. The goalkeepers, Zamora of Spain and Combi of Italy, gave exceptional performances as the tie yielded no further goals during extra time.

The replay was convened 24 hours later. Luigi Monti had given the impression that he was afflicted by a chromosomal defect in the initial match. His destructive approach was largely attributable to seven of Spain's regular players, including their goalkeeper and captain, Zamora, being absent. Italy, by contrast, fielded seven of their regular players although Pizziolo was missing, with a broken leg. Meazza scored the only goal of the game with a header from a cross.

In Bologna there was another brutal encounter between fierce rivals Austria and Hungary. Horvath scored very early in the match for Austria and Zischek extended their lead soon after the interval. Although Sarosi reduced the arrears from a penalty, Markos undermined Hungarian efforts at a comeback by being sent off as Austria won 2-1.

A meagre crowd of only 7,000, many of whom waved swastika flags, attended the Germany versus Sweden game. Sweden were a hard-working, functional, staid side. They held their own in the first half but conceded two second-half goals inside three minutes to Hohmann. Dunker scored a consolation goal for Sweden in a 2-1 defeat.

Czechoslovakia and Switzerland contested a tantalising match with the outcome never certain. Goals from Svoboda, Sobotka and Nejedly for Czechoslovakia, and Kielholz and Abbegglen III, ensured a thrilling encounter with Czechoslovakia narrowly winning 3-2.

The semi-finals paired Italy with Austria in Milan and Germany with Czechoslovakia in Rome.

Hugo Meisl's 'Wunderteam' approached the match with an enviable record, incurring only two defeats in their previous thirty games. They had, of course, beaten Italy on their home territory and were many people's pre-tournament favourites.

The Italians were clearly tired, having played three games in one week including 210 minutes of bruising football against Spain.

Hugo Meisl claimed that Italy had superior reserves to Austria, were better prepared and had a fanatical support. Whether this was a deliberate psychological ploy or he was genuinely pessimistic is a moot point. However, his gloomy prognostication appeared to transmit itself to his players.

On 3rd June 1934 it had rained heavily and the muddy playing surface conspired against Austria's delicate short-passing game. The Argentinian-born winger Guaita scrambled the only goal after eighteen minutes. Austria were a huge disappointment as they allowed the lively and energetic Italians to dominate the match.

Before the other semi-final in Rome, Czechoslovakia proudly displayed their flag, only to be greeted by a Fascist salute from the Italian crowd. Mussolini was in attendance as Czechoslovakia, playing attractive, intelligent football, gained the impetus and scored through Nejedly following an intricate, sweeping forward movement. Frantisek Planicka, their cherished goalkeeper, allowed Germany back into contention when he uncharacteristically remained motionless as a speculative long shot by Noack sailed over him. Ten minutes later

Puc restored the lead for Czechoslovakia and Nejedly scored his fourth goal of the tournament as he skilfully evaded the attentions of the German defence to complete a 3-1 victory.

The third place match was introduced for the first time and took place three days before the final.

Germany scored through Lehner after only 30 seconds. Conen, who finished as the tournament's equal top scorer, added to the lead. Horvath narrowed the deficit for Austria but Lehner gave the Germans a comfortable 3-1 lead before half-time. A long free kick by Sesta reduced the final score to 3-2 in Germany's favour, as the match degenerated into a physical confrontation.

The final took place in Rome on 10th June 1934 on a smaller than standard size pitch. A crowd of 55,000 assembled but this was less than full capacity. Mussolini, together with all the government ministers, was in attendance. A partisan crowd roared for Italy and 'Il Duce' as the Fascist government eagerly anticipated a necessary victory for prestige.

Unusually, both sides were captained by their goalkeepers – Combi of Italy and the highly impressive Planicka for Czechoslovakia. The first half was largely undistinguished. Czechoslovakia were far from intimidated and proceeded to play a neat, short-passing game. Cambal, the centre-half, was ubiquitous and Svoboda, the inside-right, occasionally tormented the Italian defence.

The match remained goalless when, with 20 minutes remaining, Puc scored, to the delight of the Czechoslovakian supporters who had travelled by road and rail. Czechoslovakia missed two further opportunities to put the tie beyond Italy's reach. Perhaps through over-anxiety, Sobotka squandered an easy chance and Svoboda hit a post.

Italy switched their forwards in a desperate attempt to avoid defeat. With only eight minutes remaining, Raimondo Orsi, an Argentinian left-winger, hit a swerving shot which was purely speculative. Somehow the bizarre and freakish flight of the ball outwitted Planicka's frantic effort to prevent a goal.

During extra time the Italians finally exhibited their skill and tactical nous. In the 97th minute Giuseppe Meazza, their star forward, although carrying an injury, received the ball on the right and crossed to Guaita. Guaita advanced before passing to Angelo Schiavio, who unleashed the winning goal.

Although it was highly regrettable that the World Cup tournament was so crudely exploited by Mussolini, it would be churlish to deny that Italy were deserving champions. They had competed in five games totalling 510 minutes of play. The physical demands placed on the players were enormous and they had displayed remarkable resilience.

The tournament was a success in terms of crowd attendance and revenue. In the 1930 World Cup little interest was stimulated in a number of games. Only 300 people watched Romania v Peru and 800 attended the United States v Paraguay tie. The lowest attendance in Italy, by comparison, was 6,000.

However, the political overtones scarcely represented Jules Rimet's ideal. Additionally, far too many of the matches exposed the unseemly side of soccer and were characterised by brutal play.

Results: Italy 1934

Italy	7	United States	1
Czechoslovakia	2	Romania	1
Germany	5	Belgium	2
Austria	3	France	2*
Spain	3	Brazil	1
Switzerland	3	Holland	2
Sweden	3	Argentina	2
Hungary	4	Egypt	2

*(after extra time, 1-1 at 90 minutes)

Quarter finals

Germany	2	Sweden	1
Austria	2	Hungary	1
Italy	1	Spain	1*
Italy	1	Spain	0**
Czechoslovakia	3	Switzerland	2

*(after extra time, 1-1 at 90 minutes)   **(replay)

Semi-finals

Czechoslovakia	3	Germany	1
Italy	1	Austria	0

Third place match

Germany	3	Austria	2

Final

Italy	2	Czechoslovakia	1*

*(after extra time, 1-1 at 90 minutes)

Italy: Combi, Monzeglio, Allemandi, Ferraris IV, Monti, Bertolini, Guaita, Meazza, Schiavio, Ferrari, Orsi.

Czechoslovakia: Planicka, Zenisek, Ctyroky, Kostalek, Cambal, Krcil, Junek, Svoboda, Sobatka, Nejedly, Puc.
Scorers: Orsi, Schiavio for Italy.
          Puc for Czechoslovakia.

1938

In 1938 Europe was in a perilous state, teetering on the on the edge of war. The long Civil War in Spain had entered its final year. The Nationalist Forces of General Franco had made sweeping territorial gains.

On 12 March 1938 German troops crossed the border into Austria, thus tearing up Article 88 of the Treaty of Versailles, under which the union of Austria and Germany – Anschluss – was forbidden.

On 14 March 1938 Adolf Hitler rode into Vienna, accompanied by goose-stepping soldiers and tanks. Hitler had contemptuously brushed aside the peace treaties. By bluster and bullying, he now presided over a Greater Germany of 74 million people.

The planned pogrom, or what the Nazi newspapers repugnantly called 'the Spring Cleaning', was about to begin in Austria. All Jewish judges and state attorneys were immediately forced out of their jobs and Jews were forbidden to leave the country or to vote in the plebiscite which took place in April 1938. Jewish shops were placarded and theatres and music halls purged of Jews, among them Max Reinhardt and Richard Tauber. In Vienna, elderly Jews were made to scrub the pavements while Nazi stormtroopers watched in amusement.

*   *   *

On 15 August 1936, shortly after the Olympic Games had ended, 40 of the 54 members at the FIFA Congress at the

Opera Kroll in Berlin endorsed France's candidature to host the World Cup. Argentina had also applied, arguing that the World Cup should take place on a different continent. Argentina's rejected bid resulted in their failure to participate in the tournament and provoked a riot outside their federation's offices in Buenos Aires. Uruguay, still beset by domestic problems, again refused to enter. England received an invitation to attend but declined.

The staging of the 1938 competition in France was a great tribute to FIFA President Jules Rimet. It was decided that Paris's Colombes Stadium would be enlarged and that other stadiums would be built in a number of French cities.

Of the record 36 countries who had initially registered, only 27 remained. Surprising and exotic qualifiers included the Dutch East Indies and Cuba. For the first time, the host country and the winner of the Cup automatically qualified for a berth. As holders, Italy were therefore exempted from the qualifying competition. In the preliminary round, Austria's withdrawal, as a consequence of being overrun by Germany, allowed Sweden a walk-over in the knock-out system which was retained from the previous series.

The first round ties were:

Italy v Norway
Brazil v Poland
Germany v Switzerland
Cuba v Romania
Czechoslovakia v Holland
Hungary v Dutch East Indies
France v Belgium

Italy were extremely fortunate to survive their opening game against Norway in Marseilles. They fielded only two survivors from 1934 – the captain Meazza and Ferrari. Although Italy scored after only two minutes through Ferraris II, Norway stormed back into the game and had several near misses before Brustad deservedly equalised. A second goal by Brustad was disallowed for offside and Oliviera made a critical save from Brynildsen in the dying seconds. During extra time,

Piola scored the winning goal but the champions had defended their title nervously.

Brazil and Poland produced a quite remarkable tie in Strasbourg. Brazil strode into a 3-1 first-half lead playing skilful, swift and fluent football as Leonidas scored a hat trick. During the interval a deluge affected the playing surface and the Poles staged an heroic comeback. There was such an abundance of mud that Leonidas requested to play barefoot. Unsurprisingly, he was not permitted to do so by the Swedish referee, Eklind. At full-time the score was 4-4. Both Leonidas and Willimowski of Poland distinguished themselves with four goals each as Brazil eventually won 6-5 after extra time. Sporting losers Poland sent Brazil a good luck telegram in advance of their quarter final tie.

Playing against Switzerland at the Parc des Princes, Germany's act of larceny in fielding leading Austrian players including Hahnemann, Raftl and Schmaus proved to be fruitless. Gauchel scored first for Germany but Abegglen III equalised before the interval. At the conclusion of extra time the score remained unchanged. Five days later the replay produced an astonishing turnaround. Germany had established a comfortable 2-0 lead by half-time with goals by Hahnemann and the hapless Lortscher, who contributed an own goal. After the interval, an impressive display of power and courage by Switzerland resulted in a 4-2 victory as Germany were, ironically, overrun.

The surprise of the first round occurred in Toulouse, where Cuba met Romania. Cuba only qualified following the withdrawal of Mexico. King Carol's Romania still had three members of their 1930 team. Although an ageing, tired side, they were nevertheless strong favourites to eliminate Cuba. The teams drew 3-3 after extra time in an exciting match, which warranted more than the meagre crowd of 6,000 present. Three days later Cuba, despite trailing to a goal by Dobai at half-time, won 2-1 with Socorro and Maquina scoring.

In Le Havre, Holland performed boldly against World Cup runners-up Czechoslovakia before eventually succumbing to goals by Kostalek, Nejedly and Zeman in extra time.

Hungary were to emerge as the highest scoring team in the tournament. Against the Dutch East Indies they swept to a 6-0 victory, with both Sarosi and Zsengeller scoring twice.

France, the hosts, met Belgium at the Colombes Stadium in Paris. They enjoyed a promising start, scoring after only 40 seconds. Veinante exploited an error by the veteran Belgian goalkeeper, Badjou, who had played in the 1930 World Cup. A rout looked possible as Nicolas scored a second after only ten minutes, but Isemborghs replied for Belgium before half-time. Nicolas ensured a 3-1 victory, scoring with 20 minutes remaining.

The quarter finals produced the following ties:

Sweden v Cuba
Italy v France
Hungary v Switzerland
Brazil v Czechoslovakia

The matches took place on 12 June with all the competing nations having to journey long distances to their next venue All teams travelled by train with the exception of the well-organised and opulent Italian squad, who luxuriated in their own plane.

Cuban hopes of a further sensation were rapidly dispelled in Antibes. Sweden demolished Cuba, with Gustav Wetterstrom scoring four times. Andersson, Keller, Jonasson and Nyberg also contributed goals as the inexperienced and exhausted Cubans meekly capitulated 8-0.

In Lille, weary Switzerland, clearly affected by their tortuous encounters with Germany, lost 2-0 to Hungary. Zsengeller again scored twice as he enhanced his reputation as a prolific striker.

The 58,544 spectators assembled at the Colombes Stadium in Paris to watch France play Italy represented the largest crowd at the 1938 tournament.

An intriguing clash unfolded between the holders and the hosts. French expectations were high as it was anticipated that Italy would be exhausted following their exacting clash with Norway. However, they confounded their critics with a goal by Colaussi after only six minutes. Colaussi crossed a ball, which was mismanaged by Di Lorto in the French goal as he allowed the ball to slip through his hands. The French riposte was immediate as Heisserer produced an exquisite goal, which was the culmination of intricate teamwork. An evenly balanced match was eventually decided by the ruthless finishing of Piola, who scored two second-half goals in a 3-1 victory for the holders.

One of the bloodiest encounters in World Cup history took place in Bordeaux between Brazil and Czechoslovakia. An unsightly and brutal battle resulted in three players being sent off, one broken leg, a broken arm and a catalogue of minor injuries as violence reigned. Procopio of Brazil launched an unprovoked attack on Nejedly and was promptly dismissed. Leonidas scored for Brazil after half an hour but the match erupted just before the interval, when Riha and Machado exchanged punches and were expelled. Weak refereeing by the Hungarian official, Hertzka, resulted in unabated indiscipline and near anarchy. On the hour mark, Domingos da Guia handled the ball and Nejedly, who was later taken to hospital with a broken leg, converted the penalty. At the end of extra time, a total of 17 players had been injured in the 1-1 draw.

Two days later the match was replayed. Brazil introduced nine new players and Czechoslovakia six. Georges Capdeville of France replaced Hertzka as the match official. In stark contrast to the original tie, the conduct of the players proved to be exemplary. Critically, Planicka, the excellent Czech goalkeeper, was absent with a broken arm.

Brazil exuded extraordinary arrogance by allowing their main party to travel to Marseilles in advance of the replay, clearly anticipating a semi-final tie against Italy. The Czechs quickly disabused Brazil of their complacency when Kopecky gave them a first-half lead. However, Brazil played delightfully and Leonidas equalised after an hour before Roberto justly scored the winner in a 2-1 triumph.

The semi-finals paired Italy with Brazil in Marseilles and Hungary with Sweden in Paris.

Brazilian confidence bordered on the incredulous as they rested two of their star forwards, Leonidas and Tim, in preparation for the Final. Brazil, indeed, fielded only three of the players who had defeated Czechoslovakia.

Although Brazil enjoyed the vocal support of the French crowd, they eventually lost 2-1. Colaussi of Italy outstripped Domingos da Guia 11 minutes into the half to score the opening goal. Piola's physical presence had an unsettling effect on the Brazilian defence. Domingos da Guia fouled Piola, who fell theatrically. The Swiss referee, Wuthrich, awarded a penalty, which Meazza converted. Although Romeo reduced the lead with three minutes remaining, it was too late for Brazil to salvage the tie.

In the other semi-final, Hungary clashed with Sweden, who were managed by the Hungarian Josephy Nagy. Although Nyberg momentarily gave Sweden hope with a goal after 35 seconds, the 'Team of Steel' were eventually smelted 5-1. By half-time Hungary had already established a 3-1 lead. They intelligently stifled Gustav Wetterstrom, who had penetrated the Cuban defence so effectively. Zsengeller scored three times and goals from Sarosi and Titkos ensured a Final appearance as the Magyars majestically strode to victory.

The third place match between Brazil and Sweden was contested in Bordeaux. Jonasson and Nyberg scored for Sweden as they established a first-half lead. But Leonidas replied with two second-half goals as Brazil won 4-2. Leonidas departed as the tournament's leading striker with eight goals.

The Final produced an intriguing encounter between two contrasting styles of play. Italy were a physical, robust and resilient team. Hungary, highly adroit, played delicate, short-passing, precision football.

Only six minutes had elapsed when Colaussi scored for Italy following a fluent move. Hungary swiftly replied when Titkos, unmarked, equalised. Meazza was inspirational for Italy and largely shaped the fate of the match, creating further goals for Piola and Colaussi. Hungary gained the initiative in midfield during the second half and the exceptionally talented

Sarosi reduced the lead. But Piola ensured a 4-2 victory with only ten minutes remaining, receiving a back heel pass from Biavati which he shot home.

Vittorio Pozzo remains the only person to have managed two World Cup winning teams. The Italian manager was renowned as a very progressive thinker who had been influenced by Manchester United's style of play. A keen scholar of the game, he often compiled meticulous dossiers on his opponents.

However, Pozzo embraced the aggressive nationalism which was prevalent in Italy. He selected Argentinian-born players on the pretext that they were liable for Italian military service. Pozzo argued that, 'If they can die for Italy, they can play for Italy.' This philosophy did not extend to Enrique Guaita, who was a member of the 1934 World Cup side. When the Abyssinian War broke out in 1936, Guaita was caught attempting to flee the border into Switzerland.

The third World Cup had been a reasonable success, with crowds averaging 21,000 per game. But the ugly political climate and the imminence of war cast a very dark shadow over the tournament.

The annexation of Austria unquestionably tarnished the 1938 World Cup. Hahnemann, Raftl, Schmaus, Skoumal, Neumer and Stroh were all Austrian players assimilated into the German team. However, the stylish Mathias Sindelar, known as 'the paper man' because of his svelte appearance, refused to play and thus became a national hero. Tragically, on 23 January 1939, following his wife's death and the official annexation of Austria, he committed suicide by inhalation of gas. Austria mourned its idol as Europe raced inexorably towards a second World War.

Results: France 1938

First Round

Switzerland	1	Germany	1*
Hungary	6	Dutch East Indies	0
France	3	Belgium	1
Brazil	6	Poland	5**
Czechoslovakia	3	Holland	0†
Italy	2	Norway	1*
Cuba	3	Romania	3††

*After extra time, 1-1 at 90 minutes
**After extra time, 4-4 at 90 minutes
†After extra time, 0-0 at 90 minutes
††After extra time, 2-2 at 90 minutes

Replays

Switzerland	4	Germany	2
Cuba	2	Romania	1

Quarter finals

Sweden	8	Cuba	0
Hungary	2	Switzerland	0
Italy	3	France	1
Brazil	1	Czechoslovakia	1*

*After extra time, 1-1 at 90 minutes

Replay

Brazil	2	Czechoslovakia	1

Semi-finals

Italy	2	Brazil	1
Hungary	5	Sweden	1

Third place match

| Brazil | 4 | Sweden | 2 |

Final:

| Italy | 4 | Hungary | 2 |

Italy: Olivieri, Foni, Rava, Serantoni, Andreolo, Locatelli, Biavati, Meazza, Piola, Ferrari, Colaussi

Hungary: Szabo, Polgar, Biro, Szalay, Szucs, Lazar, Sas, Vincze, Sarosi, Zsengeller, Titkos

Scorers: Colaussi (2), Piola (2) for Italy
         Titkos, Sarosi for Hungary

1950

It took two billion dollars, a workforce of 100,000 and several years to develop the atomic bomb. The bombs that fell on Hiroshima and Nagasaki took less than four seconds to obliterate the heart of two large cities, sending a fireball of 300,000 degrees Celsius and killing 340,000 people.

After Hiroshima and Nagasaki, nothing was ever the same again. The use of the atomic bomb was an historical turning point and changed the world more dramatically than any single event which preceded it. For the first time, human beings had discovered and unleashed a force capable of destroying life on Earth.

The Second World War was over but, despite the ever-present threat of the new atomic weapon, peace still seemed to elude the world. During 1950 North Korea invaded South Korea and China announced the movement of Peking forces into Tibet, penetrating as far as Lhasa, the Holy City.

The 1950s were the decade of Korea and of the French war in Vietnam. They were the decade of Suez and of the Hungarian uprising. In the United States the reverberations of black consciousness gave new impetus to the civil rights movement in the Deep South. In the Soviet Union the death of Josef Stalin after years of unchallenged supremacy led to a political power struggle in the upper echelons of the Soviet hierarchy, from which the mercurial Nikita Khruschev emerged victorious. The process of de-Stalinization began, but the Cold War between East and West remained unthawed.

At the end of the Second World War the European powers,

directly or indirectly, ruled virtually all of Africa and the Middle East, together with South and South-East Asia. The independence movements were already challenging the assumptions of colonial rule in the 1950s.

*   *   *

The 1950 World Cup, therefore, played to a backdrop of rapidly emerging economic, social and political change. The first FIFA Congress after the 1938 World Cup was held in Luxembourg in 1946. Brazil, which had largely been unaffected by the war, was the only candidate and therefore chosen to host the fourth World Cup. At the 1948 FIFA Congress in London, Brazil presented an alternative format which would comprise of four groups, each group containing four nations; in the second round, everyone would play everyone else and a points count would determine the winners. In reality, the tournament was hopelessly unbalanced as a depleted field of 13 teams competed, split into four groups. There was no final match, although the uneven format was to provide an unexpected and dramatic climax.

Thirty-one countries entered the qualifying tournament, including the British associations for the first time, all four having rejoined FIFA in 1946. The Home Championship was used as part of the qualification, with two nations guaranteed in the finals. Scotland lost to England 1-0 at Hampden Park, thus sulkily and ungraciously carrying out their threat to withdraw from the tournament unless they were British Champions. Sadly, Argentina again withdrew, citing difficulties with the Brazilian soccer authorities. France initially agreed to take the place of Turkey, who also withdrew, but declined on learning of their punishing tour itinerary. The Iron Curtain countries – Bulgaria, Hungary, Poland, Romania and Czechoslovakia – all absented themselves. India failed to participate when informed by FIFA that they would not be permitted to play barefooted.

Italy, the holders of the World Cup and winners in both 1934 and 1938, suffered a terrible tragedy in May 1949. An aeroplane carrying the Torino team, returning from a friendly in Lisbon and on their way to a fifth consecutive championship, crashed into the wall of a hillside monastery. The aircraft disintegrated on impact, leaving Italy's international side decimated. Every player was killed. Torino had provided as many as ten of its players for international duty. Among the renowned names who perished were Bacigalupo, the finest of goalkeepers; the pugnacious Rigamonti; the classy Castigliano; Menti, accomplished and improving with age; Mazzola, constructive and reliable; and Maroso, whose incandescent skills will never be forgotten.

Of the 13 national teams who competed for the 1950 World Cup, six were from Europe and seven from the Americas. They were grouped as follows:

> Pool 1: Brazil, Mexico, Switzerland and Yugoslavia
> Pool 2: Chile, England, Spain and the United States
> Pool 3: Italy, Paraguay and Sweden
> Pool 4: Bolivia and Uruguay

The opening game took place in the uncompleted Maracana Stadium, where Brazil played Mexico. Motorists abandoned their vehicles amidst traffic jams and walked to the stadium. Unsightly scaffolding and rubble lay strewn around the ground. Brazil were greeted by a 21-gun salute, and a cacophony of fireworks added to a highly charged atmosphere. Brazil easily defeated Mexico 4-0, with goals scored by Ademir (2), Jair and Baltazar.

Yugoslavia started promisingly, easily beating Switzerland in Belo Horizonte. Two goals by Tomasevic, together with a strike by Ognjanov, completed a 3-0 victory. Yugoslavia emerged as a serious threat to Brazil, defeating Mexico 4-1 in their next encounter in Port Alegre. Goals by Ciakowski (2), Tomasevic and Bobek sounded a warning to the hosts.

Brazil purposely included many local players against Switzerland in Sao Paulo. Switzerland introduced three changes following their defeat by Yugoslavia and proceeded to offer obdurate resistance. Although Alfredo put Brazil ahead, Fatton equalised. Baltazar re-established Brazil's lead with a stunning goal, but with only two minutes remaining, Fatton scored a precious equaliser.

Yugoslavia only required a draw to ensure qualification and the dismissal of the strong favourites. In Rio de Janeiro on 1st July 1950, 155,000 spectators assembled at the Maracana stadium. Flavio Costa, the Brazilian manager, selected a triumvirate of inside-forwards in Zizinho, Ademir and Jair. Controversy surrounded the start of the match as Yugoslavia entered the field without the injured Mitic and then returned to the dressing room. They were pursued by the Welsh referee, Mervyn Griffiths, who ordered them back, refusing to postpone the kick-off while Mitic received treatment. Yugoslavia started the match with only ten men and within three minutes had conceded a goal to Ademir. Although the travel itinerary had clearly affected the graceful Yugoslavs, they staged a laudable comeback. Rajko Mitic, sporting a white bandage, transformed his team as they attacked ferociously in pursuit of an equaliser. Zelico Ciakowski squandered a relatively easy chance and shortly afterwards Zizinho ensured victory and qualification with an excellent opportunist goal following a mazy run. In the final pool match, Switzerland defeated Mexico 2-1 with goals by Bader and Antenen.

In Pool 2, England unconvincingly beat Chile 2-0 in Rio de Janeiro, with goals by Mortensen and Mannion.

Spain surprisingly trailed for 80 minutes to a goal by Souza in their match against the United States in Curitiba. But in a hectic final few minutes, two goals by Basora and a further effort by Zarra clinched a 3-1 victory.

In their next match against the United States in Belo Horizonte, England were to suffer arguably the most humiliating defeat in their entire history. They began brightly on a bumpy, uneven surface, striking the post and shooting over the bar. The United States defended competently, with Borghi outstanding in goal. The half-back line of McIlvenny, Colombo and Bahr performed solidly.

After 37 minutes, the United States left-half, Walter Bahr, sent a seemingly innocuous cross into the goalmouth. However, the goalkeeper, Bert Williams, failed to hold the ball and Larry Gaetjens, originally from Haiti, deflected the ball into the net with his head. An increasingly neurotic England descended into desperation as they frantically attempted to retrieve the situation. When the highly improbable result of 0-1 was flashed to Fleet Street, one newspaper, convinced of an error, printed the score as 10-1 to England.

Spain comfortably defeated Chile in their next game, with goals by Basora and Zarra in the first half.

England returned to Rio de Janeiro having to beat Spain by two clear goals in order to qualify for the Final Pool. There was controversy after 14 minutes when Jackie Milburn, the England centre-forward, appeared to have scored with a header from a Finney cross. However, the Italian referee, Giovanni Galeati, disallowed the goal for offside, despite a Spanish defender clearly placing Milburn onside. Shortly after half-time, a Zarra header ensured a Spanish victory and advancement to the next round.

Chile, meanwhile, enjoyed an emphatic 5-2 win over the United States in Recife.

In Pool, 3 Sweden, coached by the Englishman George Raynor, produced a surprise victory over a seriously weakened Italian side following the aftermath of the Superaga disaster. It was an ironic triumph for the Swedes, who had lost many of their 1948 Olympic stars to Italian clubs.

Italy scored first with a goal by their captain, Riccardo Carapellese, after only seven minutes. By half-time Sweden had established a lead with goals by Jeppson and Andersson. Jeppson scored again after the interval and, although Muccinelli reduced the arrears and Carapellese hit the bar, Italy could not salvage the tie.

The second match paired Sweden with Paraguay. Sweden swept into a 2-0 lead with goals by Palmer and Sundquist. However, Paraguay staged a courageous comeback and drew 2-2, with Lopez A and Lopez F scoring. Italy consoled themselves by defeating Paraguay 2-0, with goals from Carapellese and Pandolfini, thus ensuring Sweden emerged as Pool 3 victors.

Pool 4 was absurdly restricted to a solitary match between Uruguay and rank outsiders Bolivia. The reason for this was that France withdrew, believing their schedule to be too demanding. Their itinerary would have involved firstly playing Uruguay in Port Alegre before travelling 3,500 kilometres to face Bolivia in Recife, with temperatures of 95° Fahrenheit. Brazil viewed the refusal as a hostile gesture, given that during the 1938 World Cup held in France, the South Americans had travelled from Strasbourg to Bordeaux and then onto Marseilles by train. France would at least have enjoyed the luxury of a plane.

Uruguay overwhelmed Bolivia by eight goals to nil in Recife, with only 13,000 spectators in attendance. The match signified the arrival of an outstanding talent in Juan Alberto Schiaffino, who made an unforgettable impact by scoring four goals.

Schiaffino was a modest character, born in Montevideo in 1925 of Italian parentage. He was of slight build but displayed exceptional ability from a very young age. He joined Penarol aged 18 and quickly established himself as an inside-left with speed, deft skills, intelligence and prescience. Schiaffino was to be the architect of one of the biggest upsets the World Cup has ever produced.

After a one-week rest, the Final Pool games began on 9th July. They comprised of four nations, Brazil, Spain, Sweden and Uruguay, who would compete in a six-match contest with the winner determined on a points basis.

The Final Pool consisted of the following matches:
Brazil v Sweden
Uruguay v Spain
Brazil v Spain
Uruguay v Sweden
Sweden v Spain
Uruguay v Brazil

Brazil played exquisitely against Sweden in the Maracana Stadium, with individual brilliance complementing irresistible team work. Ademir scored four, Chico two and Maneca one, as a captivating performance swamped Sweden, who could only offer an Andersson penalty goal in reply as they succumbed 7-1.

Uruguay struggled against Spain in Sao Paulo. They trailed 2-1 at half-time to goals from Basora in what transpired to be a highly physical match. During the second half, Varela of Uruguay was truly inspirational and his assertive contribution was rewarded with an equaliser 18 minutes from time.

Spain's next encounter was against Brazil in the Maracana, watched by a crowd of 172,772. Brazil's irrepressible form continued as they steamrollered their opponents 6-1. Two goals apiece by Ademir and Chico, and one each by Zizinho and Jair, contributed to another emphatic victory.

Meanwhile, Uruguay struggled against Sweden in Sao Paulo. Although Sweden had endured a more taxing programme and were less naturally gifted than Uruguay, they nevertheless led 2-1 at half-time, with goals by Palmer and Sundquist. Sweden were handicapped during the second half by an injury to Johnsson. They eventually capitulated to two goals by Miguez, the Uruguayan centre-forward, which were to prove absolutely critical in the overall context of the tournament.

Spain contested their final match in front of an embarrassingly meagre crowd of 8,000 in Sao Paulo. Sweden achieved a creditable third place with goals from Mellberg, Palmer and Sundquist which contributed to an excellent 3-1 win.

With only one match remaining in the Final Pool, Brazil led with four points, while Uruguay had struggled to amass three. Sweden had gained two points from their already completed matches and Spain one point. Brazil, therefore, merely needed to draw their final game against Uruguay to ensure they became World Champions in what is often erroneously referred to as the 1950 Final. It was, in fact, the Final Pool decider, but nevertheless generated a spectacular climax which could not have been surpassed by an official Final.

Gambling mania was rampant in Rio de Janeiro and Brazil

were an incredible 10-1 on favourites. The team were promised a staggering £10,000-a-man win bonus. A celebrating samba called 'Brazil the Victors' was composed.

The State Governor of Rio de Janeiro addressed a world record crowd of 199,854 with a nauseatingly presumptuous speech before the game: 'You Brazilians ... you players who in less than a few hours will be acclaimed champions by millions of your compatriots ... you who have no equals in the terrestrial hemisphere ... you who are so superior to every other competitor ... you whom I already salute as conquerors...'

During the first half Uruguay faced an almost relentless onslaught of offensive play by Brazil. They had to defend resolutely as Zizinho, Ademir and Jair constantly menaced their defence. Maspoli in goal gave an agile performance as he kept an almost unrelenting wave of Brazilian attacks at bay. Uruguay were rarely seen as an attacking force, but when they did produce a chance for Schiaffino, Barbosa in the Brazilian goal had to respond athletically.

Two minutes after the interval the massed Uruguayan defence was finally breached, with Friaca scoring following clever play by Ademir and Zizinho. Uruguay suddenly turned adversity to their advantage by making every pass count. They launched a series of attacks orchestrated by the industrious Rodriguez Andrade and Obdulio Varela. As they seized the initiative, Varela advanced after 66 minutes and propelled the ball to the diminutive Ghiggia, who was racing down the right wing. The winger crossed the ball to the unguarded Schiaffino, who shot first time and with consummate ease past a helpless Barbosa. With only 11 minutes remaining, Ghiggia received the ball and passed to Perez, who beat Jair, surged forward and returned the ball to Ghiggia. Ghiggia strode on to the ball and sensationally drove in a low shot for the winner inside Barbosa's near post. Brazil spent the final minute with all their players, with the exception of Barbosa, encamped in the Uruguayan penalty area.

The World Cup had returned to Montevideo, against all

expectations, after an absence of 20 years. Three Uruguayan supporters died of heart attacks while listening to a radio commentary of the game.

The 1950 World Cup produced one of the greatest ever climaxes to the tournament. Brazil had engendered considerable enthusiasm in hosting the event, although their organisation was somewhat chaotic. Their devastating and unanticipated defeat resulted in a period of national mourning. But the tournament produced many fine performances and also proved to be very lucrative. The World Cup decider was watched by a record crowd of 199,854 and the tournament boasted the highest average attendance to date of 60,772 per match.

Results: Brazil 1950

Pool 1

Brazil	4	Mexico	0
Yugoslavia	3	Switzerland	0
Brazil	2	Switzerland	2
Yugoslavia	4	Mexico	1
Brazil	2	Yugoslavia	0
Switzerland	2	Mexico	1

	P	W	D	L	Goals F	A	Pts
Brazil	3	2	1	0	8	2	5
Yugoslavia	3	2	0	1	7	3	4
Switzerland	3	1	1	1	4	6	3
Mexico	3	0	0	3	2	10	0

Pool 2

England	2	Chile	0
Spain	3	USA	1
USA	1	England	0
Spain	2	Chile	0
Spain	1	England	0
Chile	5	USA	2

	P	W	D	L	Goals F	A	Pts
Spain	3	3	0	0	6	1	6
England	3	1	0	2	2	2	2
Chile	3	1	0	2	5	6	2
USA	3	1	0	2	4	8	2

Pool 3

Sweden	3	Italy	2
Sweden	2	Paraguay	2
Italy	2	Paraguay	0

	P	W	D	L	Goals F	A	Pts
Sweden	2	1	1	0	5	4	3
Italy	2	1	0	1	4	3	2
Paraguay	2	0	1	1	2	4	1

Pool 4

Uruguay	8	Bolivia	0

	P	W	D	L	Goals F	A	Pts
Uruguay	1	1	0	0	8	0	2
Bolivia	1	0	0	1	0	8	0

Final Pool

Brazil	7	Sweden	1
Uruguay	2	Spain	2
Brazil	6	Spain	1
Uruguay	3	Sweden	2
Sweden	3	Spain	1
Uruguay	2	Brazil	1

	P	W	D	L	Goals F	A	Pts
Uruguay	3	2	1	0	7	5	5
Brazil	3	2	0	1	14	4	4
Sweden	3	1	0	2	6	11	2
Spain	3	0	1	2	4	11	1

FINAL POOL DECIDER

Uruguay: Maspoli, Gonzales M, Tejera, Gambetta, Varela, Andrade, Ghiggia, Perez, Miguez, Schiaffino, Moran

Brazil: Barbosa, Augusto, Juveval, Bauer, Danilo, Bigode, Friaca, Zizinho, Ademir, Jair, Chico

Scorers: Schiaffino, Ghiggia for Uruguay
Friaca for Brazil

1954

The French war in Indo-China entered its seventh and final year. Dien Bien Phu, the French garrison which had become the focus of the fiercest fighting of the entire war, fell to the Viet Minh communist forces of General Giap on 7 May after a 55-day siege. The defeat was a bitter blow to French morale and proved to be the final nail in the coffin of her Indo-Chinese interests. However, Vietnam was later to become an all too familiar landscape during the 1960s and 1970s as public revulsion heightened in response to full media exposure of American atrocities.

The nuclear arms race entered a new and more terrifying phase on 1 March when the United States exploded its first true hydrogen bomb on Bikini Atoll in the Pacific. Although the United States Atomic Energy Commission had already tested precursors of the new device in the Pacific in 1952, and in the Nevada desert in 1953, the new H-bomb used the solid lithium deuteride, making it much more practicable as a military weapon. The bomb was some 6,000 times as powerful as the bomb that destroyed Hiroshima, making it equivalent to 12 million tons of TNT. The explosion was so violent that it overwhelmed the measuring instruments, suggesting that the blast was considerably more powerful than expected.

On 6 May a barrier some experts once considered insurmountable was at last broken by a Briton. Roger Bannister, a 25-year-old medical student, became the first person to run a mile in under four minutes at the university track at Iffley Road, Oxford, during a match between the University and the

Amateur Athletic Association. After the pace had been set in the early laps by Bannister's fellow graduates, Chris Chataway and Chris Brasher, Bannister ran the last lap in 59 seconds to break the tape in 3 minutes 59.4 seconds – 1.9 seconds inside the Swede Gunder Haegg's nine-year-old record and just six-tenths of a second inside the magic four minutes.

* * *

Switzerland may have appeared, at first sight, a peculiar choice for staging the fifth World Cup. However, FIFA's selection was a rational and considered choice. Switzerland had not been greatly affected by the war because of its neutral status. Its economy was sound and the country was equipped with fine stadiums. Being a small country with an excellent transport system meant that travel was made easy for the competing nations. Although the organisation was haphazard and the Swiss police intemperate, there was a goals bonanza, large crowds and a Final result which outstripped the 1950 tournament on the Richter scale of shocks. The tournament in Switzerland had yet again produced another beaten favourite in the final, the most disgraceful scenes in the history of the competition and the most splendid football. By coincidence, Hungary featured in all three.

The format of the 1954 World Cup was heavily criticised as the organising committee devised a new and extraordinary elimination scheme. There were 16 participants, each obliged to play two first round matches. They were divided into four pools of four nations with two top seeds in each group. The top seeds avoided playing each other, facing only the two unseeded teams. The two winners of each pool progressed to the quarter finals, whereupon the competition progressed to a knockout basis. This system resulted in 26 games being played over 19 days. The system was never again repeated, just as the format used in Brazil was also abandoned.

The holders, Uruguay, and Brazil, who had dramatically lost the Final climactic pool decider in 1950, represented South America. Mexico qualified from Central America and South

Korea enjoyed the distinction of being the first Asian nation to compete in the finals. In addition to Switzerland, the hosts, Europe's other participants were Austria, Belgium, Czechoslovakia, England, France, Hungary, Italy, Scotland, Turkey, West Germany and Yugoslavia.

Hungary were the undisputed favourites to win the World Cup. They were holders of the 1952 Olympic title and were 27 games undefeated. The Magyars had given an exhibition of football bordering on perfection at Wembley in 1953, when they became the first foreign nation to win on English soil. They displayed exquisite short passing, precise ball control and rapid movement which, combined with cerebral power, ultimately humiliated England. Their football appeared to be derived from another planet as they outpaced, outmanoeuvred and outwitted their opponents. England looked retarded, not through incompetence, but simply because they had no response to the effervescent genius of players like Czibor, Puskas, Hidegkuti and Kocsis. The sheer artistry, speed, cunning and repertoire of skills enabled the rampant Hungarian forwards to tear the English defence asunder. The eventual margin of victory by 6-3 scarcely did justice to the all-round superiority of Hungary. Any notion that the result was a fluke was rapidly dispelled in May 1954 when the sides met again in Budapest, with Hungary winning 7-1. Their sustained brilliance and inventiveness gave them a seemingly unstoppable momentum, which made the other competing nations look like also-rans.

The seeded nations were Austria, Brazil, England, France, Hungary, Italy, Turkey, and Uruguay, placed in the following pools.

Pool 1: Brazil, France, Mexico, Yugoslavia
Pool 2: Hungary, South Korea, Turkey, West Germany
Pool 3: Austria, Czechoslovakia, Scotland, Uruguay
Pool 4: Belgium, England, Italy, Switzerland

The Pool 1 opening match paired France with Yugoslavia. France had talented half-back players in Penverne, Jonquet, Marcel and the blossoming Raymond Kopa at outside-right, together with Jean Vincent on the left wing. Yugoslavia were a side of considerable potential and had, of course, given Brazil a real fright in Rio de Janeiro in the 1950 World Cup. Ciakowski was again captain and Mitic and Bobek remained menacing inside-forwards. Zebec was a left-winger of great skill. Yugoslavia achieved an excellent 1-0 win in Lausanne with a goal scored by Milutinovic in the first half.

Brazil crushed Mexico 5-0 in Geneva. Goals from Pinga (2), Julinho, Didi and Baltazar completed a rout against the hapless Central Americans who trailed 4-0 at half-time.

France were unimpressive in their next encounter against Mexico. They suffered from a paucity of ideas as they narrowly won with a contentious penalty scored late in the game by Kopa.

One of the most engrossing pool matches took place in the scenic setting of Lausanne's Olympic Stadium, with the Savoy Alps forming a spectacular backdrop. In a pulsating match Yugoslavia initially absorbed pressure from a wave of Brazilian attacks. But their midfield gained the initiative and they took the lead just before half-time. Vukas and Mitic created an opening for Zebec to score. Brazil controlled the game thereafter and justly equalised with a powerful strike from Didi. Both sides languished in extra time, thus ensuring qualification at the expense of France.

Hungary reinforced their immense stature with a resounding 9-0 victory over South Korea in their opening Pool 2 match in Zurich. Goals from Kocsis (3), Palotas (2), Puskas (2), Czibor and Lantos completed a rout.

West Germany easily defeated the seeded Turks in Berne. Although Turkey enjoyed parity at half-time, goals from Klodt, Morlock, O. Walter and Schafer ensured a comfortable 4-1 victory.

Facing Hungary in their next match, Sepp Herberger, the West German manager, deployed an extraordinary tactical manoeuvre. He deliberately fielded an understrength team, thus virtually throwing the Hungarian match in the firm belief that his side would win a play-off against Turkey and therefore embark on an easier route to the final. Hungary produced another devastating display of artistry as they overran West Germany 8-3. Goals from Kocsis (4), Hidegkuti (2), Toth and Puskas meant Hungary had totalled 17 in their first two games. But the match marked a watershed in the tournament as Ferenc Puskas prematurely left the field, the victim of a savage kick by Werner Liebrich. Puskas later vowed that the kick, which resulted in a badly injured ankle, was deliberate.

In the final pool match, Turkey beat South Korea in Geneva 7-0, thus ensuring a play-off against West Germany. West Germany introduced seven changes and duly defeated Turkey 7-2 in Zurich, with Morlock scoring three goals and Schafer two.

Scotland, having finished second again to England in the British Championship, which doubled as a World Cup qualifying group, decided to compete. They were an impoverished and very limited side. However, in their opening game against Austria they performed tenaciously, rather unluckily losing to a goal scored by Probst in the first half.

Uruguay defended their title unimpressively on a muddy pitch in Berne against Czechoslovakia. Miguez finally broke the deadlock after 70 minutes and Schiaffino added a second with a powerful free kick.

Scotland's capacity for self-destruction could scarcely have been surpassed in their next game. Andy Beattie, the manager, rowed with the Scottish Football Association on the eve of their match with Uruguay. Beattie promptly resigned. The choice of Scotland's kit could not have been more inappropriate. Despite the 100-degree heat in Basle, the Scots wore thick woolly jerseys with long sleeves. According to wing-half Tommy Docherty, 'You'd have thought we were going on an expedition to the Antarctic.'

Many Scotland supporters would not have been averse to such a fate for their players, following a 7-0 humiliation in what was the first ever 'live' World Cup tie to feature their team.

Austria swept to a quarter final place, along with Uruguay,

following a 5-0 win over Czechoslovakia in Zurich. Probst (3) and Stojaspal (2) were the scorers.

England had scarcely eradicated an ignominious 7-1 defeat by Hungary from their mind when they took the field against Belgium in a Pool 4 match. Pol Anoul scored for Belgium after only five minutes. But England had established a lead by half-time with goals from Billy Wright and a forceful header by Nat Lofthouse. When Broadis scored a third, England appeared to be striding towards a comfortable victory. But their fragile defence was again breached by Anoul and Coppens. With the score 3-3 at full-time, the rules dictated that extra time was required. Lofthouse quickly restored England's lead but Dickinson of Portsmouth scored an own-goal as the match ended 4-4.

In Lausanne, Switzerland and Italy became embroiled in a crude physical encounter with Viana, the Brazilian referee, failing to control the indiscipline. Galli and Boniperti were subjected to over-zealous tackling in the first half. Ballaman and Boniperti each scored before the interval to give a 1-1 scoreline. Italy indulged in retribution in the second half, with Fatton being hit in the stomach and Fluckiger in the back. With only twelve minutes remaining, Giacomazzi failed to intercept a pass by Fatton which led to Hugi, the Swiss centre-forward, scoring the winner.

A largely revamped England side faced the hosts, Switzerland, in a torrid heat in Berne. Billy Wright moved to centre-half where he gave an imperious performance. Neither Matthews nor Lofthouse were fit and were replaced by Dennis Wilshaw and Jimmy Mullen his Wolverhampton Wanderers teammate. Tommy Taylor of Manchester United led the attack. The veteran Mullen scored shortly before half-time and Wilshaw added a second midway through the second half to secure a quarter final place.

Italy introduced three changes for their next match against Belgium in Lugano. They easily won 4-1 with goals from Frignani, Galli, Pandolfini and Lorenzi, thus ensuring a play-off with Switzerland for the remaining quarter-final place.

There was reported to be deep dissent within the Italian camp prior to the match in Basle. The manager, Czeizler, omitted Cappello and Galli from his side and eccentrically decided to play Segato, the left-half, in the inside left position. Perhaps not surprisingly, Italy lost heavily 4-1 to goals from Hugi (2), Ballaman and Fatton.

The quarter finals consisted of the following ties:

Austria v Switzerland
Uruguay v England
West Germany v Yugoslavia
Hungary v Brazil

Austria and Switzerland produced a truly remarkable match in Lausanne which was characterised by a goals fiesta. The first half yielded no fewer than nine as the Swiss swept into a 3-0 lead within 20 minutes. But the Austrians countered with an astonishing three goals in three minutes and five in seven minutes, establishing a 5-4 half-time lead which also featured a missed penalty. Sadly, the highly competent Swiss captain, Roger Bocquet, was largely responsible for the goal leakage. He had been suffering from a tumour and had played against medical advice, ignorant of his prognosis. Happily he survived, but his trance-like performance severely disadvantaged his team-mates. In the second half, a by now rampant Austria scored a sixth goal by Wagner. Hanappi of Austria deflected Hugi's shot past his own goalkeeper to give Switzerland a glimmer of hope, but Probst scored a marvellous individualist goal to bring a fitting climax to one of the greatest ever World Cup ties.

Uruguay and England also produced an excellent match in Basle. Uruguay were clearly endowed with far more naturally gifted players, but England worked assiduously and were obdurate in defence. In attack, Stanley Matthews was quite outstanding. But it was Uruguay who opened the scoring after only five minutes with a goal orchestrated by the exquisite skills of Schiaffino, who sold a dummy to McGarry and unleashed Borges. Borges strode away before crossing a diagonal ball to Abbadie and then received a return pass to score. England soon equalised with an intricate move culminating in a goal from Lofthouse. Only two minutes of the first half remained and England had created several opportunities when Gil Merrick, the goalkeeper, misjudged a long shot by Varela which enabled Uruguay to lead at the interval. Just after the resumption, Varela was allowed to drop kick a free kick and Schiaffino penetrated a bemused defence to score. England's pugnacious response led to Tom Finney scoring after 67 minutes to reduce the deficit. Matthews struck the post and placed Maspoli under further pressure. However, with 13 minutes left, Miguez passed to Ambrois, whose shot should have been saved by Merrick. Nevertheless, in losing 4-2, England had given a brave, battling performance which provided a stark contrast to the woeful capitulation of the Scots.

In Geneva, West Germany surprisingly defeated Yugoslavia 2-0. Although Yugoslavia had superior skill, they were overcome by West Germany's qualities of strength, stamina, commitment and willpower. Horvat, the Yugoslavian centre-forward, had the misfortune to head a ball in the direction of Beara, the goalkeeper, who had advanced off his line. The own goal had arrived after only ten minutes. West Germany ensured victory with a dubious goal by Rahn, who was almost certainly offside as he shot past the injured Beara with only four minutes remaining.

The notorious and shameful match between Hungary and Brazil, which became known as 'The Battle of Berne', remains unsurpassed in terms of psychopathic violence, disorder and anarchy. The darkest chapter in World Cup history became acrimonious as early as the third minute. Hidegkuti scored for Hungary, was mobbed by Brazilians, and had his shorts ripped off. Hungary gave no indication of being handicapped by the absence of Puskas as Kocsis scored a second goal. At this stage, Hungary both out-thought and outfought Brazil. The tackles became increasingly brutal and retaliation ever swifter. After 17 minutes a move between Didi and Indio was abruptly ended when Buzanszky felled Indio. Santos scored from the penalty spot and Hungary led 2-1 at the interval. The second half became even uglier, with the fouls being interrupted by occasional football.

Pinheiro gave away a penalty by handling Czibor's pass to Kocsis. Lantos scored from the spot-kick. Julinho then reduced the deficit with a sinuous run and forceful shot. With 15 minutes remaining, Santos and Bozsik, a Hungarian Member of Parliament, were sent off for fighting, at which point the Brazilian trainer ran on to protest and was ushered away by the Swiss police. In the final minutes Czibor streaked down the right in a lightning raid and crossed for Kocsis to head past Castilho, thus completing a 4-2 victory. In the dying seconds Brazil's Humberto was ordered off following a kick at Lorant. His departure was delayed as he melodramatically fell to his knees in front of the referee, Arthur Ellis, and begged to be allowed to stay. He finally removed himself, weeping on his way to the dressing-room, where he later joined his dejected colleagues. But even worse violence ensued in the aftermath of the match. A soda water syphon crashed into the midst of the Hungarian players rejoicing at their victory. An electric bulb was smashed and more bottles hurtled into the room as the players lay on the floor in darkness. Brazilian bodies flung themselves on the Hungarian players who were caught completely off guard, confused and bewildered. Toth was knocked unconscious and Sebes had his cheek cut open.

The semi-finals paired Austria with West Germany in Basle, and Hungary with Uruguay in Lausanne.

Austria were strongly expected to triumph over their neighbours, especially as they were considered to have superior technique and skill. Austria decided to replace their goalkeeper, Schmied, with the world renowned Walter Zeman, who had been dropped through loss of form. Unfortunately, Zeman had a wretched game and totally undermined the confidence of his defence. He erred on numerous occasions and was cruelly exposed for his positional ineptitude. West Germany displayed a degree of ruthlessness with incisive finishing which eventually overwhelmed the Austrians. Only a goal by Schafer separated the sides at the interval. Shortly after half-time a corner by Walter was headed in by Morlock. Probst momentarily gave Austria hope by scoring after Turek uncharacteristically dropped the ball. Fritz Walter scored two further goals from the penalty spot and Ottmar Walter headed two as Austria succumbed to a 6-1 thrashing.

In the other semi-final at Lausanne, played in torrential rain, Hungary and Uruguay produced an absolutely classic match. An anticipated bloodbath in the wake of 'The Battle of Berne' did not materialise and the ring of coal-scuttle helmeted soldiers surrounding the pitch proved unnecessary. The game lacked a key player in each side with the irrepressible Puskas and highly influential Varela both injured. After 13 minutes Hungary took the lead. Kocsis headed a pass by Hidegkuti to Czibor and the left-winger drove the ball past Maspoli. Just after the interval, Hungary doubled their lead when Buzanszky intercepted a clearance by Carballo and unleashed Budai and Bozsik. Budai crossed for Hidegkuti to score with a spectacular header. Uruguay staged a remarkable fight-back when all seemed lost. With only 15 minutes remaining, Schiaffino passed to Hohberg, who beat Grosics. Only three minutes from the end, the potent combination of Schiaffino and Hohberg climaxed in a second goal for Hohberg and a dramatic equaliser. The match entered extra time and Hohberg came desperately close to a third goal, striking the post from yet another pass by Schiaffino. A headed goal by Kocsis in the second period of extra time occurred with Andrade of Uruguay receiving treatment off the field.

Seven minutes from the end of the game, and with darkness descending, Kocsis scored again with a memorable header. Hungary thus won 4-2, with their manager, Gustav Sebes, claiming, 'We beat the best team we have ever met.' Uruguay had suffered their first ever defeat in the World Cup.

Austria beat Uruguay 3-1 in the third place match which Uruguay approached with insouciance.

Very few people would have dared to anticipate a result

other than a Hungarian victory, as the final took place in the Wankdorf Stadium in Berne on 4 July.

Hungary's manager, Gustav Sebes, gambled on recalling Puskas, who was declared fit after a morning test.

There was persistent rain on the Sunday, which drenched the players and a considerable number of the 60,000 spectators, approximately 20,000 of whom were vociferous Germans.

Hungary started at lightning pace and rampaged their way through the German defence. In the sixth minute Bozsik sent Kocsis through with a glorious pass. Kocsis changed direction, but the ball struck a German defender before running loose to Puskas. Puskas pounced, and his left-foot shot to the far corner put Hungary ahead. Within two minutes another thrust by the Hungarian forwards placed Kohlmeyer under pressure. His badly judged back-pass bemused Turek in goal and Czibor seized upon the chance to give his side a two-goal lead.

Perhaps Hungary were lulled into a false sense of security or simply took too much for granted. But with only 18 minutes played, West Germany, with a display of strength and drive, had drawn level. Although not capable of the sophisticated artistry of the Magyars, their fast, direct and intelligent football hauled them back from a seemingly hopeless position. After only ten minutes Morlock stuck out his right foot to divert a cross from Fritz Walter past Grosics. Eight minutes later, Rahn half-volleyed a corner kick, which was missed by Grosics, to level the match.

Turek, the West German goalkeeper, made a series of highly improbable saves which effectively turned the game. Hidegkuti's close volley and Kocsis's header from no more than six yards out were somehow stopped. Hidegkuti also hit the foot of a post. Twice in the second half Puskas had streaked through the defence, only for Turek to prevent seemingly certain goals. When Turek was finally beaten, Kohlmeyer was present to kick Toth's shot off the line, following a quite brilliant movement involving the entire Hungarian forward line. Next, Kocsis headed Czibor's centre against the German crossbar.

With only 12 minutes remaining, Czibor broke away but Turek saved his shot, hurting himself in the process. Only five minutes remained when Bozsik made a critical error. He lost possession to the challenging Schafer and, as Fritz Walter's cross was headed out, the ball ran loose to Rahn. He cleverly advanced and shot left-footed, low, past a helpless Grosics, from fifteen yards. Two minutes later Puskas hit home Toth's diagonal cross but was adjudged to be marginally offside by Mr Griffiths, the Welsh linesman.

Hungary had one final effort in the last 30 seconds, but Turek dived full length to keep a powerful shot from Czibor out of his net.

It was all over. The cup was presented and the band played 'Deutschland Uber Alles'. West Germany's victory over the fabled Hungarians ranks as the biggest World Cup Final upset in the history of the tournament.

After the World Cup many of the German players mysteriously entered rest homes, for no known reason, claiming physical problems. It has been widely speculated that drugs may have been the cause, but there was never conclusive proof.

In October 1956 there was an uprising in Hungary and the 'Malenkov new course' of economic decentralisation and de-collectivisation was pursued. The people of the capital rose against the Soviet regime, which had replaced the reforming Imre Nagy as Premier. In November Soviet tanks appeared on the streets of Budapest to put down the rising by force. All the great Hungarian players responded by leaving the country. Puskas joined Real Madrid, Kocsis and Czibor went to Barcelona and Hidegkuti to Germany.

Results: Switzerland 1954

Pool 1

Yugoslavia	1	France	0
Brazil	5	Mexico	0
France	3	Mexico	2
Brazil	1	Yugoslavia	1*

*After extra time, 1–1 at 90 minutes

					Goals		
	P	W	D	L	F	A	Pts
Brazil	2	1	1	0	6	1	3
Yugoslavia	2	1	1	0	2	1	3
France	2	1	0	1	3	3	2
Mexico	2	0	0	2	2	8	0

Pool 2

Hungary	9	South Korea	0
West Germany	4	Turkey	1
Hungary	8	West Germany	3
Turkey	7	South Korea	0

					Goals		
	P	W	D	L	F	A	Pts
Hungary	2	2	0	0	17	3	4
West Germany	2	1	0	1	7	9	2
Turkey	2	1	0	1	8	4	2
South Korea	2	0	0	2	0	16	0

Play off: West Germany 7 Turkey 2

Pool 3

Austria	1	Scotland	0
Uruguay	2	Czechoslovakia	0
Austria	5	Czechoslovakia	0
Uruguay	7	Scotland	0

	P	W	D	L	Goals F	A	Pts
Uruguay	2	2	0	0	9	0	4
Austria	2	2	0	0	6	0	4
Czechoslovakia	2	0	0	2	0	7	0
Scotland	2	0	0	2	0	8	0

Pool 4

England	4	Belgium	4*
Switzerland	2	Italy	1
England	2	Switzerland	0
Italy	4	Belgium	1

*After extra time, 3-3 at 90 minutes

	P	W	D	L	Goals F	A	Pts
England	2	1	1	0	6	4	3
Italy	2	1	0	1	5	3	2
Switzerland	2	1	0	1	2	3	2
Belgium	2	0	1	1	5	8	1

Play-off: Switzerland 4 Italy 1

Quarter-finals

Austria	7	Switzerland	5
Uruguay	4	England	2
West Germany	2	Yugoslavia	0
Hungary	4	Brazil	2

Semi-finals

West Germany	6	Austria	1
Hungary	4	Uruguay	2*

*After extra time, 2-2 at 90 minutes

Third Place Match

Austria	3	Uruguay	1

Final

West Germany   3   Hungary   2

West Germany: Turek, Posipal, Kohlmeyer, Eckel, Liebrich, Mai, Rahn, Morlock, Walter O, Walter F, Schafer

Hungary: Grosics, Buzanszky, Lantos, Bozsik, Lorant, Zakarias, Czibor, Kocsis, Hidegkuti, Puskas, Toth, J.

Scorers: Morlock, Rahn (2) for West Germany
            Puskas, Czibor for Hungary.

1958

On 6th February the whole city of Manchester was in mourning. Twenty-three people, including eight Manchester United players, were killed in a plane crash on the snow-covered Munich runway. The accident happened as the team began the last leg of their homeward trip from Belgrade after qualifying for the European Cup semi-finals. The BEA Ambassador struck a building just beyond the perimeter of the airport as it made a third attempt to take off. The plane was reduced to a tangled heap of wreckage as rescue workers fought valiantly in driving snow. Among those who perished were England regulars Roger Byrne, Tommy Taylor and Duncan Edwards, only 21, who fought desperately for his life for three weeks. When he eventually died, England lost the outstanding player of his time. The Manchester United manager, Matt Busby, after whom the team had been popularly known as the 'Busby Babes', was also seriously injured in the disaster.

A new pressure group, the Campaign for Nuclear Disarmament, more popularly known as the 'Ban the Bomb' movement, was set up. It has been considered as the founding father of all later protest movements. It was launched by philosopher and veteran peace campaigner Bertrand Russell and Canon Collins of St Paul's Cathedral.

One of the CND's first acts was to organise a protest march from London to the Atomic Weapons Research Establishment at Aldermaston in Berkshire. A crowd of around 4,000 people gathered to hear speeches by Canon Collins and other leaders before a 'hard core' of about 600 walked the 50 miles to Aldermaston.

The Middle East became extremely volatile following a chain of events which saw the monarchy in Iraq bloodily overthrown, British paratroops landing in Jordan, United States marines wading ashore at Beirut and the Soviet Union impotently rattling her sabre at the United Nations.

The crisis started with a coup by a group of young Iraqi army officers inspired by Colonel Nasser of Egypt, which destroyed the pro-Western regime of King Feisal of Iraq. The 23-year-old king was murdered, along with his powerful uncle, Crown Prince Abdulillah and General Nuri el-Said, the Prime Minister, who was kicked to death by the Baghdad mob.

The coup immediately put pressure on Jordan, Iraq's partner in the Arab Union, and on Lebanon, where President Chamoun was fighting rebels funded and armed by Nasser. Frightened by the events in Iraq, President Chamoun demanded western aid very quickly.

President Eisenhower responded to the pro-Western Lebanese President Chamoun's request by sending some 3,500 troops to the Lebanon. The arrival of the Marines was condemned by the Soviet Union and for a time the situation threatened to escalate into full-scale war.

*   *   *

Sweden was chosen to host the sixth World Cup, which was the most truly representative series staged to date. Forty-six of the 53 original entries played in 89 qualifying games watched by four million spectators. For the first time, no team other than the host nation and holders had a bye to the finals. FIFA decided that the format would comprise of four groups, each with four national teams from which two would advance with everyone playing against each other. In the event of two countries tying for second place on points, goal difference was disregarded and play-offs were used as deciders. In the next round, after straightforward play-off, the winners would proceed to the semi-finals.

Only Sweden, the hosts, and West Germany, the fortunate victors of 1954, had not fought through two years of qualifying rounds. Fourteen other countries participated in the finals.

Argentina, Brazil and Paraguay represented South America. Paraguay eliminated Uruguay, the winners in 1930 and 1950, with an astonishing 5-0 win in Asunción. Mexico, in dealing convincingly with Canada and the United States, again represented North and Central America. Europe's representatives were Austria, Czechoslovakia, England, France, Hungary, Northern Ireland, Scotland, USSR and Yugoslavia.

From the Asia/Africa section, like the conjurer's rabbit, emerged Wales. Withdrawals, caused largely by the inflamed political situation in the Middle East, led to the exclusion of Egypt and Sudan, while Indonesia was also engaged in matters more vital than football. Israel was left with no opponent. As World Cup regulations insisted that no country shall reach the finals, except the host and holder, without defeating somebody, eight nations who had finished second in their groups drew for the right to have a second opportunity. Wales were the fortunate team. They had no difficulty in defeating Israel twice by 2-0, first in Tel Aviv and later in Cardiff.

Of the 27 European countries, the two major powers who fell in the preliminary stages were Italy and Spain. Italy, who had appeared in the finals of five previous competitions, lost their proud record after a spiritless display against Northern Ireland in Belfast, in which they lost 2-1. Real Madrid were indisputably the leading club side in Europe in 1956 and in 1957, but Spain were defeated in Glasgow as Scotland unexpectedly qualified, thus ensuring all the Home Countries participated in the finals for the first time.

The countries were grouped as follows:

Group 1: Argentina, Czechoslovakia, Northern Ireland, West Germany
Group 2: France, Paraguay, Scotland, Yugoslavia
Group 3: Hungary, Mexico, Sweden, Wales
Group 4: Austria, Brazil, England, USSR

West Germany defended their title in Group 1 against Argentina in Malmo. Argentina were holders of the 1957 South American title. Significantly, three of their triumphant players, Maschio, Sivori and Angelillo, had been usurped by wealthy Italian clubs and were missing. Argentina led after only two minutes when the diminutive right-winger Corbatta scored. Rahn equalised for West Germany, who had been unimpressive since winning the World Cup, with a well-struck shot. Before half-time, Uwe Seeler had put West Germany ahead. Ten minutes from time Rahn scored a third, but the win was tarnished by a serious injury to Fritz Walter following a brutal foul by Rossi.

Northern Ireland opened their World Cup campaign against Czechoslovakia in Halmstad. Portsmouth's Derek Dougan was a surprise debut choice at centre-forward. A headed goal by Cush from a centre by McParland after 21 minutes decided the fate of the match. Northern Ireland had to survive relentless Czech attacks in the last 20 minutes.

Czechoslovakia were far more impressive in their next match against West Germany in Halsingborg. They led 2-0 at half-time with goals by Dvorak (penalty) and Zikan. Schafer reduced the deficit after an hour with a highly controversial goal. He charged the Czech goalkeeper, Dolejsi, in possession of the ball, over his line. The goal was permitted. Rahn then equalised after 71 minutes. The Czechs, denying forcibly that the ball ever crossed the line, appealed to FIFA not to allow Arthur Ellis, the English referee, to control the final match against Argentina.

Northern Ireland started brightly against their next opponents, Argentina, in Halmstad. McParland headed them into a lead with only three minutes played after Bingham and Blanchflower had confused Argentina's defence with a short corner. Argentina bemused Northern Ireland thereafter with swift, skilful forwards easily outmanoeuvring ill-prepared defenders. Corbatta equalised with a penalty two minutes from the interval. Further goals from Menendez and Avio led to a comfortable 3-1 victory.

Northern Ireland excelled against West Germany, together with their 10,000 supporters, in Malmo and all but mastered the Germans. Northern Ireland again scored first through McParland. In initiating the move from midfield, Casey was hurt. Although he only departed from the field for two minutes, West Germany had equalised through the outstanding Rahn. McParland scored a second goal after 59 minutes following a corner by Cush. Seeler struck a thunderous equaliser with a first-time shot from Schafer's pass with barely ten minutes left.

Meanwhile, at Halsingborg, Czechoslovakia's appeal was not upheld and Ellis was in control of their next match against Argentina. He awarded a penalty to the South Americans, taken successfully by Corbatta. But by this time Czechoslovakia were already 3-0 up and scored a further three in a 6-1 rout. Argentinian players had demanded an increase in pay shortly before they left for Europe and experienced an extremely hostile reception on their return to Buenos Aires, when they were pelted with rubbish.

Northern Ireland and Czechoslovakia had to play off for a place in the quarter-finals. Harry Gregg, the Northern Ireland goalkeeper, was injured and replaced by Uprichard. Scott was introduced in place of the injured centre-forward Casey. Czechoslovakia began the match as 4-1 on favourites and when Zikan headed his side ahead after 19 minutes the odds appeared to be justified. McParland equalised only seconds before half-time, meeting a loose ball after three shots by Cush had rebounded quickly from the goalkeeper. When extra time began, the Irish were reduced to only nine fit men. Uprichard, in goal, first twisted an ankle and then broke a bone in his left hand. Peacock was hobbling painfully and had to be sent upfield with only ten minutes of full-time remaining. In an incident-packed extra time, McParland scored the winning goal in the 99th minute. Blanchflower curved a free kick over the Czech defence which was met with a forceful volley. Four minutes later, Bubernik was sent off for allegedly spitting at the referee. Northern Ireland, against all expectations, had boldly secured a place in the quarter-finals. They joined West Germany, the holders, who emerged as victors of Group 1.

Scotland's World Cup quest was seriously undermined long before the tournament commenced. Matt Busby, Manchester United's outstanding manager, had been invited by the Scottish FA to take charge of his country's side only a short time before he was seriously hurt at Munich. He was never able to begin seriously the work which he regarded as a great honour.

Scotland again displayed disunity, with friction between officials and players. At Vasteras, against Yugoslavia, they gained their first ever point in the World Cup finals. Petakovic, the right-winger, scored early in the game. Murray headed a second half equaliser. Yugoslavia peppered the Scotland goal during an onslaught which Scotland narrowly survived. Bobby Collins of Celtic gave an awe-inspiring performance and emerged as the outstanding talent on the field.

Meanwhile, France overwhelmed Paraguay in Norrkoping, 7-3. The game was level at 2-2 at half-time. However, France scored a remarkable five goals during a second-half rampage. Juste Fontaine played at inside-right and scored three times. He was complemented by Raymond Kopa, named as centre-forward, but lying deep and providing penetrating, imaginative passes. The pair became known as 'le tandem terrible'. Mageregger, making wretched errors in goal, largely contributed to the landslide defeat.

Scotland had to omit Hewie, Murray and Imlach, all of whom were injured, in their next match against Paraguay in Norrkoping. The selectors made further radical changes before the kick-off. An asymmetrical side lost 3-2 to the bright, attacking play of the South Americans, who were overly physical in defence.

France, rather surprisingly, lost their next encounter, 3-2 to Yugoslavia in Vasteras. Juste Fontaine, in prolific striking form, scored a further two goals. Veselinovic also scored twice, his second proving to be the winning goal three minutes from time. At this stage France were pursuing a third goal, but

Yugoslavia counter-attacked and a mistake by Marche, the French left-back, led to the defeat.

Scotland's final match against France in Orebro afforded them a modicum of respectability despite narrowly losing to a vastly superior side. Bill Brown made his debut in goal and produced a memorable display. The new captain, Bobby Evans, was immense and Dave McKay of Hearts added much needed power to the impotent forward line. Once again Juste Fontaine scored and unluckily struck the crossbar on two further occasions. Kopa also scored. Baird replied for Scotland and Hewie missed a penalty kick But overall, Scotland performed almost as lamentably as they had done in Switzerland.

Paraguay maintained their record of scoring three goals a game in their final group match against Yugoslavia in Eskilstuna. Aguero, Parodi and Romero each scored, aided by uncharacteristic goalkeeping errors by Beara. Yugoslavia ensured qualification, along with France, with goals by Ognjanovic, Veselinovic and Rajkov which contributed to a 3-3 draw.

Sweden kicked off the tournament at the Solna stadium in Stockholm against a listless Mexico. Sweden were managed by the English-born George Raynor. He packed the team with ageing exiles brought back from Italy. Simonsson, a young, talented centre-forward, scored twice and the veteran Liedholm converted a penalty, thus completing a comfortable 3-0 victory.

Hungary's decline to an anaemic shadow of the 1954 World Cup side was perhaps the saddest feature of the tournament. Puskas, Kocsis and Czibor had not returned to their country after the 1956 uprising. Grosics, Bozsik and Hidegkuti were by now veterans. The long-standing legend of the 'Magical Magyars' was finally destroyed in Sweden.

At Sandviken, a venue not far short of the Arctic Circle, Hungary led after only four minutes against Wales. A Bozsik shot deceived Kelsey in goal. John Charles was singled out for maltreatment. But after Wales had withstood a veritable battering in the opening 20 minutes, Charles delivered retribution with a leaping header shortly before the interval, to secure a 1-1 draw. The great Hidegkuti, a pure soccer genius, was a poignant sight, reduced to complete anonymity against a courageous but extremely limited Welsh team.

Wales entered their next match against Mexico brimful of confidence. Ivor Allchurch, from a Webster corner, gave Wales a 32nd-minute lead. They held on to that advantage with only 90 seconds remaining. The Mexican right-winger, Jaime Belmonte, launched himself headlong to equalise. This was the first occasion since Mexico had entered the competition in 1930 in which they had escaped defeat in the finals.

Sweden laboured to an unimpressive 2-1 victory against Hungary in their second game. Kurre Hamrin scored both Swedish goals with Lajos Tichy of Hungary reducing the deficit with 14 minutes remaining. He was rapidly gaining a reputation for a fearsome right-foot shot.

Sweden met Wales in their final match of the preliminary group. Wales had to win in order to qualify or draw to enforce a play-off. Sweden had already qualified and rested five of their first team players. Wales endured 90 nerve-wracking minutes and were ludicrously lucky to survive a 0-0 draw. Skoglund of Sweden had the Welsh goal at his mercy on no fewer than four occasions during the second half. Four times he shot wide. Wales worked extremely hard and Jack Kelsey in goal performed heroically.

Against Mexico in Stockholm, Hungary finally came to life and Lajos Tichy enhanced his burgeoning reputation with two excellent goals. Sandor also scored and a Gonzalez own goal completed a 4-0 victory and a right to play off against Wales.

Wales met Hungary in Stockholm on 17th June. The backdrop to the game could scarcely have been more charged with tension, for only 24 hours earlier Imre Nagy, the former Prime Minister and leader of the Hungarian uprising, had been executed following a secret trial. Hungarians carrying banners draped in black demonstrated their revulsion at Communist ruthlessness. Their slow, relentless chants echoed round an almost deserted Solna Stadium.

Hungary opened the scoring when Budai burst away on his own and whipped across a centre for Lajos Tichy to score, yet again, with an unstoppable shot. Seven minutes into the second half, John Charles delivered a perfect centre for Allchurch to equalise as he smashed a glorious volley past Grosics. Sixteen minutes from time Medwin embarked on a spectacular solo run to score the winning goal. Hungary disgraced themselves six minutes from time when Sipos aimed a brutal kick at Hewitt, who was carried off on a stretcher whilst Sipos was sent off. Hungary stalked out of the stadium. From being a soccer master race they had descended to an ignoble defeat in front of only 2,823 spectators, against a Welsh side endowed with honest endeavour but little skill.

England performed dismally in their opening Group 4 match against the Soviet Union in Gothenburg. The right-winger A. Ivanov shot low and fiercely into the English goalmouth in the 14th minute. McDonald, in goal, parried the shot to the captain, Simonian, who drove in a simple goal. A. Ivanov scored a second after the interval, receiving a crossfield pass from Tsarev. Midway through the second half, England unexpectedly scored following their first genuine attack when Kevan headed beyond Yashin. With less than five minutes remaining, Haynes, in pursuit of a pass, was upended in the penalty area. The Hungarian referee, Zsolt, immediately awarded a penalty despite the fevered protestations of Lev Yashin in goal. Finney coolly equalised.

The Brazil FA, in their bid to win the 1958 competition, sent a psychiatrist to Sweden to help in the adjustment of the players' temperaments. He picked rumba records, which kept the team happy in their training camp. He also advised the selectors which of the players were the fittest, mentally, to turn out in each game. Danny Blanchflower, Northern Ireland's captain, writing in the *Observer*, said, 'anybody who consults a psychiatrist ought to have his head examined'.

Brazil met Austria on the opening day in the small town of Uddevalla. Pele was missing with a knee injury. Only months before the tournament, Edson Arantes do Nascimento had been named in the Brazilian squad. He was then no more than an 17-year-old prodigy, known as Pele, playing with the Santos club side, but he was soon to become an amazing talent who matured into arguably the finest player in soccer history. Mazzola (2) and Santos completed an easy 3-0 victory against a side who, like Hungary, had declined alarmingly.

England faced Brazil in Gothenburg with considerable apprehension. However, their meticulous preparation, based on their observations of Brazil's performance against Austria, led to the adoption of stifling tactics aimed at suppressing the clever South American forwards. England deployed additional cover in defence, with Howe and Banks successfully bolstering a defensive plan which earned a goalless draw. McDonald in goal produced a couple of excellent saves.

Austria gave the Soviet Union a serious test in Boras. Although they trailed to a goal by Illyin, they were dominating the match and were awarded a penalty after 55 minutes. Ernst Happel was their reliable penalty taker but he had been dropped. Johann Buzek, the centre-forward, shot straight at Yashin. Inevitably, seven minutes later the Soviet Union counter-attacked and scored a second through the inside-right, V. Ivanov.

Brazil's manager, Vicente Feola, had been heavily criticised by his own press for the omission of Garrincha. A deputation of Brazilian players, led by Santos, exhorted his inclusion. Feola relented and was rewarded with a breathtaking performance. Twice in the first two minutes Garrincha raced past Kuznetsov, a highly competent left-back. Each time he finished with a cracking shot which struck the post with Yashin helpless. Vava gave Brazil the lead after just three minutes, following a clever pass by Didi. Brazil played exhibition football but failed to impose their superiority until 13 minutes from time, when Vava scored a second goal receiving a pass from Pele. Over-exuberant celebrations resulted in Vava sustaining an injury. He lay prone for five minutes before receiving attention.

England met Austria in the tiny town of Boras in their third group match. After 15 minutes of preliminary sparring, Austria scored their first goal of the tournament. From a corner kick, Buzek's shot rebounded out of the penalty area and was met by Koller 25 yards from goal. He hit a stunning shot which found an unimpaired route to goal, despite a crowded goalmouth. Austria played surprisingly precise and intricate football. However, England began to create chances and shortly after the interval A'Court shot venomously. Szanwald, in the Austrian goal, could only palm the ball down in the direction of Haynes, who scored easily. Austria re-established the lead after 72 minutes with an extraordinary goal by Korner. He failed to strike the ball cleanly but McDonald, in anticipating a full-blown shot, dived prematurely. The ball eluded him, struck the post and rolled disconcertingly into the net. Within two minutes Kevan received a pass from Haynes and shot past Szanwald. Robson scored again for England but the goal was disallowed for a handling offence. The result meant that England had to play off against the Soviet Union.

Forty-eight hours later, two tired sides produced a drab, weary affair at the Ullevi Stadium in Gothenburg. England eventually emerged from their torpor and contrived to miss a number of good opportunities before half-time. In a six-minute spell after the interval, Brabrook sprinted through twice and each time unluckily struck the inside of a post. A swift counter-attack by the Soviet Union determined the fate of the match. Simonian pushed the ball to Illyin, who was unmarked on the edge of England's penalty area. As McDonald in goal advanced, Illyin shot low to the goalkeeper's right. The ball came back off the post and rolled into the other side of the net. England bombarded their opponents in the dying minutes and Yashin made a magnificent save from a shot by Kevan. It was ironic that England lost the one match they deserved to win.

The quarter-finals produced the following ties:

West Germany v Yugoslavia
France v Northern Ireland
Sweden v USSR
Brazil v Wales

Yugoslavia lost by the only goal of a hard-fought match in Malmo. Beara, their fine goalkeeper, and Sekularac, the wandering, delightful inside-left, were both absent. West Germany adopted spoiling tactics and were penalised on no fewer than 22 occasions by the Swiss referee, Wyssling. The German goal was again scored by outside-right Rahn, who raced away from Crnkovic and beat an unconvincing Krivokuca, deputising for Beara. West Germany were extremely fortunate to survive a strong penalty claim as Erhardt felled Milutinovic with nine minutes left.

Northern Ireland travelled from Malmo to Norrkoping with a squad depleted by injuries as players struggled to regain fitness for the match with France. Harry Gregg in goal, and Casey, were casualties who played nevertheless. Casey's leg wound reopened during the match. Northern Ireland held out for 43 minutes, but when Wiesnieski scored they were overrun. France's mobile, darting forwards toyed with an overworked and exhausted defence. Fontaine, Kopa and Piantoni were an electrifying trio. Fontaine (2) and Piantoni goals after the interval completed a 4-0 victory. Harry Gregg had travelled to Sweden by boat after surviving the Munich air disaster. He suddenly decided to depart by the quickest mode of transport from Bonn airport. Gregg had shown on the tour how completely he had regained his nerve. Now he did it in the air, too.

The Sweden versus Soviet Union confrontation at Stockholm was a close affair. Igor Netto, the Soviet captain, hurt against England, was unable to play. Hamrin opened the scoring for Sweden with a header four minutes from half-time. The tie was placed beyond the Soviet Union's reach two minutes from the end when Simonsson scored a second goal created by Hamrin.

Wales performed quite magnificently in Gothenburg and provided perhaps the most exacting test for Brazil on their path to the final. Unfortunately, John Charles was unable to play, bruised and battered in his encounters with robust Hungarian defenders. But Wales fought courageously, defending superbly against an increasingly desperate Brazilian attack. Mel Hopkins policed Garrincha and Dave Bowen was an inspirational captain. Jack Kelsey, in goal, gave another outstanding performance. He was eventually beaten by a Pele goal after 73 minutes. Kelsey appeared untroubled by the shot until it cruelly deflected past him off the foot of Williams. Wales had given a highly creditable performance and unquestionably emerged as the highest achievers of the four Home Countries.

The semi-finals paired Sweden against West Germany in Gothenburg and Brazil against France in Stockholm.

In Gothenburg the fervour of the crowd was whipped up to the highest pitch by bands of organised cheerleaders, allowed on the field before the match. This practice was condemned by FIFA, who banned it for the Final.

West Germany were under almost constant siege during the first half, in which a superior Swedish side were extravagantly wasteful in squandering numerous opportunities. West Germany scored first in the 25th minute when Schafer met a pass from Uwe Seeler and volleyed a magnificent goal. Skoglund equalised after 33 minutes following a move initiated by Nils Liedholm, who clearly handled the ball.

The tough German side moved relentlessly forward in the second half. Uwe Seeler shot right across the face of an empty goal in meeting a long centre from Eckel. Sweden had to endure unrelieved pressure until a moment of foolhardiness turned the match. In the 58th minute Erich Juskowiak, the German left-back, was sent off by Istvan Zsolt, the Hungarian referee. Juskowiak had been fouled by Hamrin and retaliated by kicking him. For minutes Juskowiak argued with Zsolt and angrily pushed away his colleagues Fritz Walter and Hans Schafer, who had attempted to escort him to the touchline.

West Germany, reduced to ten men, had lost the initiative at a time when their power and stamina were threatening to grind down Sweden's increasingly stretched defence. The outside-left, Cieslarczyk, dropped back into defence but West Germany, surprisingly, held the balance of power until their hopes receded with a further blow. Fritz Walter was carried off the field following an extremely harsh tackle by Sigvard Parling, Sweden's left-back. Although absent for only three minutes, Walter, the 37-year-old architect of West Germany's attack, was considerably reduced in efficiency.

Only ten minutes remained when Sweden broke away to score a decisive goal. After Hamrin had struck the post, West Germany launched a counter attack which resulted in a free kick on the edge of the penalty area. A shot by Walter rebounded from the massed defence to Rahn, unmarked. But he deliberated and lost possession to Skoglund. Skoglund raced down the park complemented by Hamrin. They penetrated the German defence and a final shot was parried by Herkenrath. The ball fell to 37-year-old Gunnar Gren, who scored with a fearsome shot. Hamrin scored a further impudent goal three minutes from time. He walked the ball to the touchline before proceeding to waltz past three defenders, beating Herkenrath with contemptuous arrogance.

West Germany thus relinquished their title as World Champions. Herberger's side were far below the standard of the 1954 team. Their reliance on strength and direct thrusts had failed to overpower a Swedish side who embraced more delicate skills.

The second semi-final in Stockholm tilted decisively in Brazil's favour following an injury to Jonquet when the match was evenly balanced at 1-1. Vava scored a cleverly contrived goal after only two minutes. Seven minutes later, Juste Fontaine claimed the first goal of the tournament conceded by Brazil. The admirable French, with Kopa in particular, were both formidable and elegant. Injured after 37 minutes, Jonquet limped ineffectively amongst his forwards. The side reorganised and the fine balance of the French attack was disrupted. Thereafter, Brazil's rampant forwards displayed ruthless efficiency in scoring four goals in a 40-minute period. An excellent long range shot by Didi put Brazil ahead only two minutes after Jonquet's injury. Pele reinforced his mushrooming stature as he ran amok with three second-half goals. Piantoni's late goal was scant consolation as France were swept aside 5-2.

The third place match took place in Gothenburg on the eve of the final. Juskowiak of West Germany was not able to play because of FIFA's ruling that a player ordered off during the Championship would be barred automatically from his country's next match. The manager, Sepp Herberger, decided to switch Erhardt from centre-half to left-back. Erhardt had been instrumental in providing stability to the midfield. Eckel and Fritz Walter, two of the four remaining members of the 1954 side, were absent and Uwe Seeler failed to recover from a leg injury. Kwiatkowski played in goal, therefore representing five changes from the semi-final defeat.

The French forwards were unstoppable, with Juste Fontaine scoring four times as they achieved a remarkable 6-3 win. In just six games France had totalled 23 goals, with the Moroccan-born Juste Fontaine achieving a record-breaking 13. Only eight months before the tournament started, France had been trounced 4-0 by England at Wembley. Their preparation in Sweden was excellent. The combination of Kopa working in perfect harmony with Fontaine exhilarated the crowds and enhanced the tournament as a spectacle.

The final between Sweden and Brazil took place on the afternoon of Sunday, 29th June, in the Rasunda Stadium in Stockholm, with 49,737 in attendance. Sweden sought revenge for their 7-1 defeat in 1950. It rained solidly for 24 hours before the Final and this was thought to favour Sweden.

Brazil lost a goal to Nils Liedholm after only four minutes. The goal was quite exceptional, involving seven passes. A long throw from Svensson led to short passes between Bergmark, Borgesson and Simonsson. Liedholm took on two or three Brazilians single-handedly, eluding tackles before shooting obliquely into the bottom corner of the net. For the first time in the tournament Brazil were behind. Vava quickly replied with a goal in the ninth minute following a low, hard cross from Garrincha. In the 32nd-minute an almost identical goal put Brazil ahead. Pele also hit the inside of a post with a brilliant swinging drive from 20 yards. The third goal scored by Pele in the 54th minute contained one of the most remarkable examples of individual skill ever to grace a football field. Santos crossed a long centre which Pele caught on his broad expanse of chest. From there, he transferred the ball to his knee as Gustavsson, Sweden's centre-half, challenged. Quickly, Pele flicked the ball off his knee over Gustavsson's head and promptly ran around the defender to volley his shot just inside the post. A fourth goal arrived 13 minutes later. Bergmark, the right-back, tried to dribble the ball out of his own penalty area but was dispossessed by Zagalo, who promptly scored. With only 11 minutes remaining, Liedholm passed to Simonsson, who advanced to score easily. Sweden could have given themselves a glimmer of hope six minutes later when Hamrin robbed Bellini in his own penalty area. The Swedish winger evaded Gilmar in goal, but his shot was too acute. Pele provided the perfect climax to a wonderful performance when he outjumped Sweden's defenders to head a fifth goal from Zagalo's long centre at the very conclusion of the match.

Brazil had finally won the World Cup and became the first nation to win the tournament outside their own continent. The captain, Bellini, led his joyous team on a lap of honour, holding aloft a vast blue and yellow flag of Sweden. The Brazilian team received a tumultuous accolade from the sporting Swedish crowd.

Results: Sweden 1958

Group 1

West Germany	3	Argentina	1
Northern Ireland	1	Czechoslovakia	0
West Germany	2	Czechoslovakia	2
Argentina	3	Northern Ireland	1
West Germany	2	Northern Ireland	2
Czechoslovakia	6	Argentina	1

	P	W	D	L	Goals F	A	Pts
West Germany	3	1	2	0	7	5	4
Northern Ireland	3	1	1	1	4	5	3
Czechoslovakia	3	1	1	1	8	4	3
Argentina	3	1	0	2	5	10	2

Play-off

Northern Ireland	2	Czechoslovakia	1

(after extra time 1-1 at 90 minutes)

Group 2

Yugoslavia	1	Scotland	1
France	7	Paraguay	3
Paraguay	3	Scotland	2
Yugoslavia	3	France	2
France	2	Scotland	1
Paraguay	3	Yugoslavia	3

	P	W	D	L	Goals F	A	Pts
France	3	2	0	1	11	7	4
Yugoslavia	3	1	2	0	7	6	4
Paraguay	3	1	1	1	9	12	3
Scotland	3	0	1	2	4	6	1

Group 3

Sweden	3	Mexico			0	
Hungary	1	Wales			1	
Mexico	1	Wales			1	
Sweden	2	Hungary			1	
Sweden	0	Wales			0	
Hungary	4	Mexico			0	

	P	W	D	L	F	A	Pts
					Goals		
Sweden	3	2	1	0	5	1	5
Wales	3	0	3	0	2	2	3
Hungary	3	1	1	1	6	3	3
Mexico	3	0	1	2	1	8	1

Play-off

Wales	2	Hungary	1

Group 4

USSR	2	England			2	
Brazil	3	Austria			0	
Brazil	0	England			0	
USSR	2	Austria			0	
Brazil	2	USSR			0	
England	2	Austria			2	

	P	W	D	L	F	A	Pts
					Goals		
Brazil	3	2	1	0	5	0	5
USSR	3	1	1	1	4	4	3
England	3	0	3	0	4	4	3
Austria	3	0	1	2	2	7	1

Play-off

USSR	1	England	0

Quarter-finals

West Germany	1	Yugoslavia	0
France	4	Northern Ireland	0
Sweden	2	USSR	0
Brazil	1	Wales	0

Semi-finals

Sweden	3	West Germany	1
Brazil	5	France	2

Match for third place

France	6	West Germany	3

Final

Brazil	5	Sweden	2

Brazil: Gilmar, Santos D, Santos N, Zito, Bellini, Orlando, Garrincha, Didi, Vava, Pele, Zagalo

Sweden: Svensson, Bergmark, Axbom, Borjesson, Gustavsson, Parling, Hamrin, Gren, Simonsson, Liedholm, Skoglund

Scorers: Pele (2), Vava (2), Zagalo for Brazil
Liedholm, Simonsson for Sweden

1962

On 3rd July, 132 years of French rule in Algeria came to an end with a brief declaration signed by Charles de Gaulle. He 'solemnly recognised' the independence of the North African country that had been considered to be an integral part of France, so ending a conflict which recalled him from retirement to rule the Republic again.

The recognition followed a referendum on 1st July when six million Algerians voted almost unanimously for independence in co-operation with France. Both Muslim and French citizens were enfranchised. The final vote in favour was 99 per cent. Jubilant Algerians cheered Benyoussef Ben Kheddah, their new Prime Minister, on his return to Algiers, but Ahmed Ben Bella, his quarrelsome deputy, refused to appear and flew off in a huff to Egypt to see his ally, President Nasser.

In October the world seemed closer to nuclear war than at any time before or since. Following the previous year's Bay of Pigs fiasco, the Kennedy administration obtained conclusive proof that the Soviet Union was building offensive missile bases in Cuba which could have doubled the number of American cities and bases threatened by Soviet attack. After rejecting the option of an immediate military strike against the installations, Kennedy ordered a naval blockade against Soviet ships bringing military equipment to the island, with the threat of retaliation if the blockade was broken. The situation threatened to escalate into full-scale conflict between the superpowers as Khruschev considered whether to accept the challenge thrown down by the Americans. In the end, six days after the US ships moved into the path of the Soviet vessels, Khruschev ordered his convoy to turn back and agreed to dismantle the Cuban bases.

Adolf Eichmann, the 'transport manager' of the Holocaust, in which six million Jews died, was executed in Israel just before midnight. When told his appeal for clemency had been refused, he asked for a bottle of wine, wrote letters to his family and was visited by the Reverend William Hull, a nonconformist minister. When he was taken to the scaffold, he refused the black hood, sent his greetings to Germany, Austria and Argentina, 'the countries I shall not forget', and told the official witnesses: 'We shall meet again. I have believed in God. I obeyed the laws of war and was loyal to my flag.'

*　　*　　*

On 10th June 1956, at the FIFA Congress in Lisbon, it was decided that Chile would host the Seventh World Cup. This was largely the result of efforts by the FA President Carlos Dittborn, born in Rio de Janeiro, but of Chilean descent. Unfortunately, on 28th April 1962, one month before the opening of the World Cup, Dittborn died.

The 1962 competition in Chile is remembered as the one everyone wants to forget. Chile had been devastated by an earthquake a year previously. A new stadium in Santiago had been completed in December, another more modest ground was located at the coastal town of Vina del Mar, while Rancagua and Arica completed the four sites. However, apart from Chile's matches, which were the best attended of all, only Brazil's group attracted crowds of more than four figures. High admission prices did not help. Poor standards, defensive football and vicious tackling all contributed to a disappointing tournament.

A new record of 52 participants reflected the growing interest in the tournament. The format was the same as 1958, with four groups of four nations each playing one another, with the top two progressing to the quarter-finals. On this occasion, however, unlike previous tournaments, in the event of a tie, goal difference would determine the qualifiers.

With Chile, the hosts, and the holders, Brazil, automatically assured of a place, 14 other countries participated in the finals. Argentina, Colombia and Uruguay also represented South America. Mexico represented North and Central America. Europe's participants were Bulgaria, Czechoslovakia, England, Hungary, Italy, Spain, Switzerland, USSR, West Germany and Yugoslavia.

The greatest shock, perhaps, was caused by the failure of Sweden, hosts and runners-up in 1958, to qualify. The Swedes, having been drawn in the same group as Switzerland and Belgium, must have been confident of a visit to Chile. But their team had not been one of the youngest in the 1958 campaign and there had been a steady drain of their talented players to Italy. Switzerland defeated Sweden 2-1 in a play-off in Berlin.

France, semi-finalists four years earlier, were also unexpectedly beaten by Bulgaria in a play-off in Milan, 1-0. The superbly fit, well-disciplined Bulgarians formed part of a formidable contingency of Iron Curtain qualifiers.

The countries were grouped as follows:

Group 1: Colombia, Uruguay, USSR, Yugoslavia
Group 2: Chile, Italy, Switzerland, West Germany
Group 3: Brazil, Czechoslovakia, Mexico, Spain
Group 4: Argentina, Bulgaria, England, Hungary

In Group 1 Uruguay faced Colombia in remote Arica, at the renamed Carlos Dittborn Stadium. Colombia were appearing in their first ever World Cup, having surprisingly defeated Peru in a qualifying round. They started very well and established a half-time advantage with a penalty by Zuluaga, despite absorbing considerable pressure. Coll almost doubled the lead when he struck a post. Luis Cubilla, the outside-right, equalised for Uruguay following a clever run and Sasia scored the winner with a powerful shot.

The Soviet Union and Yugoslavia contested a grim struggle.

Yashin excelled for the Soviet Union as he successfully repelled Yugoslavian attacks with his dexterity in goal. Shortly after half-time Ponedelnik, the sinewy centre-forward, rattled a free kick against the bar and Ivanov beat Soskic, the Yugoslavian goalkeeper, to the rebound. Ponedelnik himself scored in the dying minutes. The match was marred by a serious incident, with Dubinski breaking his leg in a collision with Mujic, the Yugoslavian outside-right. A few days later the Yugoslavian delegation announced that they had suspended Mujic for twelve months.

Yugoslavia and Uruguay strove for supremacy in yet another ugly brawl. Cabrera put Uruguay ahead briefly before Skoblar equalised with a penalty and Galic established an interval lead for the Eastern Europeans. The centre-forward, Jerkovic, scored in the second half to put the match beyond Uruguay's reach. But numerous fouls committed by two desperate teams resulted in the Czech referee, Galba, dismissing Cabrera of Uruguay and Popovic of Yugoslavia midway through the second half.

The Soviet Union started off like world beaters against Colombia and established a remarkable 3-0 lead within the first 11 minutes, with goals by Ivanov (2) and Chislenko. Aceros reduced the lead before half-time. A further goal by Ponedelnik gave the Soviet Union a 4-1 lead which they maintained until midway through the second half. But after a corner kick by Coll had rolled luckily into the net, Colombia launched a tremendous rally which brought them two more goals through Rada and Klinger, thus producing an astonishing 4-4 draw. Lev Yashin's obituary was being compiled, somewhat prematurely, after the finest goalkeeper in the world had erred and allowed Colombia to stage a highly improbable comeback.

The Soviet Union, in facing Uruguay in their final group match, required a point to ensure a place in the last eight. They topped their group with the aid of a last-minute goal by Ivanov. Uruguay, who had started the tournament as second favourites to Brazil, disappeared ignominiously. The Soviet

Union scored first through Mamikin but Sasia equalised. Uruguay were reduced to ten men by injury.

Yugoslavia romped into second place with an emphatic 5-0 victory over Colombia. Goals by Jerkovic (3), Galic and Melic ensured a third consecutive quarter-final meeting with West Germany.

In their opening game in Group 2, Chile met Switzerland in the National Stadium, Santiago, with the Andes forming a breathtaking backdrop. Chile gained a satisfactory 3-1 win in front of 65,500 spectators. Wuthrich put Switzerland ahead with a long-range shot. Leonel Sanchez equalised just before half-time. The English referee, Ken Aston, then had to call on his wealth of international experience as the game threatened to explode. Chile had gained a two goal advantage within ten minutes of the second half, with goals by the right-winger Ramirez and Leonel Sanchez.

The next match between West Germany and Italy was typical of the tournament as a whole. The goalless draw between the sparring opponents was quite abysmal, with strong defensive play justifiably provoking a torrent of criticism.

Group 2 was then host to the most violent game of the tournament between Chile and Italy, which became known as the Battle of Santiago. Four minutes after kick-off, Aston had ordered the Italian inside-forward Ferrini off the pitch. Amid ear-splitting whistles and jeers from the hostile crowd, Ferrini refused to obey that order. Consequently, the game was held up for nearly ten minutes before the obdurate Italian was escorted to the dressing-room by armed policemen.

Despite Aston's drastic action, the game failed to improve. Indeed, the pitch quickly became a battlefield as players forgot the ball and concentrated on kicking the nearest opponent. Shortly before half-time, David, Italy's right-half, and Chile's left-winger, Leonel Sanchez, savagely attacked each other. Sanchez, the son of a professional boxer, planted a left hook that was televised around the world. The referee and linesmen were somehow unsighted as the aggressor went unpunished. Shortly after the resumption, David joined Ferrini in the dressing room for a retaliatory kick at Sanchez. Years later Sanchez admitted he had not been kicked. Italy were thus obliged to carry on with only nine men. They held out until the 73rd minute, when Ramirez headed Chile into the lead following a free kick. Three minutes from time, Toro brought thunderous cheers, not only from the Santiago crowd, but from every man, woman and child at the other stadia who possessed a transistor radio, by clinching victory with another goal.

West Germany's workmanlike 2-1 triumph over Switzerland at a much more peaceful National Stadium was overshadowed by an injury to Eschmann, the Swiss inside-left, who was taken to hospital with a broken ankle. West Germany opened the scoring just before the interval with a goal by Brulls. Uwe Seeler added a second, but Schneiter pulled a goal back in a game dominated by defenders.

The group concluded with West Germany again working assiduously and achieving an impressive 2-0 win over Chile. A penalty midway through the first half by Szymaniak enabled West Germany to absorb considerable pressure and counter-attack. Uwe Seeler added a second goal with eight minutes remaining to secure first place.

Brazil retained nine of their 1958 side but adopted a more cautious 4-3-3 pattern, with winger Zagalo dropping back. They were now coached by Moreira, who replaced the sick Feola. At Vina del Mar, Mexico were the opponents in the Group 3 opening match. Brazil gave an economical performance in winning 2-0. Zagalo headed the first goal from a Pele cross. Pele excelled and fittingly scored a splendid second as he beat four defenders and Carbajal in goal.

Di Stefano, one of the greatest centre-forwards of his generation, was injured and replaced by the former Hungarian captain, Ferenc Puskas, in Spain's encounter with Czechoslovakia. Czechoslovakia had come perilously close to elimination on the road to Chile. They lost 3-2 to Scotland at Hampden Park before eventually winning a play-off in Brussels after Scotland had led with only minutes remaining.

With such artists as Suarez and Del Sol, Spain were a huge

disappointment, resorting to brutal tactics. Czechoslovakia's organisational skills helped to withstand intense Spanish pressure. The Czechoslovakian right-winger, Stibranyi, scored the only goal of the game ten minutes from time.

Brazil and Czechoslovakia treated each other with great respect in a dull, defensive game without any goals. Brazil's galaxy of stars failed to find the target and were further troubled when Pele strained a thigh muscle and was considered unlikely to return for a crucial game against Spain.

Spain enjoyed remarkable luck as they were chased all over the pitch by the lively Mexicans. Then Gento broke free from his own penalty area in the last minute, ran the length of the pitch and crossed the ball to the limping Peiro, who snatched the only goal.

Spain and Brazil produced arguably the most exciting game of the preliminary series. Defeat by Spain would have sent Brazil home in disgrace. They started the game without their greatest asset, Pele. His place at inside-left was taken by Amarildo, a man of 22, who had never before played in a World Cup tie. As his predecessor had done in Sweden, Amarildo rose to the occasion.

Spain's manager, Herrera, had boldly dropped Suarez and Del Sol, his star forwards, and also left out Santamaria, Real Madrid's centre-half. Instead, he chose three comparatively unknown players. Adelardo and Collar, both of Athletico Madrid, came into the attack as a new right-wing pair and Echevarria, the Bilbao centre-half, replaced Santamaria. Herrera's gamble came desperately close to succeeding. In the 35th minute Adelardo put Spain ahead. Thereafter, Spain mastered midfield until well into the second half. In the 72nd minute Zagalo whipped over a low centre and Amarildo flung himself forward to hit the ball into the net. Spain continued to look the better side and constantly threatened to eliminate the champions. Then, five minutes from the end, Puskas, who had been outstanding, challenged the goalkeeper, Gilmar, for a high ball. Both fell as Gilmar punched the centre away. The ball ran loose to Verges who blasted it, shoulder-high, towards the net. Gilmar launched himself off the turf to make the greatest save of his distinguished career. As the ball was cleared, it bounced to the feet of Garrincha, who promptly raced upfield and slipped a pass to Didi. The inside-forward flicked the ball onto Amarildo, who calmly nodded in the winner.

The following day Mexico produced one of their finest ever World Cup performances in beating the already qualified Czechoslovakia, 3-1. Carbajal, the Mexico goalkeeper, one of the outstanding characters in the competition, enjoyed his 33rd birthday, at least momentarily, before Masek, the left-winger, raced away and scored within the first minute. From that moment the determined, ball-playing Mexicans dominated their dour, defensively minded opponents with a joyful exhibition of attacking football. Diaz equalised to inspire a courageous comeback. Czechoslovakia were conscious of the need to avoid conceding another goal in order to avert a tough confrontation against Hungary in the quarter-finals. But Mexico launched a wave of attacks and Del Aguila, a right-winger, gave them a lead before half-time. H. Hernandez added a third goal as Mexico achieved their first ever victory in the World Cup finals. .

Argentina started impressively in their opening Group 4 match against Bulgaria in Rancagua. They led after only three minutes with a well contrived goal. Marzolini, the left-back, beat two defenders and crossed the ball for Facundo to drive home the only goal of the game. Argentina's miscreants proceeded to display a wide repertoire of thuggery, resorting to every conceivable trick as they abandoned any semblance of a moral code. A total of 69 free kicks were awarded as the Spanish referee, Gardeazabal, whistled almost incessantly.

England met their old rivals, Hungary, and were deservedly beaten 2-1 after an uninspiring performance. The England players had attained a high level of fitness under the well prepared tutelage of Walter Winterbottom. Although Hungary were a pale imitation of the 1954 side, they played neat, controlled football which placed England on the defensive.

Springett in goal made only one mistake during the match, but it proved to be very costly. In the 17th minute Rakosi robbed Haynes in midfield and passed to Lajos Tichy, who hit his customary long-range, venomous right foot shot. Springett appeared to completely misjudge the shot as it lodged in the roof of the net from 25 yards. England equalised after an hour, courtesy of another goalkeeping error. Grosics dropped a corner from Douglas and Greaves let fly at the loose ball, which Matrai handled on the line. Flowers scored from the penalty spot. Ten minutes later Flowers slipped on intercepting a pass and Albert galloped past Springett to put Hungary ahead.

England underwent something of a transformation in conquering Argentina 3-1. Winterbottom took a calculated risk by dropping Hitchens and bringing in the largely untried Alan Peacock, of Middlesbrough, at centre-forward. Peacock, taller and larger than Hitchens, was felt better equipped to withstand the anticipated battering from Navarro. In the 16th minute Peacock soared above the Argentinian defence to head a centre from Charlton under the bar. The ball appeared to have crossed the line before Navarro pushed it out with his hand, but the Soviet referee, Latychev, awarded a penalty which the unflappable Flowers converted. Just before the interval, Armfield scurried along the right touchline before thumping the ball against the bar. Flowers pounced on the rebound, side-stepped a tackle and passed to Charlton, who shot right-footed past a helpless Roma in goal. With 14 minutes remaining, Douglas feinted to slip a pass through the middle to Peacock, sent the defence the wrong way, then drove a hard shot at Roma. The surprised goalkeeper could only parry the ball and Greaves appeared from nowhere to bang the loose ball home.

Iliev and Diev were missing for Bulgaria as their weakened team were thrashed 6-1 by Hungary. Four of the goals arrived in a remarkable first 12 minutes. The scorers were Albert (3), Tichy (2) and Solymosi. Sokolov's strike was scant consolation for Bulgaria.

In their final group tie against Argentina, Lajos Baroti, the wily Hungarian coach, already knew his side were almost certain of heading the group. His players were therefore content not to over-exert themselves. A drab goalless draw ended with Hungary astride the top of the table with five points, leaving Argentina with three, one more than England, who were due to meet Bulgaria the following day.

England approached their game in the knowledge that they had a superior goal average to Argentina and required only one point to reach the quarter-finals. A weary England side played nervously, with Jimmy Greaves squandering a couple of simple chances.

After an absolutely wretched game had finished goalless, it was widely suggested that the Bulgarians had deliberately allowed England to enter the last eight. The meagre crowd who jeered both sides off the pitch obviously thought that Winterbottom's team had been given a helping hand. Their suspicions had been aroused when Kostov, Bulgaria's right-winger, headed a cross from inside-left Kolev yards wide, though he was standing in front of the goal. Speculation was rife that Bulgaria were so annoyed by Argentina that they chose to gain revenge by aiding England.

The preliminary ties had been characterised by violence, ill temper, serious injury and an absence of artistic football. Dubinski of the Soviet Union, Colombia's captain Zuluaga, and Eschmann of Switzerland were all in hospital with broken legs. Fouilloux of Chile had fractured an ankle and Belen of Argentina nursed rib injuries. Diev of Bulgaria and the Spanish full-backs Rivilla and Reija all departed from the tournament prematurely through injury. Pele's participation ended in attempting an impossible shot against Czechoslovakia in Brazil's second game.

The general situation was best summed up by the Santiago newspaper *Clarin*, whose crimson banner headlines said tersely, 'World War'. The situation had become so ugly that the World Cup organising committee called the 16 team managers together to impress on them that the savagery must stop. On the eve of the third series of group matches, Sir Stanley Rous, President of FIFA, had made an impassioned appeal to the 16 nations for a return to sportsmanship. Although the battles for survival remained keen, they were reasonably clean. No more players were sent off, and none was seriously injured. Unfortunately, the standard of football did not rise to the heights expected, for the emphasis remained on defensive tactics.

Europe dominated the quarter-finals. Brazil and Chile, indeed, were the only non-European representatives. The 'Communist' bloc fared particularly well, with Czechoslovakia, Hungary, the Soviet Union and Yugoslavia all qualifying. England and West Germany carried the flag for Western Europe.

The quarter finals produced the following ties:

West Germany v Yugoslavia
Chile v USSR
Brazil v England
Czechoslovakia v Hungary

Yugoslavia's 1-0 victory over West Germany in Santiago was clinched by Radakovic with only four minutes left. It eradicated the memory of two quarter-final defeats in previous World Cup tournaments against the Germans.

Yugoslavia's young forwards were inspired by Sekularac, the only survivor of the 1958 side. They tormented the solid, powerful but unimaginative defence. Herberger's side rode their luck as the vivacious East Europeans bombarded the German goal, but were let down by erratic shooting. But as full-time approached, Galic, the inside-left, raced along the touchline to the by-line and pulled the ball back into the middle. The right-half, Radakovic, galloped into the penalty area to thump the only goal past a surprised Fahrian in goal.

In Arica, Chile beat the Soviet Union in a game many were convinced would see the elimination of the hosts. Lev Yashin, the most reliable goalkeeper of his era, cost his country a place in the last four with two uncharacteristic errors. The first occurred after only ten minutes when Voronin fouled Leonel

Sanchez on the edge of the penalty area. Sanchez took the free kick himself and sent the ball hurtling past a leaden-footed Yashin. Despite this setback, the Soviet Union adhered to a 4-2-4 formation and refused to panic, equalising in the 26th minute. Left-winger Meschki pushed the ball accurately into an opening, Ivanov seized onto it and passed to Ponedelnik, who drove the shot at Escuti in goal. The Chilean goalkeeper pushed the shot away, and as the ball bounced in the goalmouth, Chislenko placed it into the net. Within a minute Chile had re-established the lead. Rojas latched onto a loose ball and from 35 yards out blasted it under Yashin's diving body. The Soviet Union, thereafter, squandered a couple of good opportunities to equalise.

The Chilean victory led to unprecedented demonstrations of national fervour. For two nights the streets of Santiago were taken over by thousands of flag-waving, dancing, chanting men, women and children. Cars and their passengers were stranded for hours on end, their drivers pleased if eventually they returned home with vehicles not too badly damaged. Bars and hotels were packed to suffocation by Chileans, who, even if they had never seen a football match in their lives, were determined to celebrate this notable occasion in their country's history with the traditional Pisco Sour or local champagne.

Brazil and England produced the best quarter-final tie at Vina del Mar. England announced an unchanged side. But as the teams emerged it soon became apparent that Hitchens had replaced Peacock, who had a slight muscle strain. England made a promising start and created a couple of half chances. Hitchens narrowly failed to meet an Armfield cross and Douglas miskicked a centre from Hitchens. The Brazilian forwards began to exercise their power and a drive by Garrincha was cleared off the line by Armfield. Garrincha's ball control was quite outstanding and he was a relentless source of torment to the overstretched England defence. In the 31st minute Zagalo drove a corner kick into the penalty area and Garrincha arrived with lightning pace to head the ball past Springett. Only seven minutes later, England rocked Brazil when Haynes' free kick was headed against the post by Jimmy Greaves and the rebound fell to Hitchens, who equalised.

Within 15 minutes of the second half Garrincha had decisively determined the fate of the match. In the 54th minute Flowers fouled Vava just outside the penalty area. While the England players formed a wall in front of goal, Didi stood by the ball as though he intended taking the kick. Instead Garrincha scurried forward and swept the ball through the narrowest gap so powerfully that Springett could only push it to Vava, who nodded the ball home. Garrincha then turned a formidable task for England into an impossible one. He received a pass from Vava 25 yards from goal and sent a shot which appeared to be heading wide of the right-hand post. Suddenly, the ball dipped and swung in under the bar. Springett was later harshly criticised for misreading the flight of the ball.

Hungary and Czechoslovakia fought a dour battle at the half-filled stadium in Rancagua. Czechoslovakia broke away in the 14th minute and Scherer grabbed a goal. Florian Albert and Latos Tichy were suffocated by an indomitable defence, assisted by the brilliance of their goal keeper, Schrojf. Hungary, whose forwards were devastating against Bulgaria and controlled against England, were stifled by their defence-orientated opponents.

The semi-finals paired Czechoslovakia with Yugoslavia in Vina Del Mar and Brazil with Chile in Santiago.

An embarrassingly meagre crowd of around 5,000 watched the Iron Curtain clash in the Sausalito Stadium. Czechoslovakia retained the side which had eliminated Hungary, with Pospichal retaining his place on the right-wing instead of Stibranyi, who had played in the three group matches. Yugoslavia attempted to resolve their right-wing problem which had troubled them since their decision to suspend Mujic following their opening game against the Soviet Union. Melic, Ankovic and Kovacevic had already been tried there and now Sijakovic was given his first chance.

As Czechoslovakia had scored only three goals in four games, it was something of a surprise when they moved purposefully into attack for the opening minutes. But it was not long before Yugoslavia's intelligent forwards were sweeping upfield with precise passing movements which even Brazil scarcely bettered.

The game became an intriguing struggle between Europe's best defence and Europe's most artistic attack. Galic created a wonderful opening for Jerkovic, who unaccountably missed an easy opportunity. Three minutes after the interval, the Yugoslavian defence twice failed to clear a bouncing ball and Kadraba, the Czech centre-forward, headed a goal. As Yugoslavia became increasingly anxious, the game descended into pettiness and the referee, Dienst of Switzerland, was obliged to call the captains together. In the 70th minute Jerkovic atoned for his earlier miss by spectacularly heading the ball over Schrojf whilst standing with his back to the goal. Yugoslavia, thereafter, mounted a succession of attacks. Schrojf made an excellent save from Skoblar. Ten minutes from time, Scherer enjoyed a free passage to goal and promptly scored. A handling offence by Markovic led to another goal by Scherer from the ensuing penalty. Czechoslovakia had thus reached the World Cup Final for the second time in their history.

Chile met Brazil at the National stadium watched by the largest crowd of the tournament. The match was an exhibition of attacking football at its best, with both sides prepared to take risks in their endeavour to score goals.

Realising that in the continued absence of Pele Brazil's most dangerous forward would be Garrincha, Chile's coach, Riera, gambled boldly by dropping his captain, Navarro, and bringing in Rodriguez at left-back. Rodriguez had successfully contained Garrincha in two previous internationals. The strategy came unstuck after only nine minutes. Zagalo beat Eyzaguirre out on the left and crossed the ball. Amarildo missed it with an attempted scissors kick, but Garrincha ruthlessly despatched the ball in the net from the edge of the box with his left foot.

Within minutes Chile had penetrated Brazil's somewhat sluggish defence and Rojas struck a thunderous shot against the post. Brazil strode upfield seconds later and thought they had doubled their lead. An exquisite pass from Amarildo found Vava, who delicately flicked the ball round Sanchez before shooting past Escuti. But the linesman flagged for offside. After 32 minutes Garrincha rushed to meet a Zagalo corner-kick and hurled himself between two defenders to head past Escuti. Chile fought back tenaciously and scored three minutes before half-time. Landa was fouled 25 yards from goal and Toro blasted the resultant free kick past Gilmar. Three minutes after the resumption, Garrincha delivered a corner kick which was met by the unmarked Vava, who headed the ball wide of Escuti. After 62 minutes Leonel Sanchez converted a penalty to rekindle Chilean hopes. Brazil remained calm and completed a 4-2 victory with 13 minutes left. A swift left-wing thrust by Zagalo and Garrincha culminated in Vava curling a left-foot shot into the far corner of the net. A thoroughly engrossing spectacle was tarnished in the last ten minutes. Landa of Chile was ordered off by Yamasaki, the Peruvian referee. The Chilean forward appeared to be guilty of dissent after tackling Zito robustly but legitimately. Only moments later, Garrincha, one of the most sporting professionals in the game, was sent off after he uncharacteristically lashed out at Rojas. Sadly, the man known as 'Little Bird', who had captivated audiences with his wonderful artistry, was pelted with a torrent of missiles.

On the eve of the Final, Chile met Yugoslavia in the third place match. Chile's attack was led by Campos, who replaced the suspended Landa. Extra time looked inevitable until Chile scored the most extraordinary goal of the tournament in the 90th minute. Rojas raced upfield to the edge of the penalty area and toe-ended the ball goalwards. Soskic, in goal, moved confidently to his right to gather the gentle shot when it struck Markovic's heel and trickled into the other side of the net.

The possibility of Garrincha being suspended for the Final

preoccupied the thoughts of the artistically minded for 24 hours following Brazil's semi-final triumph. Sir Stanley Rous decreed that Garrincha would merely be cautioned, taking into account his previous impeccable record and acknowledging that he had been greatly provoked.

It was widely anticipated that Czechoslovakia would adopt purely negative tactics. However, they endeared themselves to the crowd by setting out to play attacking football. In the opening minutes Kadraba had the ball snatched away by the diving Gilmar and then Kvasnak shot over from six yards. Brazil composed themselves and Garrincha raced down the right before crossing the ball to Vava, who volleyed it against the post. Zagalo then beat Tichy out on the left and curled the ball into the box. Only Schrojf's agility denied Garrincha's effort.

In the 15th minute a swift exchange of short passing between Scherer and Pospichal fragmented the Brazilian defence. Masopust advanced and seized onto a meticulous pass from Scherer. Gilmar was left helpless as the ball nestled into the net. Within two minutes Amarildo collected the ball near the goal line. He duped Schrojf in the Czech goal into believing he intended to centre the ball. Instead, he impudently struck the ball behind the nonplussed goalkeeper into the far corner of the net. Despite conceding the goal, Czechoslovakia continued to look the more mobile, methodical and controlled side. All they lacked was the necessary ruthlessness near goal.

During the first 15 minutes of the second half, Czechoslovakia tormented the Brazilian defence as Masopust, Scherer and Pospichal imposed themselves. Scherer headed just over the bar when it seemed easier to score. Kvasnak deliberated in front of goal, thus allowing Gilmar to turn the shot round the post. Brazil were reeling, but somehow survived a Czech onslaught. In the 68th minute Zito, who had rarely ventured over the half-way line, sent a perfect pass to Amarildo near the left corner flag. He juggled the ball on his left foot before curling over a centre which was met by Zito, who charged in to chest the ball over the line. A few minutes later Djalma Santos appeared to handle a shot by Jelinek, but the Soviet referee, Latychev, dismissed the penalty claim. Masopust was then unlucky that his header scraped over the bar. Brazil had, by now, gained in confidence and their ageing team began to impose its supremacy. With only minutes remaining, Garrincha lobbed the ball goalwards, Schrojf dropped it and Vava scored.

Without Pele, the world's most complete footballer, Brazil failed to attain the heights of Sweden four years earlier. The vivacity, artistry and panache was less in evidence. Nevertheless, Brazil had withstood a strong European representation and their elderly team had mastered the Czech challenge with two flashes of the old Brazilian magic.

Results: Chile 1962

Group 1

Uruguay	2	Colombia	1
USSR	2	Yugoslavia	0
Yugoslavia	3	Uruguay	1
USSR	4	Colombia	4
USSR	2	Uruguay	1
Yugoslavia	5	Colombia	0

	P	W	D	L	Goals F	A	Pts
USSR	3	2	1	0	8	5	5
Yugoslavia	3	2	0	1	8	3	4
Uruguay	3	1	0	2	4	6	2
Colombia	3	0	1	2	5	11	1

Group 2

Chile	3	Switzerland	1
West Germany	0	Italy	0
Chile	2	Italy	0
West Germany	2	Switzerland	1
West Germany	2	Chile	0
Italy	3	Switzerland	0

	P	W	D	L	Goals F	A	Pts
West Germany	3	2	1	0	4	1	5
Chile	3	2	0	1	5	3	4
Italy	3	1	1	1	3	2	3
Switzerland	3	0	0	3	2	8	0

Group 3

Brazil	2	Mexico	0
Czechoslovakia	1	Spain	0
Brazil	0	Czechoslovakia	0
Spain	1	Mexico	0
Brazil	2	Spain	1
Mexico	3	Czechoslovakia	1

	P	W	D	L	Goals F	A	Pts
Brazil	3	2	1	0	4	1	5
Czechoslovakia	3	1	1	1	2	3	3
Mexico	3	1	0	2	3	4	2
Spain	3	1	0	2	2	3	2

Group 4

Argentina	1	Bulgaria	0
Hungary	2	England	1
England	3	Argentina	1
Hungary	6	Bulgaria	1
Hungary	0	Argentina	0
England	0	Bulgaria	0

	P	W	D	L	Goals F	A	Pts
Hungary	3	2	1	0	8	2	5
England	3	1	1	1	4	3	3
Argentina	3	1	1	1	2	3	3
Bulgaria	3	0	1	2	1	7	1

Quarter-Finals

Yugoslavia	1	West Germany	0
Chile	2	USSR	1
Brazil	3	England	1
Czechoslovakia	1	Hungary	0

Semi-Finals

| Czechoslovakia | 3 | Yugoslavia | 1 |
| Brazil | 4 | Chile | 2 |

Third place match

| Chile | 1 | Yugoslavia | 0 |

Final

| Brazil | 3 | Czechoslovakia | 1 |

Brazil: Gilmar, Santos D, Mauro, Zozimo, Santos N, Zito, Garrincha, Didi, Vava, Amarildo, Zagalo

Czechoslovakia: Schrojf, Tichy, Novak, Pluskal, Popluhar, Masopust, Pospichal, Scherer, Kvasnak, Kadraba, Jelinek

Scorers: Amarildo, Zito, Vava for Brazil
Masopust for Czechoslovakia

1966

On 8th January the United States launched the biggest offensive ever in the Vietnam war. The 'Iron Triangle', a Viet Cong jungle stronghold 20 miles north-west of Saigon, was attacked by 8000 United States troops. The area, riddled with tunnels, was pounded by B-52 heavy bombers and artillery before the troops stormed in.

The World Cup went missing from a stamp exhibition in Westminster Central Hall on 20th March. It subsequently became the subject of a ransom demand to the Football Association. On 27th March it was found in a south London garden by a mongrel called Pickles. David Corbett, a Thames lighterman, saw his dog tearing at an object wrapped in newspaper. The bundle contained the solid gold Jules Rimet trophy, whose loss had caused great embarrassment to the football hierarchy. On 31st March Labour won a landslide victory in the British election with an overall majority of 96. Harold Wilson said on his return to 10 Downing Street, 'Now we have a clear mandate.' The Rhodesian crisis was at the top of the agenda. Prime Minister Wilson believed that the illegal Smith regime would be readier for a settlement now that it had to abandon hopes of dealing with a Conservative government.

In August, Chairman Mao Tse-tung launched the Great Proletarian Cultural Revolution to bring the country closer to the ideal communist state. The new campaign was formed by millions of young Chinese brandishing copies of the 'Little Red Book', with quotations from Mao's works. Their aim was to arouse townspeople and villages to recapture the victorious 1949 revolutionary zeal and eradicate all those who departed from Mao's ideals, including revisionists and Western sympathisers.

Dr Hendrik Verwoerd, Prime Minister of South Africa and leader of the Nationalist Party, was assassinated by a Bible-quoting white extremist in the House of Assembly on 6th September. Demetrio Tsafendas, of Greek and Portuguese parents, pulled a long stiletto from his belt and stabbed Verwoerd four times in the chest.

At 09.30hrs on the morning of 20th October, tragedy struck the small Welsh mining village of Aberfan when a slag heap collapsed, resulting in an avalanche which engulfed and demolished the village school. The disaster left 147 dead and virtually wiped out an entire generation of schoolchildren. An army of rescue workers toiled throughout the day and night in tunnelling through 45 feet of slag in an effort to reach the victims. Hardened reporters and policemen broke down in tears as the first bodies were carried out of the mud and the full extent of the tragedy began to become clear.

*   *   *

Seventy countries registered with FIFA for the Eighth World Cup. On 30th January 1964, the groups for the qualifying matches were decided in Zurich, the site of FIFA's former headquarters. Brazil, the 1962 champions, and England, the hosts, were guaranteed finalists. Of the remaining 14 places, nine were to be allocated to Europe, three to South America, one to North/Central America/Caribbean and just one to Africa/Asia/Australia.

There was a mass withdrawal of all 16 African countries, who protested that one place should be reserved exclusively for them. South Africa was suspended by FIFA for violating anti-discrimination codes in the FIFA charter. This meant that only three teams in the sprawling Africa/Asia/Australia zone competed. However, South Korea boycotted a tournament in Cambodia to determine the qualifier, on the pretext that they preferred to concentrate on the 1968 Olympics. North Korea ensured their place in England by defeating Australia twice, 6-1 and 3-1, in Phnom Penh.

It was ironic that for the first time since all the Home Countries had been eligible for the World Cup none actually qualified for the finals. Scotland lost heavily in Naples against Italy, who won their group. Wales were eliminated in a group won by the Soviet Union. Northern Ireland acquitted themselves well before narrowly failing to surpass Switzerland.

South America was represented by Brazil, the World Champions, Argentina, Uruguay and Chile. Mexico, by winning subgroup C of the North and Central Americas, proceeded to eliminate Jamaica, winners of subgroup A, and Costa Rica, victors of subgroup B. Europe included the hosts, England, plus Bulgaria, France, Hungary, Italy, Portugal, Spain, Switzerland, the USSR and West Germany. The major surprise in the European qualifying matches was Portugal's advancement in a difficult group which included Czechoslovakia and Romania.

The competition adhered to the format of 1962, with four groups of four nations. The two winners of each group progressed to the quarter-finals, whereupon the tournament proceeded on a knock-out basis.

On 6th January 1966 at the Royal Garden Hotel in London, FIFA determined the following groups:

Group 1: England, France, Mexico, Uruguay
Group 2: Argentina, Spain, Switzerland, West Germany
Group 3: Brazil, Bulgaria, Hungary, Portugal
Group 4: Chile, Italy, North Korea, USSR

The opening match of the tournament between England and Uruguay took place at Wembley Stadium on Monday 11th July. Although Uruguay were considered to be the most potent group threat to England, a number of their leading players exiled in Argentina were missing, including Silveira, Pavoni, Matosas, Sasia and Cubilla. However, the highly adroit Pedro Rocha, Cortes, Troche and Mazurkiewicz in goal made them highly respected opponents.

The Uruguayans adopted negative, unadventurous tactics, with the emphasis on a nine-man defence. England dominated play and forced 16 corners to 1 for Uruguay but were never overtly threatening. They displayed petulance in response to harsh tackles. Nobby Stiles threw a punch and was lucky to remain on the field. Jimmy Greaves and Roger Hunt were ineffectual and Bobby Charlton directionless in an uninspiring game bereft of ideas. England were jeered off the park and departed abruptly and boorishly.

France met Mexico in Group 1 two days later. They were expected to win, but Mexico played with more authority. Borja came close to scoring after only five minutes and had a goal disallowed in the 18th minute for offside. France gave an unsynchronized performance and it was no surprise when Enrique Borja gave Mexico a lead after 49 minutes. Hausser equalised after an hour to give France a most unsatisfactory draw.

White City greyhound racing stadium was the extraordinary venue for the next Group 1 match between France and Uruguay. The ironic reason was that Wembley was holding a greyhound meeting. France rid themselves of the lassitude that had haunted their performance against Mexico. Their lively forwards exposed a defensive vulnerability that Uruguay had failed to reveal against England.

Manicera's wild tackle on Herbet appeared to have taken place outside the penalty area. De Bourgoing scored to put France ahead from the dubious spot-kick. This had the effect of galvanising Uruguay, who had established a lead by half-time with goals from Rocha and Cortes. After the interval Uruguay presented themselves as a solid and cohesive unit which France were unable to breach.

England's next encounter, against Mexico, was yet another sterile affair. The manager, Alf Ramsey, replaced Ball and Connelly with Paine and Peters. Geoff Hurst was again omitted. Mexico's approach was not dissimilar to Uruguay's, with a massed defence intent on keeping England at bay. Shortly before half-time, with the crowd growing increasingly impatient, Bobby Charlton gathered the ball and, with defenders retreating, unleashed a thunderous right-foot shot from all of 25 yards which hurtled into the Mexican net. It had taken England 128 minutes to score their first World Cup goal. In the second half Bobby Charlton delivered a pass to Greaves, whose shot rebounded, allowing Roger Hunt to add a second goal.

Mexico recalled Carbajal, the 37-year-old goalkeeper participating in his fifth World Cup, in their final match against Uruguay. Uruguay played cautiously, fully aware that a draw would enable qualification. Mexico had an early foray which carried no real menace. Nevertheless they delighted their colourful supporters with an unexpected goalless draw in a dire game.

England faced France in their final group match. Unless France won emphatically, England were assured of qualification. Ramsey replaced Terry Paine with Ian Callaghan. Ball and Hurst were again absent. Herbin of France was injured early in the game and moved to centre-forward. France attacked boldly but succumbed to a goal in each half scored by Roger Hunt. The first occurred with Hunt clearly offside. The second coincided with Simon of France flat out on the ground, the victim of a deplorable foul by Nobby Stiles which Ramsey failed to condemn. Two officials of the Football Association strongly voiced their disapproval of Stiles' contemptible play and exhorted Ramsey to withdraw him from the team. Ramsey's response was that if Stiles departed, he would follow. The 2-0 victory ensured that England won the group with Uruguay second.

West Germany gave an impressive display of attacking football in their Group 2 encounter with Switzerland at Hillsborough, Sheffield. Switzerland dropped two of their leading players, Leimgruber and Kuhn, for breaking a curfew. They subsided playing a fluent German side capable of ruthless finishing. Beckenbauer displayed remarkable maturity for a twenty-year-old and scored twice, as did Haller. Held also scored in a 5-0 rout.

The following day at Villa Park, Birmingham, Argentina faced a Spanish side boasting Del Sol, Gento and Suarez. Suarez was the victim of some brutal tackling early in the game. The hugely disappointing tie was goalless at half-time. Two goals by Artime ensured a victory for the South Americans. Pirri, in his debut for Spain, scored with an arched header.

Leimgruber and Kuhn were recalled for Switzerland's next game against Spain in Sheffield. Switzerland were clearly traumatised by their overwhelming defeat at the hands of West Germany and adopted a defensive approach from the outset. Their strategy was effective during the first half as they restricted Spain to minimal opportunities and scored through Quentin. Midway through the second half, Sanchis collected the ball on the halfway line and evaded a series of tackles before unleashing a glorious equaliser. Amancio snatched victory for Spain with an exquisite header.

Argentina held West Germany to a goalless draw at Villa Park, Birmingham. West Germany lost much of their impetus by deploying Beckenbauer to guard the inventive Onega. Albrecht of Argentina was sent off after 65 minutes for a foul on Weber. He had previously rugby-tackled Haller. Argentina were warned by FIFA for their overly physical style of play.

In their final group match against Switzerland, Argentina faced a hostile crowd at Hillsborough. They gave an inhibited performance in winning 2-0, with second-half goals from Artime and Onega.

Spain were required to beat West Germany in order to reach the quarter-finals. They looked capable of doing so when Fuste gave them a first-half lead. West Germany launched a wave of attacks after the interval. Emmerich equalised with a highly improbable goal. He pursued a seemingly irretrievable ball and struck a powerful shot from the by-line into the roof of the net. In the dying minutes Uwe Seeler scored to secure West Germany first place, with a superior goal difference to Argentina.

Brazil were so confident that they would win the trophy for a third time, and therefore outright, that they actually had another made to donate in its place, to be known as the Winston Churchill Cup.

Pele enjoyed the distinction of scoring the first goal of the competition against Bulgaria at Goodison Park, Everton. A fulminating free-kick after 14 minutes of the Group 3 encounter exorcised the general torpor of the tournament. Zhechev of Bulgaria policed Pele, often inflicting harsh treatment. Garrincha scored a second goal with another swerving free kick after being fouled. But he was now a jaded, slower, less effective figure.

Hungary and Portugal met at Old Trafford, Manchester, the following day in an intriguing match. Hungary were disadvantaged by an injury to their goalkeeper, Szentmihalyi, virtually from the kick-off. Jose Augusto scored for Portugal after Szentmihalyi erred in dealing with a corner kick. Hungary were unlucky to be trailing as they had produced a series of penetrating attacks with both Bene and Farkas striking the bar. They deservedly equalised after 61 minutes with a goal by Bene. But a further mistake by their goalkeeper allowed Augusto to re-establish Portugal's lead. Torres scored a remarkable third goal in the dying seconds from a seemingly impossible angle. In the end, Hungary had been outmanoeuvred by the clever midfield inventiveness of Mario Coluna, together with the formidable Torres and agile Eusebio. Nevertheless, the 3-1 scoreline flattered Portugal, who were aided by goalkeeping frailties.

Hungary and Brazil clashed at Goodison Park, Everton, in the second round of matches. What unfolded was one of the most exhilarating games in the tournament's history. Pele had sustained an injury to his right knee and was replaced by Tostao. Gerson was drafted into midfield and Denilson dropped. Hungary also made significant changes. Gelei replaced Szentmihalyi in goal and Szepesi and Mathesz replaced Sovari and Nagy. Hungary swept into the lead after only three minutes with the graceful Florian Albert striking a shot past Gilmar from a narrow angle. Hungary excelled with competent defenders and a cohesive, fluid attack. In 15 minutes

Tostao equalised against the run of play. During the second half, Hungary deservedly scored with an exquisite goal. Albert surged forward, exposing the vulnerability of the Brazilian defence, before despatching the ball to Bene with a meticulous pass. Bene advanced down the right and a low cross allowed Farkas an uninhibited volley. A penalty by Meszoly ensured that Brazil suffered their first World Cup defeat since 1954, when their conquerors had also been Hungary.

Portugal's next match was against Bulgaria at Old Trafford. Vutzov scored a bizarre own goal after only five minutes. Further goals by Eusebio and Torres ensured a 3-0 victory.

For their final group match against Portugal, the ten-man Brazilian selection committee introduced an astonishing nine new players. Pele was recalled despite being unfit. He was literally kicked out of the tournament, repeatedly fouled by Vicente and Morais before eventually being forced to retire. Pele later claimed he would never play another World Cup match. Manga, the replacement Brazilian goalkeeper, performed nervously and was largely responsible for Portugal taking a 2-0 lead within 25 minutes. First he tamely punched out Eusebio's centre, presenting Simoes with a headed goal. A free kick was then allowed to be nodded back from the far post by Torres and Eusebio headed a second. After the interval Rildo, the Brazilian left-back, scored at a time when Eusebio was tormenting his opponents with his punishing speed and athleticism. It was fitting therefore that he should serve as executioner, with a venomous shot five minutes from time.

Hungary ensured qualification and the elimination of Brazil by defeating Bulgaria 3-1 at Old Trafford. Asparoukhov opened the scoring for Bulgaria. But goals from Meszoly, Bene and an own goal by Davidov completed a 3-1 win.

In Group 4 the inscrutable and exotic North Koreans displayed boundless enthusiasm but predictably lost to the Soviet Union, 3-0, at Ayresome Park, Middlesbrough. Malafeev (2) and Banischevski were the scorers.

Italy gave a strangely languid performance against Chile at Roker Park, Sunderland. Mazzola and Barison each scored to complete an unimpressive 2-0 victory.

Chile met North Korea in their second group match. Marcos scored for Chile in the first half. North Korea had clearly endeared themselves to the appreciative Middlesbrough crowd and gained in confidence as the match progressed. They salvaged a splendid draw with only two minutes remaining when Pak Seung-zin equalised.

The Soviet Union met Italy at Roker Park, Sunderland. The Italians lacked cohesion against a powerful Soviet side. The Italian defence was embarrassingly easily infiltrated, failing to contain the right-winger Chislenko, who scored the only goal.

North Korea then produced the biggest World Cup upset since England's ignominious defeat by the United States in 1950. Fabri, the Italian manager, introduced seven changes for the final group match at Ayresome Park, Middlesbrough. In order to counteract the swiftness of the North Koreans, he paradoxically selected sluggish defenders in Guarneri and Janich. Italy were reduced to ten men after 35 minutes when Bulgarelli departed with torn knee ligaments. Seven minutes later Pak Doo-ik scored with a stunning strike. Italy were eliminated and faced a hostile reception on their return home.

The Soviet Union defeated Chile 2-1 in the final Group 4 match, thereby gaining maximum points, with North Korea second. Porkujan, a left-winger, was introduced and scored both goals. Marcos replied for Chile, who finished bottom.

The eight quarter-finalists were Argentina, England, Hungary, North Korea, Portugal, Uruguay, USSR and West Germany, and produced the following ties.

> England v Argentina
> Uruguay v West Germany
> North Korea v Portugal
> Hungary v USSR

England were the only nation still to concede a goal as they faced Argentina in brilliant sunshine at Wembley. The match highlighted the tensions that existed between Latin American and European football. Brazil had already departed from the tournament understandably angry at weak refereeing, which exposed their players to brutal assault.

England introduced Geoff Hurst for the injured Jimmy Greaves and Ball replaced Callaghan. Argentina recalled Albrecht after suspension. The game was interrupted by a number of fouls as the German referee, Herr Kreitlein, struggled to exercise control. Rattin, the Argentinian captain, fouled Bobby Charlton and was promptly booked. The game reached a climax after 37 minutes when Rattin remonstrated in response to the booking of a colleague. Initially, the referee took no action, but Rattin continued to argue and his persistent petulance and unwavering contempt led to Kreitlein ordering him off. Rattin protested and refused to leave the field. He lingered for eight minutes as officials on the sideline tried to restore order. At one point, Albrecht appeared to beckon his entire team to depart from the field of play.

The fouling continued unabated. Embarrassingly for England, they were frequently outclassed, especially when the mischievous Onega was in possession. With only twelve minutes remaining, Peters, out on the left, sent in a high cross. Hurst ran into empty space and glanced a header into the right-hand corner of the net to put England in the semi-final. After the final whistle, Alf Ramsey, incensed by Argentina's behaviour, intervened to prevent the customary swapping of jerseys. He later, despicably, branded Argentinians as animals. A letter from Lord Lovat to *The Times* a few days later interestingly pointed out that Argentina had committed 19 fouls compared to England's 33.

At Hillsborough, Sheffield, further controversy surrounded a South American nation. Uruguay started promisingly against West Germany, striking the bar and generally controlling the first half. Jim Finney, the English referee, incensed the Uruguayan players when he denied them a penalty after Schnellinger handled on the line. West Germany's confidence grew as they rode their luck. Haller, with a fortuitous deflection from a Held shot, gave the Germans a lead they scarcely merited. West Germany's tactics were thoroughly contemptible as they provoked the Uruguayans into retaliation. Shortly after half-time Emmerich kicked Troche, the Uruguayan captain, who foolishly responded with a kick to the stomach which resulted in an ordering off. Five minutes later Silva was somewhat harshly dismissed for scything Haller. Reduced to nine men, Uruguay yielded three further goals to Beckenbauer, Seeler and Haller in the final 20 minutes.

The North Korea v Portugal tie at Goodison Park, Everton, was an epic. North Korea sensationally scored in the first minute. As the Portuguese players retreated, Li Dong-woon, in possession, drove the ball forcefully at a massed defence. It bounced to Han Bong-jin on the right wing. He pushed the ball inside to Pak Seung-zin, who hit a rising shot into the top left-hand corner of the net.

Portugal were completely bewildered by the pace of the North Koreans, who within 20 minutes had doubled their lead. Pak Doo-ik passed to Yan Seung-kook, who in turn passed for Li Dong-woon to perfectly steer a second goal. The shell-shocked and mesmerised Portuguese defenders conceded a third only moments later. Yang Seung-kook received the ball from Han Bong-jin, and following a sinuous run past two bemused defenders, drove a right-foot shot into the roof of the net.

Portugal refused to panic and, inspired by the genius of Eusebio, staged a remarkable comeback. Eusebio passed to Simoes, collected the return and waltzed past defenders in pursuit of an opening before scoring. Critically, North Korea conceded a further goal shortly before half-time. Shin Yung-kyoo tripped Torres as he burst through the defence. Eusebio blasted the ensuing penalty past Li Chan-myung's despairing dive. In the second half Eusebio sent Simoes down the left and, as the cross came over hard and low, Eusebio met it, agilely leaping to fire home a right-footed shot. Eusebio was by now unstoppable. He darted down the left wing leaving three North Koreans in his wake and, as he neared goal, was felled when he was about to shoot. He composed himself before scoring from another penalty kick. Portugal were ahead for the first time and guaranteed their victory with the irrepressible Eusebio orchestrating the fifth goal. He ventured down the left and delivered a centre which Torres, positioned by the far post, nodded back across goal for Augusto to head in. North Korea had captivated the English with their inventiveness, generosity of spirit and courage. Portugal had shown considerable character allied to marvellous technique.

The last quarter-final tie between Hungary and the Soviet Union was played at Roker Park in Sunderland. The Soviet Union, in deference to Albert's vast array of skills, assigned Voronin to man-mark him. Gelei presented the Soviet Union with a goal after only five minutes as his blunder allowed Chislenko to score. A powerful Soviet side intimidated their meeker opponents. Porkujan added a second goal just after the interval. Bene reduced the deficit and Rakosi missed a good opportunity to equalise as Hungary staged a late rally. Yashin produced an excellent save from a thunderous free kick by Sipos. Perhaps the 2-1 result in favour of the Soviet Union would have been reversed had the splendid Yashin played in goal for Hungary. The semi-finals paired the Soviet Union against West Germany at Goodison Park and England against Portugal at Wembley.

The Soviet Union v West Germany tie was a hugely disappointing match. A battle of attrition developed into an ill-tempered affair. Sabo, in attempting to foul Beckenbauer, injured himself and was reduced to a passenger for the remainder of the game. Yashin kept the German forwards at bay with a display of highly competent goalkeeping. But with only seconds of the first half remaining, Schnellinger dispossessed Igor Chislenko, injuring him in the process. He ran on to deliver a perfect cross-field ball to Haller, who latched onto it and scored. Chislenko, by now nursing an injury, was recalled to the pitch. He was again dispossessed, this time by Held. In frustration he kicked Held and was immediately sent off. In doing so he was the fifth player to be dismissed, the fourth against West Germany. Beckenbauer scored a delightful second goal with a deftly executed left-foot shot which swerved round the Soviet wall of defenders. In the final minutes Tilkowski, in the German goal, failed to hold a cross and Porkujan scored a consolation goal. West Germany had reached their second World Cup Final in a most unsatisfactory match.

England and Portugal produced a refreshingly clean and sporting contest in contrast to so many of the brutal encounters which had plagued the tournament. Portugal excluded Morais and Vicente, the defenders who had maltreated Brazil, and Pele in particular. Nobby Stiles was assigned the unenviable task of marking Eusebio. Stiles had successfully suppressed Eusebio's supreme talents while performing for Manchester United in the European Cup against Benfica.

England played well for the first time in the competition. Bobby Charlton excelled with a superb performance. After half an hour, Wilson sent through Hunt. Pereira, in goal, parried the shot and in a scene of confusion Bobby Charlton coolly placed the ball in the net. England had created further opportunities by half-time and were largely inspired by the indefatigable Ball. Portugal enjoyed their best spell during a 15-minute period after the interval. Banks made fine saves as the impeccable Moore, tenacious Stiles and indomitable Jack Charlton resisted Portuguese efforts. With only 11 minutes left, Bobby Charlton struck a fearsome second goal. Three minutes later, as Portugal assailed the English goal, Torres rose to meet a cross from Simoes and headed over Banks. Jack Charlton punched the ball out and Eusebio inevitably scored with the resultant penalty. Portugal desperately pursued another goal and Banks had to tip a final effort by Coluna over the bar. Eusebio departed from the pitch in tears, a poignant figure who had captured the imagination of the English public.

The match for third place between Portugal and the Soviet Union took place two days later. Although apathy often surrounds this match, a crowd in excess of 70,000 converged on Wembley. Eusebio scored with a penalty, but Malafeev had equalised by half-time. Torres scored the winning goal, giving Portugal a thoroughly merited third place.

The England versus West Germany Final was played on the afternoon of Saturday 30th July, 1966. The course of history favoured England as West Germany had never, in 65 years of trying, beaten England. Matters were made worse for the Germans with Tilkowski, the goalkeeper, having incurred a shoulder injury against the Soviet Union. Helmut Schoen, the manager, could not replace him as Sepp Maier, his young and highly talented deputy, was also injured. There was much speculation about the return of a fit Jimmy Greaves. But Alf Ramsey decided to adhere to his principles and favoured a harder working Roger Hunt. By now, Hurst had established himself and was deemed to be irreplaceable. Both England and West Germany fielded unchanged sides.

England started brightly against nervous opponents. A high centre by Stiles troubled Tilkowski before Hottges headed the ball away. It was briskly returned by Bobby Charlton and Tilkowski, in punching the ball off Hurst's head, knocked himself out. England dominated the early moments but it was West Germany who opened the scoring after 13 minutes. Haller seized onto a weak headed clearance by Ray Wilson, the full-back, and scored with a low accurate shot. Only six minutes had elapsed before England equalised. Charlton passed to Moore, who was fouled by Overath. Moore chipped the ball thirty yards, allowing it to drop perfectly onto the head of Hurst, who was inexplicably unmarked. Hurst guided a faultless header past the stranded Tilkowski.

Towards the end of the first half West Germany were on the ascendancy, with Overath an inspiration in midfield orchestrating many of the dangerous moves. The rain fell at the beginning of the second half. The dynamic Alan Ball was by now establishing himself as the most influential player on the pitch. But there was a long period of deadlock before England thought they had won the World Cup with only twelve minutes remaining. Ball took a curling corner kick which was headed away by Weber. The ball ran to the feet of Hurst, who shot tamely at Tilkowski. However, the German full-back Hottges instinctively kicked the ball away when off-balance. The ball leapt invitingly to a line of English players. Peters strode forward and drove the ball between a disconsolate Tilkowski and Schnellinger into the net. With only four minutes left, England could have ensured victory. As West Germany committed themselves to attack, Ball pierced their defence, sending Hunt clear on the left. Bobby Charlton and Hurst were on his right and only Schulz stood between them and the goal. It was a three against one situation. Hunt's pass was badly delivered and Bobby Charlton's hurried effort was sliced well wide of goal. In the final minute Jack Charlton recklessly challenged Held in heading the ball away. Emmerich took a gentle free kick about 35 yards from goal on the left side of the field. The ball slid past a wall of defenders and fell to Held. He shot at goal and the ball struck Schnellinger on the arm unintentionally. The ball deflected between Seeler and Wilson, arriving at Weber, who lunged out his right leg to score powerfully at the far post.

West Germany had dramatically equalised with only 15 seconds of the match remaining. Arriving when it did, the goal would have broken most teams. But Ramsey strolled onto the field and told his players, 'You've won it once, now do it again.' He also asked his players to look at the exhausted Germans and remarked, 'Look at them, they're finished.'

Alan Ball ran even faster in extra time and produced a shot which Tilkowski turned over the bar. With ten minutes of extra-time played, one of the most controversial moments in the entire history of the game occurred. Alan Ball received the ball on the right wing following a pass by Stiles. Ball accelerated before crossing the ball to Hurst, standing about eight yards from goal. Hurst controlled the ball, swivelled and, whilst leaning back, delivered a forceful drive which struck the underside of the crossbar and bounced down. Weber headed the ball away as Roger Hunt stood with his arms raised in acknowledgement of a goal. There was a moment of indecision as England players claimed a goal. The Swiss referee, Herr Dienst, was besieged by German players dismissing the claim. Herr Dienst ran to the sideline and consulted with the Russian linesman, Tofik Bahkramov, before emerging to the centre circle to the anguish of the shattered Germans.

West Germany had no alternative but to commit themselves to attack, thus exposing their defence. The referee had his whistle in his mouth as Moore sent a long precise pass which found Hurst. Hurst advanced as Overath closed in on him. Tilkowski remained on his goal-line. Hurst blasted the ball in an effort to gain respite, but the rising left-footed shot was outrageously accurate and exploded into the roof of the net. Geoff Hurst had become the first player to score three goals in a World Cup Final. England were the first hosts to win the World Cup since Italy in 1934. Alf Ramsey was later awarded a knighthood for his achievement.

Results: England 1966

Group 1

England	0	Uruguay	0
France	1	Mexico	1
Uruguay	2	France	1
England	2	Mexico	0
Uruguay	0	Mexico	0
England	2	France	0

	P	W	D	L	F	A	Pts
					Goals		
England	3	2	1	0	4	0	5
Uruguay	3	1	2	0	2	1	4
Mexico	3	0	2	1	1	3	2
France	3	0	1	2	2	5	1

Group 2

West Germany	5	Switzerland	0
Argentina	2	Spain	1
Spain	2	Switzerland	1
West Germany	0	Argentina	0
Argentina	2	Switzerland	0
West Germany	2	Spain	1

	P	W	D	L	F	A	Pts
					Goals		
West Germany	3	2	1	0	7	1	5
Argentina	3	2	1	0	4	1	5
Spain	3	1	0	2	4	5	2
Switzerland	3	0	0	3	1	9	0

Group 3

Brazil	2	Bulgaria			0	
Portugal	3	Hungary			1	
Hungary	3	Brazil			1	
Portugal	3	Bulgaria			0	
Portugal	3	Brazil			1	
Hungary	3	Bulgaria			1	

	P	W	D	L	Goals F	A	Pts
Portugal	3	3	0	0	9	2	6
Hungary	3	2	0	1	7	5	4
Brazil	3	1	0	2	4	6	2
Bulgaria	3	0	0	3	1	8	0

Group 4

USSR	3	North Korea	0
Italy	2	Chile	0
North Korea	1	Chile	1
USSR	1	Italy	0
North Korea	1	Italy	0
USSR	2	Chile	1

	P	W	D	L	Goals F	A	Pts
USSR	3	3	0	0	6	1	6
North Korea	3	1	1	1	2	4	3
Italy	3	1	0	2	2	2	2
Chile	3	0	1	2	2	5	1

Quarter finals

England	1	Argentina	0
West Germany	4	Uruguay	0
Portugal	5	North Korea	3
USSR	2	Hungary	1

Semi-finals

| West Germany | 2 | USSR | 1 |
| England | 2 | Portugal | 1 |

Third Place Match

| Portugal | 2 | USSR | 1 |

Final

| England | 4 | West Germany | 2* |

*After extra time, 2-2 at 90 minutes

England: Banks, Cohen, Wilson, Stiles, Charlton J, Moore, Ball, Hunt, Charlton R, Hurst, Peters

West Germany: Tilkowski, Hottges, Schulz, Weber, Schnellinger, Haller, Beckenbauer, Overath, Seeler, Held, Emmerich

Scorers: Hurst (3), Peters for England
Haller, Weber for West Germany

1970

Four students were killed and nine others injured when National Guardsmen opened fire on a student demonstration at Kent State University, Ohio. The shootings occurred during a wave of campus protests against the entry of American troops into Cambodia on 1st May. On 4th May, between 1,500 and 3,000 students gathered on the college campus at Kent State University, contravening an order by the State Governor banning all meetings, whether peaceful or otherwise. At about midday tear gas was used to break up the demonstration. When some students threw back the canisters and started to hurl stones, the National Guard opened fire without warning. The four students killed – two women and two men, aged 19 and 20 – were not involved in the demonstration itself.

On 22nd May there was outrage in Israel when a bus carrying children from school was shelled by Arab guerrillas on the Israel-Lebanon border. Eight children and three adults were killed and 21 were injured when the guerrillas fired bazookas at the vehicle from a distance of 20 yards. The Popular Front for the Liberation of Palestine claimed responsibility, and within hours Israeli forces had shelled four Lebanese villages in reprisal.

On 12th September three airliners were blown up by Arab guerrillas after a triple hijack. The British, Swiss and American planes were seized by members of the Popular Front for the Liberation of Palestine who had been holding about 300 passengers hostage at Dawson's Field, a desert airstrip near

Amman. After days of negotiation, the hostages were finally released in exchange for seven Arab detainees.

In mid-November more than 150,000 people died in the typhoon and tidal wave which brought death and disaster to East Pakistan. The tidal wave, as high as a two-storey building, changed the map of the delta, sweeping away islands and creating others. Whole communities, together with their livestock, were killed.

*   *   *

Mexico, at first sight, appeared to be an injudicious choice for staging the ninth World Cup, particularly as Argentina had made a bid. The FIFA Congress, with Sir Stanley Rous presiding, took into consideration Mexico's stronger currency and the existing infrastructure after the 1968 Olympic Games. Nevertheless, there were grave fears relating to heat and altitude. The 1968 Olympics had demonstrated, only too clearly, the problems of top-class athletes competing at high altitudes. Few parts of central Mexico were at less than 6-7,000 feet above sea level. What could have been prevented was the insensitive selling-out of the tournament to financial interests. Far too many games were played in noonday heat merely to satisfy European television companies.

There were 71 entrants out of 138 FIFA members registered for qualifying matches, divided into 16 groups. The only withdrawal was North Korea, who refused to meet Israel and were forced to pull out by FIFA. The late registrations of Cuba, Albania, Congo and Ghana were not accepted by the 1968 FIFA Congress which met in Casablanca. There it was decided that Europe would have eight places, South America three, Central and North America one, Asia and the Pacific one and Africa one. The Africans had obtained their objective by boycotting the 1966 World Cup. There were two important innovations introduced at the 1970 tournament. First, each team would be allowed to make two substitutions at any time and for any position during a match. Second, a card cautioning system came into operation, with a yellow card denoting a booking and a red card a sending-off.

Four of the eight quarter-finalists from the 1966 World Cup were surprisingly eliminated during the qualifying competition. Portugal, third in 1966, and regarded as one of the rising nations of European soccer, finished bottom of their group behind less fancied nations Romania, Greece and Switzerland. They were, by now, a veteran side and Eusebio was not fully fit. Hungary had retained their Olympic title in Mexico City in 1968 and, being accustomed to the rarefied atmosphere, were considered to be strong challengers for the World Cup. However, they had to play off against Czechoslovakia after a surprise defeat by Denmark. Czechoslovakia easily triumphed 4-1 and for the first time since 1950 the Magyars were absent from the Finals.

Italy, desperately keen to atone for the humiliation of 1966, only ensured qualification in their final qualifying match against East Germany in Naples, winning with three first-half goals.

Of the Home Countries, only England, as champions, travelled to Mexico. Wales lost all four matches in their clashes with Italy and East Germany. Scotland lost their final two games against West Germany and Austria. Northern Ireland were defeated in their critical final group game against the Soviet Union, 2-0 in Moscow. George Best was absent, having been injured two days earlier playing for Manchester United.

Argentina, who were favourites to qualify from their three-nation group, lost to Bolivia and Peru. The former Brazilian hero Didi managed the Peruvian side who progressed to Mexico. Brazil were the only nation to qualify with a 100 per cent record, impressively scoring 23 goals in six qualifying matches and conceding just two. Tostao scored nine of the goals. The game between Brazil and Paraguay at the Maracana Stadium on 31st August 1969 attracted a record crowd of 183,341 for a qualifying game. Uruguay completed the complement of South American nations. The reigning South

American champions did not concede a single goal in their four matches.

Israel competed in their first finals after beating Australia in the Asia-Oceania Final. Morocco were also debutants and became the first African nation since Egypt in 1934 to contest the final stages.

El Salvador's journey to their first participation in the Finals could scarcely have been more turbulent or dramatic. They emerged as winners of the CONCACAF group after ten matches and a war with Honduras. Honduras and El Salvador played each other for the right to take part in the 1970 World Cup in Mexico. The first match took place in Tegucigalpa, the Honduran capital, on 8th June 1969. The Salvadoran team had to endure a sleepless night as psychological warfare was waged by the Honduran fans. A sleep-deprived El Salvador lost 1-0.

Roberto Cardona, a Honduran striker, scored a final-minute winning goal. This was too much to bear for 18-year-old Amelia Bolanios, who was watching the match in front of the television at her parents' home in San Salvador. She seized her father's pistol and shot herself through the heart. The whole capital participated in her televised funeral.

One week later, at the return match, the Honduran team spent a sleepless night as screaming fans broke the windows of the hotel, and threw rotten eggs and dead rats. Portraits of the national heroine, Amelia Bolanios, were displayed by the mob that lined the route to the stadium. El Salvador won 3-0 and the Honduran team were escorted back to the airport by armoured cars. Two visiting fans died and many more were kicked and beaten as they fled to the border.

Four days before the qualifying play-off, diplomatic ties were dramatically severed. This, however, was trivial compared with the aftermath of El Salvador's 3-2 extra-time victory on 15th June 1969. Within 24 hours the so-called 'soccer war' had broken out. Three days of bitter fighting then followed which left 3,000 dead. The violence reflected a long-standing hostility, with Hondurans resentful towards the influx of Salvadorans across the border into their sparsely populated farmland. El Salvador claimed that Honduras had persecuted these settlers.

El Salvador eventually ensured their qualification by beating Haiti 1-0 in a play-off in Kingston, Jamaica.

On 10th January 1970 the groups were selected at the Maria Isabel Hotel in Mexico City. The groupings were:

Group 1: (Mexico City) Belgium, El Salvador, Mexico, USSR

Group 2: (Toluca and Puebla) Israel, Italy, Sweden, Uruguay

Group 3: (Guadalajara) Brazil, Czechoslovakia, England, Romania

Group 4: (Leon) Bulgaria, Morocco, Peru, West Germany

The opening match, a goalless draw, between Mexico and the Soviet Union on 31st May replicated the curtain-raiser at Wembley four years earlier in its sheer tedium. A crowd of 107,000 watched the hosts play defensively against a cautious Soviet side. Alberto Onofre, an accomplished Mexican half-back, was missing, having broken a leg in a practice match four days earlier. Enrique Borja, a highly rated striker, was another notable absentee. Kurt Tschenser, the West German referee, set a precedent by cautioning four Soviet players, thus sending a potent message to the 16 participating nations. The FIFA directive ensured there was no repetition of the vicious thuggery which had clouded the tournaments of 1962 and 1966. Indeed, not a single player was to be sent off in Mexico. Pusatch of the Soviet Union made history when he replaced Shesterniev at half-time to become the World Cup's first substitute.

Mexico's status as hosts exempted them from qualifying, thus allowing El Salvador an improbable place in the finals. Although El Salvador endeared themselves to the Mexican crowd with their enthusiasm and tireless running, they were easily overcome by Belgium. Magana, in goal, performed well in a damage limitation exercise. Van Moer scored twice for Belgium and Lambert, with a penalty, completed a 3-0 victory.

Belgium were overwhelmed in their next match against a powerful Soviet side. The Soviet Union imposed themselves from the kick-off and scored after 15 minutes when a 30 yard drive by Bishovets carried under Piot's body. Further second-half goals by Asatiani, Bishovets and Khmelnitski contributed to a comfortable win. Lambert scored a late consolation goal for Belgium, who now needed to defeat Mexico to qualify for the quarter-finals.

The Mexico versus El Salvador encounter was overshadowed by an extraordinary refereeing decision. With the match goal-less and half-time approaching, Ali Kandil, the Egyptian match official, blew for a foul to El Salvador. But the Mexican, Padilla, took the kick and his pass found Valdivia, who scored. El Salvador argued and protested for four minutes, two players were booked, but Kandil remained unmoved. After the interval a demoralised El Salvador conceded a further three goals to Valdivia, Fragoso and Basaguren, who made World Cup history by becoming the first substitute to score and to replace a substitute.

El Salvador had the unfortunate distinction of being the only side to fail to score in the tournament. Nevertheless, they battled bravely against the Soviet Union, who took 51 minutes to eventually break the deadlock with a goal by Bishovets. A further goal by Bishovets in the 74th minute completed a 2-0 win.

The final Group 1 match paired Mexico with Belgium. Mexico assailed the Belgian goal in a pulsating match watched by a crowd of 105,000. The only goal of the game arrived in the 15th minute. Valdivia ran into the prostrate Jeck in the penalty area. The Argentinian referee, Angel Coerezza, awarded a highly dubious penalty which Pena converted. Mexico had reached the quarter-finals for the first time in their history. The Soviet Union headed the group on the basis of scoring one more goal.

Group 2 matches were played in Puebla and Toluca, which at 8,792 feet above sea level was the highest venue. Uruguay, who qualified with consummate ease, were less impressive against the amateurs of Israel. Luis Cubilla was a constant source of threat but Vissoker, the Israeli goalkeeper, performed competently to prevent a landslide defeat. Uruguay lost the highly talented Pedro Rocha after only 13 minutes with a groin injury. Sadly, it was the end of his World Cup participation. A header by Maneiro midway through the first half and a second-half strike by Mujica ensured a 2-0 win for Uruguay.

Italy, the European Champions, met Sweden in the rarefied atmosphere of Toluca. The Italian captain, Rivera, was omitted and replaced by Mazzola. Italy attacked boldly in the first half, during which Domenghini scored the decisive goal following a mistake by the reserve goalkeeper, Hellstrom.

Uruguay and Italy played out a grim goalless draw in Puebla. The match was one of almost unremitting tedium, with both sides displaying their mastery of defensive football.

Israel and Sweden met at Toluca in front of an embarrassingly meagre crowd of 9,000. Sweden introduced five changes following their narrow defeat by Italy and recalled Sven Larsson in goal. Turesson eventually broke the deadlock after 57 minutes with a goal for Sweden. However, three minutes later Spiegler gained a creditable 1-1 draw as he strode through the defence before unleashing a wonderful shot from 25 yards.

In order to qualify, Sweden needed to defeat Uruguay by two clear goals in Puebla. Before the match started, rumours emanated that the Brazilian referee, De Moraes, had been offered a bribe. The rumours were later to be proved unfounded. Nevertheless, the match official was replaced by Henry Landauer of the United States. Uruguay again elected to adopt a defensive strategy aimed at stifling the Swedish attack. A goalless draw looked inevitable until Grahn of Sweden, a substitute who had been on the pitch for little over five minutes, scored with a header in the dying seconds.

Italy played cautiously and nervously against Israel, mindful of their humiliating defeat by North Korea in 1966. The few chances they created were dealt with outstandingly well by the Israeli goalkeeper, Vissoker. Gianni Rivera, the captain, was a second-half replacement for Domenghini. A goalless draw ensured Italy topped the group despite scoring only one goal in three games. Uruguay, rather luckily, edged ahead of Sweden to join Italy.

Group 3 was perhaps the most intriguing as it comprised of the champions, England, and the favourites, Brazil, together with impressive qualifiers in Romania and Czechoslovakia. Brazil entered the finals just three months after an internal upheaval had unseated manager Joao Saldanha and installed Zagalo, a World Cup winner of 1958 and 1962, in his place. Brazil, with a forward line rivalled only by its predecessor in 1958 and Hungary's in 1954, contributed to arguably the most memorable of all World Cups. (1954 would have its advocates.) Jairzinho, Pele, Tostao and Rivelino embellished the tournament with their exhilarating, attacking football.

England, whilst retaining leading players from 1966 in Bobby Moore, Geoff Hurst and Gordon Banks, reinforced the side with newer talents in Francis Lee, Colin Bell and Terry Cooper. The phlegmatic captain, Bobby Moore, had even survived the trauma of being placed under house arrest in Colombia on a trumped-up charge of stealing a bracelet from a jeweller's shop. He owed his place in the World Cup to a flurry of diplomatic activity which secured his release for the Championship.

However absurd the allegations against Moore, England failed to endear themselves to the Mexican public. For this, Sir Alf Ramsey must be held largely culpable. His gauche, hostile and boorish handling of local journalists whipped up a frenzy of anti-English feeling in the Mexican media.

In the opening Group 3 match against Romania, England were loudly jeered by the Mexican crowd. Ramsey criticised the Jalisco Stadium pitch, thus heightening antipathy towards England. Dembrowski should have scored for Romania in the first half when an easy opportunity struck the crossbar. A tough-tackling, robust Romanian side eventually succumbed

119

to a Geoff Hurst goal in the second half. Hurst scored with a low, left-footed drive.

Pele returned to the Brazilian side, despite his threat to retire after being kicked out of the 1966 tournament. Pele, embroiled in a power struggle with Saldanha, largely shaped the manager's fate after Saldanha contemplated dropping him. Since 1966, Brazil had developed many talented players including Carlos Alberto, Clodoaldo and Tostao, who recovered from a severe eye injury.

Although Brazil were strongly fancied to win the World Cup, much criticism was levelled at their fragile defence. Against Czechoslovakia in their opening game, their vulnerability was exposed after only eleven minutes when Petras scored. Brazil equalised after 24 minutes from a free kick when Jairzinho went on a 'dummy' run whilst Rivelino bent the ball around the Czechoslovakian defensive wall. The most memorable moment of the match arrived with half-time approaching. Pele, in possession in his own half a full 60 yards from goal, spotted the Czechoslovakian goalkeeper, Viktor, off his line. He elected to strike a high ball goalwards. Viktor frantically scrambled back to his goal but was left helpless as the ball soared only inches wide of the post. It was a marvellous piece of improvisation, quite unique to Pele. Brazil imposed their superiority during the second half. Pele received a long pass from Gerson on his chest and scored with a volley. Jairzinho scored a third goal which looked suspiciously offside. However, there was no doubting his second and Brazil's fourth goal late in the game when he ran past four men before scoring, thus completing an emphatic 4-1 victory.

Czechoslovakia introduced five changes for their next game against Romania and recalled Kvasniak, who had played in the 1962 final. Petras again distinguished himself for Czechoslovakia. A diving header after only three minutes was not enough to win the game as Romania asserted themselves, abandoned the physical approach and proceeded to display fluent football. Neagu equalised after 52 minutes. With 15 minutes remaining, Neagu was fouled inside the penalty area and Dumitrache converted the spot-kick to give Romania victory.

England's status as World Champions had been met with an enduring scepticism. The manner of their victory four years earlier had left many people disgruntled. On the eve of England's critical encounter with Brazil, several thousand youths congregated outside the Hilton Hotel where the team were staying. They contrived to make sufficient noise to ensure that the players would take the field sleep-deprived. The match was staged at midday with temperatures approaching 100° Fahrenheit. The Jalisco Stadium in Guadalajara was packed to capacity and the large crowd were treated to a classic game.

The midfield artistry and panache of Gerson was missing, injured in his side's opening match. England were without Keith Newton, who was also injured. During the opening ten minutes England dominated possession. Then came what is generally considered to be the greatest save ever witnessed. Jairzinho received the ball from Carlos Alberto down the right. The winger accelerated past Cooper to the bye-line. He swept the ball forcefully to the far post beyond the reach of Labone, Moore and Banks, who were guarding the goal area. Pele pounced, leaping over Mullery. He arched his back and neck, thereby gaining maximum velocity as he unleashed a ferocious header downward. The ball hurtled towards the net at the far post. Banks was positioned at the near post in anticipation of Jairzinho's cross. The entire stadium and the viewing millions had already acclaimed an exceptional goal. But Banks somehow twisted over to the right of goal and, with his legs askew, the ball struck the ground two or three feet from his line. It travelled at frightening speed but Banks' groping hand miraculously scooped the ball over the bar.

The game was thoroughly absorbing and quite beautifully balanced. Brazil's incandescent skills were matched by the intelligence of England's football, which produced swift breaks.

With more ruthless forwards, England would surely have gained a draw.

The deciding goal in the 59th minute had Tostao as its architect. He rather fortunately played the ball through Bobby Moore's legs. He then cleverly weaved around converging defenders and centred the ball to Pele. As Labone and Cooper advanced, Pele deftly stroked the ball to his right. Jairzinho, on his outside, met the ball to perfection and blasted his cross-shot into the net.

With 20 minutes remaining, Alf Ramsey substituted Astle for Lee and Bell for Charlton. Astle had a perfect chance to equalise when Everaldo erred, rolling the ball to Astle near the penalty spot. A goal seemed certain, but the ball fell to his weaker left foot and it slid past Felix's left-hand post. Two further chances fell to Alan Ball but he failed to convert either.

Brazil omitted both Rivelino and Gerson for their final group match against Romania. Both Mocanu and Dinu resorted to brutal defending and the former was particularly fortunate to remain on the field. Pele opened the scoring with a free kick and Jairzinho added a second midway through the first half. At that point, Romania replaced their goalkeeper, Adamache, with Radacanu, who had been disciplined for violating a curfew. Dumitrache reduced the deficit before half-time. As Brazil applied pressure, after the interval, Pele scored again before Dembrowski headed a second goal near the end. Brazil won 3-2 without being seriously stretched, thus gaining maximum points.

England required a draw against Czechoslovakia to ensure a quarter-final place. Bobby Charlton equalled Billy Wright's record of 105 caps. His brother Jack was recalled to a re-organised side containing many reserve players. England proceeded to give a wretched display. A dubious penalty decision for an alleged handling offence by Hagara afforded Allan Clarke the only goal during the second half.

The opening Group 4 match between Peru and Bulgaria was marred by a terrible tragedy which had occurred two days earlier. A devastating earthquake in Peru had killed 50,000 people. A one-minute silence was observed in memory of those who perished. The Peruvian players, wearing black armbands, were visibly affected by the appalling disaster.

Bulgaria quickly made capital against a deeply traumatised side and Dermendiev enjoyed the distinction of scoring the first goal of the tournament. Peru's cause looked hopeless as they surrendered a second goal four minutes after the interval, when Rubinos, in goal, failed to hold a shot from Bonev. But Peru staged a quite remarkable comeback. In the 50th minute Gallardo crashed a shot off the underside of the bar to reduce the lead. Only five minutes later their captain, Hector Chumpitaz, struck a free kick which eluded a massed defensive wall on its route to the net. With only 17 minutes left, Peru sensationally won the match amidst cathartic scenes of emotion. The young inside-left Cubillas scored a brilliant solo goal to provide the perfect climax to a marvellous drama.

Morocco were the first African nation to qualify for the finals since Egypt in 1934. They were 500-1 outsiders to win the World Cup. West Germany, by contrast, were amongst the strong favourites. Despite the apparent mismatch, it was Morocco who led the Group 4 encounter with a goal by Jarir after 21 minutes. The second half commenced in extraordinary circumstances. Laurens Van Ravens, the Dutch referee, signalled the restart with Morocco short of a full complement of players. The goalkeeper, Allal Ben Kassu, was absent for nearly a minute as play continued. West Germany eventually equalised in the 56th minute when Seeler scored from a pass by Muller following intense German pressure. With only 12 minutes left, Loehr headed against the bar and Gerd Muller gave West Germany an unjust 2-1 victory.

Morocco battled courageously in their next game against Peru, keeping the South Americans at bay during the first half. The game turned decisively in Peru's favour during a ten-minute spell midway through the second half. Cubillas seized on to a bad clearance by Ben Kassu in goal to open the scoring. Two minutes later he provided the groundwork for Challe to add a second. With 15 minutes remaining, Cubillas netted arguably the most outstanding goal of the tournament.

Helmut Schoen, the West German manager, introduced Libuda against Bulgaria. The Balkan side started promisingly and scored after 12 minutes when Nikodimov broke away. Libuda equalised in the 20th minute following a misjudgement by Simeonov in goal. Muller scored from a cross by Libuda to give West Germany a half-time lead. Muller then converted a penalty after Libuda had been fouled. He contributed to the fourth goal, passing to Seeler, who drove home. Muller's third goal arrived two minutes from time before Kolev gained a consolation goal as a rampant West Germany won 5-2.

Peru and West Germany had already qualified prior to their meeting in Leon. A total of four goals were scored during a 25-minute period in the first half. Gerd Muller netted a hat-trick in a highly entertaining match. Cubillas reduced the arrears a minute from the interval. Peru pursued further goals but were denied by the able Sepp Maier in goal. Victory ensured West Germany would remain in Leon for their quarter-final match, whereas Peru would have to travel to Guadalajara.

Bulgaria and Morocco fought for the right to gain their first point in the final game of Group 4. Bulgaria made radical changes. No fewer than 20 players participated in their three matches. They established a lead five minutes from the interval when Zhechev scored. After an hour, Ghazouani equalised, thus earning Morocco a well-merited draw.

The quarter-finals produced the following ties:

Soviet Union v Uruguay
Italy v Mexico
Brazil v Peru
England v West Germany

Uruguay and the Soviet Union contested a dour struggle in a half-empty Azteca stadium. Morales returned to the Uruguay side following a knee injury. The Soviet Union were the more enterprising side but their attacks were consistently repelled by a highly competent Uruguayan defence. The game produced no goals after 90 minutes. During extra time the Soviet players visibly tired. Nevertheless, Bishovets scored but his goal was disallowed. The deciding goal three minutes from the end of extra time was marred by controversy. Victor Esparrago had entered the pitch as a substitute with more than 100 minutes played. Cubilla, the Uruguayan right-winger, crossed the ball which was met by the head of Esparrago. The ball appeared not to have crossed the goal-line but, amidst vigorous Soviet protests, the goal stood.

Mexico's advancement to the quarter-finals was met by mounting hysteria. The rejoicing of their success was gaining a frightening momentum which was abruptly halted by Italy in Toluca. Mexican expectations were heightened when Gonzalez scored after only 13 minutes following exquisite play by Fragoso. Domenghini equalised with a somewhat fortuitous goal after 25 minutes when his shot deflected off Pena into the goal. Valcareggi, the Italian coach, pulled off a masterstroke at half-time, replacing Mazzola with Luigi Riva, their captain. Italy finally rid themselves of their inhibitions and Riva and Rivera complemented each other quite brilliantly. Riva gave a dazzling performance. He exchanged passes with De Sisti and crossed to Rivera, who scored with a well-executed left-foot shot. Five minutes later an intricate move initiated by Riva led to the striker scoring a third. Finally, Riva received the ball from Rivera, evaded two tackles and placed the ball past Calderon in goal at the second attempt, to complete an emphatic 4-1 victory.

Brazil and Peru engaged in an enchanting encounter at Guadalajara. There were close parallels between the two sides, who were renowned for their exhilarating, exuberant football but also notorious for defensive weaknesses. The Peruvian coach, Didi, who had inculcated his team with Brazilian values, was briefly reunited with his former colleagues. Gerson and Rivelino returned to the Brazilian side. Tostao played splendidly for Brazil and was instrumental in the first goal, creating an opportunity for Rivelino who struck a low, swerving shot past Rubinos after only eleven minutes. Only four minutes later Brazil had doubled their lead with another interchange between Rivelino and Tostao, the latter scoring from an acute angle. After half an hour Peru reduced the deficit when Gallardo scored from a narrow angle with Felix out of position. Seven minutes after the interval, a long shot by Pele was deflected by Tostao to re-establish a two-goal lead. A plucky Peru fought back and Sotil, who had replaced Baylon, advanced and shot. Brito failed to clear the ball and Cubillas scored from 20 yards. Jairzinho brought the game to a fitting climax when he received a defence-shattering pass from Tostao and netted, thus maintaining his enviable record of scoring in every game.

West Germany faced England in Leon with the knowledge that they had an appalling record against their opponents. Eleven previous full internationals played since 1901 had resulted in nine victories to England and one draw. After 67 years, an understrength England were finally defeated, in a friendly match of no significance, in Hanover in 1968.

A dramatic development occurred before the start of the game when Gordon Banks was declared ill. Peter Bonetti, his replacement, was about to make a World Cup debut. Banks was thought to be suffering from 'Montezuma's Revenge' which left him white, nauseous and eternally grateful for access to a toilet.

England played quite magnificently during the opening half hour before deservedly taking the lead, with a splendidly executed goal. Cooper, in his customary left-back position, pushed the ball inside to Mullery, who exchanged passes with Lee. He then directed the ball across the width of the pitch to the right where Newton was positioned. Mullery then raced diagonally to the far post and received Newton's low centre, which he perfectly placed past a bemused Maier. His first goal in over 30 internationals had been worth the wait. Four minutes after the interval England appeared to have secured a semi-final place. Moore dispossessed Seeler and passed to Ball who, in turn, found Hurst. Hurst advanced in the inside-right position and passed to Newton, who surged forward on the outside and again delivered an excellent cross which was met by Peters, who scored.

Helmut Schoen, the German manager, made an astute substitution after 58 minutes when Libuda was replaced by Grabowski. His runs severely punished Cooper, who was wilting in the oppressive heat and altitude. In the 68th minute Beckenbauer advanced, picked up a rebound, and struck a low, right-footed, seemingly harmless shot from the edge of the penalty area. Bonetti was slow to respond as the ball travelled under his dive into the side of the net.

Within a minute of the goal, Ramsey substituted Bobby Charlton, making his record 106th appearance for England, with Colin Bell. Ball unleashed Bell, who delivered a far post low cross which was met athletically by Hurst. He flicked a header which appeared netbound inside the far post. At the last moment, the ball flew across the goal, to the relief of a stranded Maier. Peters was then replaced by the combative Norman Hunter, thus radically changing the composition of the midfield. The substitution seemed ill-advised, particularly as it occurred when Newton was on the ground nursing an injury.

England were visibly tiring and, with less than a quarter of an hour remaining, West Germany equalised. Labone failed to clear the ball decisively and Schnellinger seized the opportunity to deliver a left-footed cross to Seeler, who was marginally onside. He slipped behind Mullery and leapt with his back to goal to send the ball on a remarkable parabola over Bonetti, who was out of position.

During extra time West Germany were on the offensive and produced a succession of corners. But there was a moment of high controversy before the fate of the match was finally decided by Muller. Lee evaded Schnellinger on the by-line and delivered a perfect cross which Hurst drove home. The goal was inexplicably disallowed. In the 108th minute Grabowski on the right wing beat Cooper, crossed, and Loehr headed the ball back from the left. Muller took off in anticipation of the ball at the far post. But he suddenly launched his agile frame and, with Bonetti again out of position, struck a mid-air volley to cruelly eliminate the Champions. West Germany had staged a truly remarkable comeback. England declined inexorably, at international level, thereafter.

The semi-finals paired Italy with West Germany in Mexico City and Brazil with Uruguay in Guadalajara.

In the Azteca Stadium, Italy and West Germany fought a memorable contest which produced five goals during extra time. That extra time took place was only made possible by a dramatic West German equaliser in injury time.

Italy established a lead after only eight minutes when Boninsegna scored with a left-footed shot following a rather fortunate rebound. Italy were lucky to escape a strong penalty claim when Beckenbauer spurted past four players into the penalty area, only to be sent sprawling in a collision with Facchetti.

At half-time Italy replaced Mazzola with Rivera. West Germany dominated the play as Italy adopted a defensive strategy. Three incidents compressed into a six-minute spell of fierce German pressure nearly resulted in an equaliser. First, Overath struck the bar. Then, when Beckenbauer was felled, the referee awarded a free kick just outside the penalty area. The Germans claimed the offence occurred in the area. Lastly, in a frantic goalmouth scramble, Bertini appeared to scythe Seeler.

With Italy seemingly on their way to their first Final since 1938, West Germany launched a last desperate attack. In the third minute of injury time, Grabowski crossed from the left and Schnellinger, a veteran of four World Cups, slid the ball into the net. Sepp Maier raced the length of the field to dive on Schnellinger amidst uncontained scenes of joy.

Franz Beckenbauer had by now been playing for half an hour with a dislocated shoulder but he refused to leave the pitch, continuing heavily strapped. Five minutes into extra time, West Germany took the lead when an innocuous header by Seeler resulted in a defensive mix-up by Poletti which

Muller capitalised on. A free kick by Rivera enabled Burgnich to score following another defensive lapse. Two minutes before the end of the first period of extra-time, Domenghini broke on the right and passed to Riva, who struck a low shot into the far corner.

With ten minutes remaining, a corner to West Germany was met at the far, left-hand post by Seeler, who nodded it across goal and Muller dived low to score. This was Muller's tenth goal of the tournament and he was to finish the top scorer. Almost immediately from the restart, Boninsegna, taking the ball out to the left, evaded Schulz and crossed for Rivera to drive the wining goal. Once again Rivera had been a decisive influence in the later stages of a game.

The Uruguayans complained to FIFA before their semi-final with Brazil, as they considered their opponents to have 'home advantage' in Guadalajara. In the opening minutes Uruguay cleverly contained Gerson, thereby reducing Brazil's fluency. Uruguay scored first after 18 minutes when Morales delivered a long pass to the diminutive Luis Cubilla, who scored from an acute angle with Felix out of position.

Brazil equalised right on half-time when Tostao advanced before releasing an exquisite pass to Clodoaldo, who scored from the penalty box. The second half resumed with Brazil dominant. However, Uruguay almost regained the lead when a forceful Cubilla header was brilliantly saved by Felix. With only 14 minutes left, Jairzinho scored, completing a move he had orchestrated in his own half. He passed to Pele, who in turn gave the ball to Tostao. He laid it into the path of the marauding Jairzinho, who blasted the ball into the net from an acute angle. A left-foot shot from Rivelino in the last minute, following a pass from Pele, gave the 3-1 scoreline a flattering quality as Uruguay had fought with courage and ingenuity. Pele then produced another moment of outrageous inventiveness. He pursued a long ball towards goal and, as Mazurkiewiecz rapidly advanced, Pele allowed the ball to bypass him. He then darted around a bewildered goalkeeper before shooting marginally wide.

The third place play-off in the Azteca Stadium on the eve of the Final was watched by an astonishing attendance of 104,000. West Germany scored a fine goal by Overath midway through the first half. A thrilling movement between Libuda, Muller and Seeler culminated in the goal. Thereafter, both sides attacked, producing an entertaining game. Overath, in the absence of Beckenbauer, skilfully marshalled the midfield. It was the first time during West Germany's campaign that Gerd Muller had failed to score.

The World Cup Final, played on 21st June, promised to be an intriguing contrast of styles. Brazil, easily the most gifted side, were vulnerable in defence and Felix in goal hardly inspired confidence. Italy had a strong, *catenaccio* defence. They had also improved in front of goal as the tournament progressed. Both countries had won the World Cup twice and whoever won would be permanent holders of the Jules Rimet Trophy.

It was, appropriately, Pele who gave the Brazilians the lead after 18 minutes when he scored his country's 100th World Cup goal. A Tostao throw-in found Rivelino, who delivered a well-judged cross. Pele rose beyond Bertini and launched himself spectacularly to head the ball powerfully past Albertosi's left side. He thus emulated Vava by scoring in two World Cup Finals.

Although Mazzola of Italy was quite outstanding and covered vast tracts of ground, the side carried little menace and appeared to lack self-confidence. It was something of a surprise, therefore, when they equalised eight minutes from half-time. Clodoaldo foolishly attempted to back-heel the ball to Everaldo deep in his own half. Boninsegna pounced, gained possession and sprinted into the penalty area. Carlos Alberto and Brito attempted to converge on him, but Felix dashed out of goal and collided with Brito. Boninsegna regained his composure and concentrated on the path of the ball. Had he missed the opportunity, Riva was in attendance and would have scored.

Gerson, a compulsive cigarette smoker, masterminded Brazil's handsome victory with a majestic second-half performance. In the 65th minute he sent a pass to Everaldo on the wing. Everaldo pushed the ball straight ahead to Jairzinho, who in turn found Gerson. Gerson struck a thunderous low, left-footed shot which left Albertosi helpless.

Five minutes later World Cup history was created. A foul on Pele resulted in a free kick to Brazil. Everaldo delivered a short pass to Gerson. Gerson crossed precisely, over the head of Burgnich, to Pele. Pele unselfishly elected to head the ball down to Jairzinho, who messily scored running the ball into the net. In doing so became the first player to score in every round.

With four minutes remaining, Brazil scored a fourth goal. Clodoaldo initiated an attack with a mesmerising run. He passed the ball forward to Jairzinho, who in turn found Pele. Pele rolled the ball to Carlos Alberto, who was hurtling forward, on the right. He hit a thunderous right-foot shot inside Albertosi's right-hand post.

Brazil had won the Jules Rimet Trophy for the third time and so it became their permanent possession. It was a popular victory which demonstrated that enterprise, panache, exuberance, intuitive genius, and attacking football could be rewarded with success. The two previous tournaments had filled people with a sense of foreboding, as many of the games had been characterised by negativity and violence. Brazil had captured the imagination with their triumph of creativity over cynicism. Despite the difficult conditions, the 1970 World Cup developed into arguably the best ever.

Results: Mexico 1970

Group 1

Mexico	0	USSR	0
Belgium	3	El Salvador	0
USSR	4	Belgium	1
Mexico	4	El Salvador	0
USSR	2	El Salvador	0
Mexico	1	Belgium	0

	P	W	D	L	Goals F	Goals A	Pts
USSR	3	2	1	0	6	1	5
Mexico	3	2	1	0	5	0	5
Belgium	3	1	0	2	4	5	2
El Salvador	3	0	0	3	0	9	0

Group 2

Uruguay	2	Israel	0
Italy	1	Sweden	0
Uruguay	0	Italy	0
Sweden	1	Israel	1
Sweden	1	Uruguay	0
Italy	0	Israel	0

	P	W	D	L	Goals F	Goals A	Pts
Italy	3	1	2	0	1	0	4
Uruguay	3	1	1	1	2	1	3
Sweden	3	1	1	1	2	2	3
Israel	3	0	2	1	1	3	2

Group 3

England	1	Romania	0
Brazil	4	Czechoslovakia	1
Romania	2	Czechoslovakia	1
Brazil	1	England	0
Brazil	3	Romania	2
England	1	Czechoslovakia	0

	P	W	D	L	Goals F	A	Pts
Brazil	3	3	0	0	8	3	6
England	3	2	0	1	2	1	4
Romania	3	1	0	2	4	5	2
Czechoslovakia	3	0	0	3	2	7	0

Group 4

Peru	3	Bulgaria	2
West Germany	2	Morocco	1
Peru	3	Morocco	0
West Germany	5	Bulgaria	2
West Germany	3	Peru	1
Bulgaria	1	Morocco	1

	P	W	D	L	Goals F	A	Pts
West Germany	3	3	0	0	10	4	6
Peru	3	2	0	1	7	5	4
Bulgaria	3	0	1	2	5	9	1
Morocco	3	0	1	2	2	6	1

Quarter-finals

Uruguay	1	USSR	0*
Italy	4	Mexico	1
Brazil	4	Peru	2
West Germany	3	England	2**

*(after extra time 0-0 at 90 minutes)
**(after extra time 2-2 at 90 minutes)

Semi-finals

Italy	4	West Germany	3*
Brazil	3	Uruguay	1

*(after extra time 1-1 at 90 minutes)

Third Place play off

West Germany	1	Uruguay	0

Final

Brazil	4	Italy	1

Brazil: Felix, Carlos Alberto, Brito, Piazza, Everaldo, Clodoaldo, Gerson, Jairzinho, Tostao, Pele, Rivelino

Italy: Albertosi, Cera, Burgnich, Bertini (Juliano), Rosato, Facchetti, Domenghini, Mazzola, De Sisti, Boninsegna (Rivera), Riva

Scorers: Pele, Gerson, Jairzinho, Carlos Alberto for Brazil
            Boninsegna for Italy

1974

On 3rd March all 346 passengers and crew on a Turkish Airlines flight from Paris to London perished in one of the world's worst air disasters. The wide-bodied DC10 was on the last leg of its journey from Ankara to London when the accident happened.

Eye witnesses reported that the jet descended very fast and very low before exploding into a massive fireball. The plane was totally destroyed after it plummeted into the thick Forest of Ermonville, 30 miles north-east of Paris, cutting a swathe nearly a mile long. Rescue workers and accident investigators found wreckage and the remains of bodies strewn over several miles of countryside. Among the dead were at least 200 Britons, 49 Japanese and 40 Turks.

On 17th May the Northern Ireland conflict extended to Dublin when three car bombs went off during the rush hour, killing 23 people and seriously injuring more than 100. An hour later, another car vanished in a huge explosion which killed a further five and injured 20 in the border town of Monaghan. All four cars had Northern Ireland registrations; two of them had been hijacked from Protestant areas in Belfast. In Dublin a police witness said: 'Blood was flowing down the pavement. I never believed such horror could exist.' Dublin was declared a disaster area.

Twenty-nine people were killed and hundreds were injured when a massive explosion ripped through a chemical plant at Flixborough, Lincolnshire, on 1st June. The factory was reduced to a mass of tangled wreckage by the force of the blast. The

135

explosion devastated acres of surrounding countryside and some 2,000 houses were damaged. The village of Flixborough was evacuated as a vast acrid cloud of poisonous cyclohexane gas escaped.

President Richard Nixon, facing impeachment by Congress for 'high crimes and misdemeanours' in the Watergate scandal, became the first ever President of the United States to resign his office. The announcement came on 8th August after a series of damaging revelations about the role of the President and his advisors in the break-in at the Democratic Party's National Headquarters, the Watergate Building, in Washington DC on 17th June 1972, and in the cover-up which followed.

*　　*　　*

At the 1964 FIFA Congress in Tokyo, Mexico had been chosen to stage the 1970 World Cup and West Germany the 1974 World Cup. Coincidentally, West Germany, like Mexico, was to host the Olympics two years before staging the World Cup.

Security for the 1974 World Cup was tighter than ever before following the massacre of 11 Israeli athletes by a band of 'Black September' Arab guerrillas on 5th September 1972. Unprecedented security measures were introduced, which included heavily armed police, ubiquitous guard dogs, and accommodation facilities akin to fortified prisons.

Three days before the opening ceremony, FIFA voted for its presidency. Sir Stanley Rous, after 13 years in the post, was succeeded by Joao Havelange of Brazil. For the first time in 70 years the post was held by a non-European. The newly-elected President was reputed to have spent a considerable sum of money on his campaign to achieve the most prestigious and coveted title in world soccer.

FIFA, in addition to having a new President in 1974, also replaced the Jules Rimet trophy, which now resided permanently in Brazil. In Zurich, more than 53 projects were studied before finally on 5th April 1971, the work of the Italian sculptor Silvia Gazzangia was chosen. The new World Cup trophy, two athletes holding the world in their arms, stands 20 inches high, weighs around 11 pounds and is made of 18-carat gold. It was produced by the Bertoni firm in Milan at a cost of one million Swiss francs. Names such as the Stanley Rous Trophy and Churchill Cup were put forward, but FIFA decided to call it the 'FIFA World Cup'. It stays with the winner for four years, after which they receive a smaller replica. There will no longer be the opportunity to gain permanent ownership of the trophy after three Cup victories. The original World Cup trophy was stolen in Rio de Janeiro and a substitute had to be made by the Brazilians.

For the first time since 1950, the knock-out format was partly discarded. Sixteen teams would take part in four groups, but this time the top two teams in each group proceeded into two further groups, instead of entering a knockout phase. The group winners became the finalists and the runners-up would meet in a third place match.

There were 95 original entrants registered for the qualifying competition. Gabon, Jamaica, Madagascar and Venezuela withdrew after the draw for the qualifying competition. The final qualifying tie between the winners of Europe Group 9 and South America Group 3 was not completed. The USSR and Chile had drawn 0-0 in Moscow but the Soviet Union refused to play the return in the National Stadium in Santiago. It had been used to house political prisoners when the military overthrew the democratically elected Marxist head of state, President Salvador Allende. FIFA ruled that the match should go ahead and Chile kicked off and scored into the vacant Soviet net. The non-appearance of the Soviet Union led to Chile advancing to the finals. The decision by FIFA was callous beyond belief, given that thousands of Allende's supporters had been herded into the stadium, tortured and killed.

Scotland were the only Home Countries' representative, qualifying for the first time since 1958. During their qualification they underwent a change of personnel, with Tommy Docherty preferring the coveted post of Manchester United manager. Willie Ormond was installed as his successor and could scarcely have had a worse start. On St Valentine's Day, 1973, his side lost 5-0 at home to England. On 26th September 1973, 100,000 spectators packed Hampden Park and saw Joe Jordan head a dramatic late winner against Czechoslovakia after Nehoda had given the Czechs the lead.

England failed to qualify for the finals for the first time since entering the tournament in 1950. They were unexpectedly held 1-1 at Wembley by Wales. England then travelled to Chorzow and lost 2-0 to Poland as a consequence of the brilliance of Lubanski, together with uncharacteristic defensive frailties. England required a victory in the final group match against Poland at Wembley. Poland had been Olympic champions only two years previously and had several excellent players including Lato, Deyna and Gadocha. Despite almost unrelenting second-half pressure by England, Jan Tomaszewski gave a quite remarkable, if unorthodox, exhibition of goalkeeping to secure a 1-1 draw. On 14th February 1974 an 'inquest' began into the failure to qualify. On 1st May Sir Alf Ramsey was asked to resign, refused, and was therefore dismissed.

Northern Ireland were in Group 6, paired with Bulgaria, Portugal and Cyprus. The 'Troubles' in Northern Ireland meant that they played their matches in England. They performed abysmally, winning only once against Cyprus. In Sofia, against Bulgaria, winners of the Group, George Best was sent off.

Sweden, Austria and Hungary completed Group 1, sharing the remarkable feat of identical points. Sweden and Austria had the same goal difference, superior to that of Hungary, and thus played-off. On a snow-covered pitch in Gelsenkirchen, Sweden triumphed 2-1.

Italy reached their eighth finals without conceding a goal. Belgium also avoided conceding a goal, but were eliminated as Holland enjoyed a vastly superior goal difference.

Yugoslavia's qualification was extremely contentious. They required a victory by two clear goals against Greece in Athens to secure a play-off with Spain. A 4-2 victory was snatched with a last-minute goal. Subsequent rumours of bribery proved to be unfounded. Yugoslavia won the play-off in Frankfurt, thus ensuring their place in the finals for the first time since 1962.

Brazil, as holders, won their place automatically, as did the hosts, West Germany. The other teams to qualify from South America were Argentina, Chile and Uruguay. Peru, one of the most exciting and talented participants in Mexico, were eliminated in a play-off with Chile in Montevideo.

The unlikely winners of the Central and North America zone were Haiti, who benefited from the final pool of 15 matches all taking place in Port au Prince. Mexico, strong favourites to qualify, only finished third. Trinidad raised grave suspicions about impartiality when they had four goals disallowed against Haiti. The El Salvadoran referee, Enriquez, was subsequently suspended.

Zaire emerged as the first black African nation to reach the World Cup finals. They had already qualified for the finals when Morocco refused to play their home game as a protest against the refereeing of the match in Zaire. The final qualifiers were Australia, who emerged as the winners of the Asia-Oceania group.

On 5th January 1974, in Frankfurt, the 16 national teams were divided into the following groups:

Group 1: Australia, Chile, East Germany, West Germany

Group 2: Brazil, Scotland, Yugoslavia, Zaire

Group 3: Bulgaria, Holland, Sweden, Uruguay

Group 4: Argentina, Haiti, Italy, Poland

West Germany began the tournament as 2-to-1 favourites. The squad was essentially that which had won the European Nations Cup in 1972. Beckenbauer was now playing the role of attacking sweeper, Breitner was an excellent full-back, Uli Hoeness inspirational in midfield and Muller a ruthless goalscorer. Nevertheless, West Germany had declined since playing the dazzling, fluid football of 1972. Gunter Netzer, who had been hugely influential, no longer featured in the side.

In their opening Group 1 match in Berlin against Chile,

West Germany were unimpressive and laboured to a 1-0 victory. The South Americans worried the hosts and exposed their lack of composure in midfield. Chilean left-wingers demonstrated on the terraces. It was something of an irony, therefore, that Paul Breitner, a Marxist, should have scored the winning goal with a tremendous long-range shot after 17 minutes. Carlos Caszely of Chile was sent off after 67 minutes for kicking Bertie Vogts.

On the same day, in Hamburg, both Australia and East Germany made their World Cup debuts. Australia had a cosmopolitan side managed by the Yugoslavian Rasic. East Germany adopted a highly robust style and had three players booked. In the second half an own goal by Colin Curran and a venomous volley by Streich gave the Iron Curtain side a 2-0 victory.

West Germany were again unconvincing in their next match against Australia. They appeared to be conserving energy for their final Group 1 encounter with East Germany. The Hamburg crowd were impatient and vituperative, particularly towards Beckenbauer. Goals from Overath, Cullmann and Muller secured a 3-0 win against resilient opposition, who were unlucky not to score when Abonyi hit an upright.

Chile performed creditably against East Germany in Berlin. In Reinoso they had a midfield player of speed and intelligence; in Figueroa they possessed one of the most competent defenders in the tournament. Hoffmann scored from a rebound for East Germany in the 56th minute following a free kick. Ahumada converted a cross from Reinoso to give Chile a merited draw.

The encounter between East and West Germany had been keenly anticipated since the draw was made. The historic first-ever clash between these two nations took place before a sell-out 60,200 crowd at Hamburg's Volkspark Stadium, amid tight security. Around 3,000 East German fans had been granted permission to cross the border following strict security vetting.

There were stories emanating from the West German camp of internal disharmony, with Franz Beckenbauer allegedly undermining and, indeed, usurping the authority of Helmut Schoen, the manager. West Germany's defeat to a late goal by Sparwasser did nothing to dispel the rumours as East Germany emerged as group victors. West Germany had already qualified and it was strongly suggested that the defeat was convenient, given their wish to avoid Holland in the next phase of matches.

The Australia against Chile clash was played in torrential rain and had to be suspended for a short while. Chileans again demonstrated and the police arrested several people. The game ended as a scoreless draw. The dismissal of Raymond Richards seven minutes from time was curious. After receiving a second yellow card from the Iranian referee, Jafar Namdar, the Australian remained on the field for a further five minutes. Only when a linesman drew the referee's attention to the law did Richards exit.

The Group 2 inaugural match between the holders Brazil and Yugoslavia took place in the Wald Stadium, Frankfurt. Pele was unswerving in his decision not to compete in what would have been his fifth World Cup. Clodoaldo, Tostao and Gerson, all stars of 1970, were injured.

For the third successive World Cup, the opening game ended goalless and was a truly wretched affair. Brazil, with fewer gifted players in attack, adopted a cautious, defensive strategy. Oblak, in midfield for Yugoslavia, displayed deftness, speed and guile. A real moment of controversy occurred two minutes from the interval when Acimovic was felled in the penalty area and no action was taken. Brazil's style scarcely endeared them to the Frankfurt crowd, their football unrecognizable from that of the side who played with such panache and *joie de vivre* in Mexico.

Scotland's recurrent off-the-field problems were a considerable source of both mirth and embarrassment. The exploits of Jimmy Johnstone and Billy Bremner, in particular, were met by the wrath of Scottish officials who wanted to send the players home. Willie Ormond successfully pleaded for them to stay.

Against Zaire, Ormond, conscious of the need to pursue goals, recalled Dennis Law. Zaire were one of the weakest sides in the competition. They were coached by the Yugoslavian Vidinic, once his country's goalkeeper. Scotland gave an outrageously inhibited performance which they were later to regret. Zaire started adventurously before Scotland found a degree of composure. After 26 minutes Jordan headed to Lorimer, who scored with a spectacular volley. Six minutes later Jordan headed a free kick by Bremner, which slipped past Kazadi in goal. Thereafter, Scotland relaxed and could score no further goals in the remaining 58 minutes.

Brazil met Scotland in Frankfurt, with Piazza, Rivelino and Jairzinho the only survivors from 1970. Brazil played well during the opening 20 minutes. Thereafter, with Bremner orchestrating midfield, Scotland dominated the match. Along with the indefatigable Bremner, David Hay had an inspired game. Both Holton and Buchan gave strong performances in defence. In the second half, Bremner, Lorimer and Jordan all had good opportunities to score. Scotland believed themselves to be the moral victors in a goalless draw.

Yugoslavia achieved a record-equalling 9-0 victory over Zaire in Gelsenkirchen. They scored three times within the first 18 minutes through Bajevic, Dzajic and Surjak. The Zaire coach decided to replace his goalkeeper, Kazadi, with Tubilandu. His initiation was to recover the ball from the net after Katalinski scored a fourth. Mwepu of Zaire aimed a kick at the referee but, in a case of mistaken identity, N'daye was sent off. Further goals by Bajevic and Bogicevic gave Yugoslavia a 6-0 half-time lead. They netted three more in the second half through Oblak, Petkovic and Bajevic. Zaire's players were so disheartened that they wanted to head for home straightaway. FIFA eventually talked them into staying.

Scotland faced Yugoslavia, requiring a win unless Brazil won by only two clear goals against Zaire. The game was goalless at half-time, which appeared to be satisfactory as

Brazil led by a single goal against Zaire. Scotland fell behind ten minutes from time when Dzajic crossed for Karasi to head the ball past Harvey. In the last minute Scotland equalized when substitute Tommy Hutchison, a replacement for Kenny Dalglish, pulled the ball back for Jordan to score. Scotland had to wait a further three minutes before knowing their fate.

Brazil finally scored their first goal of the tournament after 192 minutes with a low shot by Jairzhino. A thunderous 25-yard drive from Rivelino midway through the second half led to a tense finale. The deciding goal which eliminated Scotland was scored 11 minutes from time. A speculative shot by Valdomiro rolled under Kazadi's body. Scotland emerged unbeaten, alone among the 16 teams. Yugoslavia were group winners on the basis of a vastly superior goal difference to Brazil. After Zaire had been eliminated, a representative of the German company responsible for providing each squad with a luxury coach called to collect his bus. The Zairean team had already departed, speeding down the autobahn towards Africa with their newly acquired means of transport.

Holland were thought by many experts to have a side which was on a parallel with the great Brazilian teams of 1958 and 1970. They had qualified for the finals for the first time since 1938. Their qualification had by no means been straightforward, ousting their fierce rivals Belgium on goal difference. They had assembled a team whose interchangeable defensive and attacking football spawned the term 'Total Football'. This meant forwards would, when necessary, become defenders and, conversely, defenders would become forwards. A blurring of roles was made possible by the versatility and flexibility of players. The Dutch had a glut of highly gifted players which included Cruyff, Van Hanegem, Neeskens and Krol. Johan Cruyff was born into a poor area of Amsterdam in 1947. He joined Ajax of Amsterdam at the age of 10. By the age of 17 he had made his first team debut, and by 19 his international debut. Although of slight build, he displayed deft skills, passing the ball with unerring speed and accuracy. He was endowed with exquisite ball control and quite remarkable speed of thought. By 1973 he had won three European Cups for Ajax and was voted European player of the year on two occasions. He scored 215 goals in Dutch league games before enjoying further success with Barcelona. Cruyff had taken over the mantle of the world's greatest player from Pele.

In a Group 3 match, Holland met Uruguay in Hanover. It was obvious from an early stage that Rinus Michels, the Dutch manager, had fashioned an immensely talented collection of players. Holland scored after only seven minutes when a delightful right-wing chip from Suurbier was met by Rep's head. Uruguay showed their ugly side by adopting a confrontational approach which reduced them to ten men after 70 minutes. Castillo was sent off for punching Resenbrink in the stomach. Resenbrink gained his retribution when, three minutes from time, he exposed the goalkeeper, Mazurkiewicz, and delivered a ball for Rep to score his second. The 2-0 victory scarcely did justice to a Dutch side who were embarrassingly superior.

Although Bulgaria and Sweden shared a goalless draw in Dusseldorf, the game was far from dull. Sandberg and Edstrom, prolific goalscorers, posed a sustained threat for Sweden. The captain, Bonev, and winger, Denev, gave distinguished performances for Bulgaria.

Sweden, somewhat surprisingly, also achieved a goalless draw against Holland in Dortmund. Their relaxed approach, together with solid, composed defending, temporarily subdued Holland. Nevertheless, Cruyff displayed remarkable virtuosity, creating good opportunities which were squandered by extravagant finishing.

Bulgaria and Uruguay shared a 1-1 draw in Hanover. Bonev, the Bulgarian captain, was again impressive in midfield and appropriately scored with a spectacular header 15 minutes from time. Bulgaria were only three minutes from their first finals victory when they conceded a soft goal to Pavoni.

Holland ensured top place in their group with an emphatic

4-1 win against Bulgaria in Dortmund. The irrepressible skills of Cruyff left Bulgaria floundering. Neeskens scored two first-half penalties in the fifth and 45th minutes. Rep added a third before Krol scored an own goal. De Jong, a substitute for Neeskens, completed a comfortable victory.

The final group match between Sweden and Uruguay in Dusseldorf was not without interest. Sweden required a draw to advance, whereas Uruguay had to win. Sweden finally scored after 226 minutes of football with a strike by Edstrom. Further goals by Sandberg and Edstrom exacerbated Uruguay's humiliation. The highly gifted Pedro Rocha made a sad exit from the international arena, having played his fourth tournament in succession. The Uruguayan manager, Roberto Porta, publicly apologised for his side's ignominious displays and promptly resigned.

In Group 4, probably the weakest side in the tournament, Haiti faced the twice-world-champions Italy in the Olympic Stadium, Munich. One minute into the second half, the Haitian centre-forward Sanon scored. He thus became the first player to beat Dino Zoff, the Italian goalkeeper, for 1,142 minutes. The goal inevitably evoked memories of Italy's humiliation against North Korea in 1966. Rivera quickly equalised to relieve the tension. Midway through the second half, Benetti, with the assistance of a deflection, established the lead and substitute Anastasi completed a 3-1 victory. A dope test on the Haitian full-back Ernst Jean-Joseph later proved positive. Jean-Joseph was the first player to be suspended from the World Cup for taking an illegal substance. He protested his innocence, but this did not prevent him being beaten and dragged from his base by Haitian officials. The manner of his undignified exit reflected the iniquitous regime run by Haitian President Duvalier and his cohort of thugs.

The notion that Poland had been underestimated by England was borne out by their performance against Argentina in Stuttgart. Deyna was a cunning strategist in midfield. Lato replaced the injured Lubanski and would emerge as the leading scorer of the tournament. Gorgon was an imperious defender and Tomaszewski, a maverick goalkeeper, enhanced his burgeoning reputation.

Poland raced into a two-goal lead inside eight minutes, with goals by Lato, after Carnevali dropped the ball, and Szarmach. In the second half Argentina replaced Brindisi with the diminutive winger Rene Houseman. Heredia reduced the arrears before another error by Carnevali allowed Lato to restore the two-goal advantage. Babington scored a second goal for Argentina in a highly entertaining game.

Rene Houseman was truly inspirational in his side's next encounter against Italy in Stuttgart. A perfect pass by Babington resulted in a delightful goal by Houseman after 19 minutes. Italy equalised when Perfumo deflected Benetti's pass beyond Carnevali.

Haiti were simply overwhelmed by Poland in Munich. Poland led 5-0 at half-time as Haiti attempted a damage-limitation exercise. Goals from Szarmach (3), Lato (2), Deyna and Gorgon completed a 7-0 rout and ensured Poland's progress to the next round.

Argentina faced Haiti in the knowledge that a win was essential. Even then qualification was incumbent upon Poland defeating Italy. Yazalde and Houseman scored before the interval. Ayala increased the lead before Sanon notched his second goal of the tournament for Haiti. Yazalde completed a 4-1 win.

Italy required a draw against Poland in Stuttgart to ensure their survival in the competition. Their manager, Valcareggi, dropped Riva and Rivera following a poor performance against Argentina. Italy were comprehensively beaten. Szarmach scored one of the outstanding goals of the tournament when he hurtled forward to meet a Kasperczak cross. Kasperczak also contributed to the second goal a minute from the interval when he beat two defenders before delivering a cross which Deyna met with a splendid volley. Capello scored a late consolation goal which flattered Italy, who were eliminated on an inferior goal difference to Argentina.

The two surviving second-round groups comprised of Argentina, Brazil, East Germany and Holland in Group A and Poland, Sweden, West Germany and Yugoslavia in Group B.

The Group A opening match pitched Brazil with East Germany in Hanover. The only goal of the game arrived after an hour. A free kick was awarded to Brazil. Jairzinho joined the East German defensive wall and then moved out of the way to allow a Rivelino drive to find an unobstructed path to the net.

Holland gave an effervescent display of quite breathtaking football against Argentina in Gelsenkirchen. They overran an Argentinian side missing the influence of Babington, who was suspended. The Dutch established a lead after only 11 minutes. Van Hanegem elected to chip a ball to Cruyff, who displayed deft control before rounding the keeper to score. Following a corner, Krol struck a thunderous shot to double the lead after 25 minutes. Heavy rain probably decelerated Holland's superiority. Nevertheless, two second-half goals by Rep and Cruyff, in a 4-0 win, gave some indication of the discrepancy between the sides. Holland were now installed as the tournament favourites.

Holland remained in Gelsenkirchen to face East Germany, who decided to deploy Weise to mark Johan Cruyff. Although the strategy was effective, Holland had too many talented players to be seriously inconvenienced. Resenbrink created an opportunity which Neeskens converted for his fourth goal in five games. Resenbrink doubled the lead after an hour.

In an all-South American clash in Hanover, Brazil and Argentina met for the first time ever in a World Cup tie. Rivelino scored first with a fulminating shot. Brindisi equalised three minutes later when his free kick found Leao out of position. Jairzhino decided the fate of the match with a header early in the second half.

The Holland versus Brazil encounter in Dortmund would determine which of them went through to the World Cup Final. Brazil needed a victory, but a draw would be adequate for Holland. Holland had played at a consistently high level from the outset, whereas Brazil had improved gradually. Brazil's reputation for bright, positive, attacking football was severely punctured as they degenerated into a highly cynical side who indulged in ferocious tackling. The thoroughly reprehensible fouling was by no means solely confined to Brazil. Holland, frequently provoked, were not shy in seeking retribution. Holland were marginally the better side during the first half. After the resumption they imposed their superiority. In the 50th minute Neeskens sprinted down the middle, found Cruyff on the right, received the return pass, swivelled and lobbed the ball over Leao for a wonderfully executed goal. Brazil had no alternative but to venture forward in pursuit of two goals. In the 65th minute Cruyff ensured his side would be contesting the final when he struck an excellent volley from a Krol cross. Six minutes from the end of an unsavoury match, Pereira was sent off by the West German referee, Kurt Tschenscher, for a wild tackle on Neeskens. Five other players were booked as Brazil tarnished memories of their exuberant football of 1970.

The Argentina versus East Germany match was rendered meaningless as neither side had gained a single point. Nevertheless, a large crowd watched a hugely disappointing match. Streich gave East Germany the lead after 14 minutes but Houseman equalised in the 20th minute. A nondescript match ended 1-1, leaving Argentina at the bottom of the group as they had an inferior goal difference to East Germany.

Poland met Sweden on a saturated pitch in Stuttgart in the opening Group B contest. Sweden missed easy chances which fell to Grahn and Tapper. The only goal was scored two minutes from the interval. Szarmach headed back a Gadocha cross and Lato seized onto the opportunity with a near-post header. The first goal that Sweden had conceded proved to be very costly. Sweden had a golden opportunity to equalise when Gorgon fouled Torstensson, but Tomaszewski pushed Tapper's spot-kick round the post.

West Germany and Yugoslavia met, yet again, in a critical

World Cup match in Dusseldorf. Milan Miljanic, the Yugoslavian manager, adopted a defensive strategy. Paul Breitner, the Marxist full back, appeared to be demonstrating that the seeds of destruction lay in his own shooting boots. He scored the opening goal, six minutes from half-time, with a venomous drive. Thirteen minutes from time a cross by Uli Hoeness was met by the irrepressible Muller, who slid the ball into the net to complete a 2-0 victory.

Poland won their second successive game, against Yugoslavia, in Frankfurt but again carried a degree of good fortune. Karasi needlessly conceded a penalty after 25 minutes, fouling Szarmach. Deyna scored from the penalty spot. Just before half-time Karasi atoned for his indiscretion. An intricate movement involving Bogicevic and Jerkovic ended with Karasi rounding Tomaszewski to equalise. The Lato-Gadocha partnership, which was becoming almost telepathic, contrived to score the winning goal. A corner from Gadocha, and Lato's delicate near-post header, left Poland the only remaining unbeaten side in the tournament.

Arguably the best match of the Championship unfolded in a rain-drenched Dusseldorf. Sweden's play had been characterised by exciting, attacking football. Prior to their match against West Germany they had yielded only one goal in four matches. West Germany had steadily improved and the introduction of the driving midfielder Bonhof, of Borussia Moenchengladbach, gave them considerable impetus.

Edstrom gave Sweden a lead after 26 minutes with a splendid volley. Sweden, critically, lost Larsson through injury six minutes later, thus disrupting the equilibrium of the side. Five minutes after the resumption, Overath equalised with a low drive following a Hellstrom punch from a Beckenbauer shot. A minute later West Germany took the lead with an extraordinary goal by Rainer Bonhof. His shot rebounded from both uprights before crossing the line. Sweden displayed admirable resilience and Sandberg equalised, thus completing a spell of three goals in three minutes. Grabowski, a replacement for Herzog, scored in the closing stages following good

149

play by Muller. Muller was then brought down in the penalty area and Hoeness converted the spot-kick to complete a 4-2 victory in a highly exciting match.

Neither Sweden nor Yugoslavia could reach the final, or indeed qualify for the third place play-off as they had each incurred two losses. Surjak gave Yugoslavia the lead but Edstrom swiftly equalised. With only four minutes remaining, Torstensson scored the winning goal for Sweden.

West Germany only required a draw against Poland to ensure a place in the 1974 World Cup Final. Although both sides had attained maximum points in the group, West Germany had a superior goal difference. A rainstorm meant that the kick-off had to be delayed. A quagmire of a pitch disadvantaged Poland, who were accustomed to a fast, attacking game. Maier in the West German goal acquitted himself well with an improbable double save from firstly Lato, then Gadocha. The only goal of the game was almost inevitably scored by Gerd Muller. With 14 minutes remaining, Bonhof ventured into the penalty area and, as he was being tackled, passed to Muller whose explosive finish decided the fate of an entertaining match. Hoeness later missed a penalty kick which was struck feebly.

The third place play-off has been largely viewed as a tedious and pointless affair. It was ironic, therefore, that on the eve of the Final a capacity crowd watched Brazil play Poland in the Olympic Stadium, Munich. Brazil were unfortunate when a shot by Rivelino struck a post. Brazil's substitute, Mirandinha, then appeared to be held back unfairly by Kasperczak inside the Polish penalty area. The only goal of the game was fittingly scored by Lato 14 minutes from time. He struck a low shot past Leao. Although a linesman flagged for offside, the goal stood, much to the consternation of Jairzhino, who was booked for his protestations. Lato missed an easy opportunity in the final minute. Poland had achieved a creditable third place, qualifying for a World Cup final tournament for the first time since 1938. The Olympic Champions had made a deep impression on the footballing world.

The all-European Final on 7th July resonated with expectation. Holland and West Germany were old enemies and there was intense rivalry between both their footballers and their supporters. It was fitting that these two sides should be contesting the Final. They had consistently produced the highest ratio of penetrating attacks in what was a particularly low scoring tournament. Holland, thrilling exponents of Total Football, were unquestionably the most talented side in the competition. West Germany had a group of technically accomplished players who were skilful, but had reached their zenith in the European Nations Cup. Holland were the marginal favourites to win.

Before an assembled crowd of 77,833 at the Olympic Stadium, Munich, and a worldwide television audience of one billion, Jack Taylor, the English referee, was about to start the game when he noticed the corner flags were missing. Holland started sensationally. They completed a movement of 16 passes which had a dramatic finale. Their possession football from the kick-off smacked of nothing more than arrogance until the ball penetrated the German half. Cruyff, playing behind the forward line, thrust forward at lightning pace. He evaded Bertie Vogts, who was assigned to man-mark him, but was tripped by Hoeness inside the penalty area. Jack Taylor, without hesitation, pointed to the spot. Johannes Neeskens calmly placed the penalty kick beyond the reach of Sepp Maier. Holland had scored in the first minute without a single German player making contact with the ball. It was the first time ever in a World Cup final that a penalty had been converted.

Holland, thereafter, rather unwisely indulged in relaxed, complacent football which suggested they were merely content to lead. It was to prove very costly as West Germany equalised with a penalty. Overath threaded a delightful ball for Holzenbein, who was felled by Jansen. Breitner beat Jongbloed with a well placed spot-kick. This was the tenth World Cup Final. The previous nine had never yielded a penalty score and yet, remarkably, two had arrived within 25 minutes. The incident marked a watershed in the game. Bonhof was forceful, ably supported by Beckenbauer as West Germany went on the offensive. During a period of intense German pressure, Holland broke away. Cruyff and Rep left Beckenbauer hopelessly exposed in defence but Rep failed to capitalise when he hesitated, allowing Maier to dive at his feet. Two minutes from half-time, Grabowski passed the ball to Bonhof, who sped past Haan. His cross was met to perfection by Muller, who turned almost 180 degrees before sweeping the ball past Jongbloed. Muller's tally of goals in World Cup finals was now 14 and therefore surpassed Just Fontaine's previous record. Cruyff confronted Jack Taylor at half-time and demanded greater protection from Bertie Vogts. This resulted in a booking.

After the interval Holland largely dominated the play. The Dutch were handicapped by injuries to Resenbrink and Rijsbergen, both of whom had to be substituted. Van de Kerkhof almost equalised when his long cross eluded the German defence, but Neeskens' volley was blocked by Maier. Muller appeared to have notched his 69th goal for his country but was ruled to be marginally offside.

As in 1954, West Germany had endured defeat on the way to winning the trophy. And, also as in 1954, they had trimphed over more skilful and gifted opposition in the Final. Their sheer will to win, resilience, organisation and efficiency made them worthy winners of the new FIFA World Cup. Holland captured the imagination of the footballing public and gave a vast degree of pleasure to lovers of the game.

Results: West Germany 1974

Group 1

West Germany	1	Chile	0
East Germany	2	Australia	0
West Germany	3	Australia	0
Chile	1	East Germany	1
East Germany	1	West Germany	0
Australia	0	Chile	0

	P	W	D	L	Goals F	A	Pts
East Germany	3	2	1	0	4	1	5
West Germany	3	2	0	1	4	1	4
Chile	3	0	2	1	1	2	2
Australia	3	0	1	2	0	5	1

Group 2

Brazil	0	Yugoslavia	0
Scotland	2	Zaire	0
Brazil	0	Scotland	0
Yugoslavia	9	Zaire	0
Scotland	1	Yugoslavia	1
Brazil	3	Zaire	0

	P	W	D	L	Goals F	A	Pts
Yugoslavia	3	1	2	0	10	1	4
Brazil	3	1	2	0	3	0	4
Scotland	3	1	2	0	3	1	4
Zaire	3	0	0	3	0	14	0

Group 3

Holland	2	Uruguay	0
Bulgaria	0	Sweden	0
Holland	0	Sweden	0
Bulgaria	1	Uruguay	1
Holland	4	Bulgaria	1
Sweden	3	Uruguay	0

					Goals		
	P	W	D	L	F	A	Pts
Holland	3	2	1	0	6	1	5
Sweden	3	1	2	0	3	0	4
Bulgaria	3	0	2	1	2	5	2
Uruguay	3	0	1	2	1	6	1

Group 4

Italy	3	Haiti	1
Poland	3	Argentina	2
Argentina	1	Italy	1
Poland	7	Haiti	0
Argentina	4	Haiti	1
Poland	2	Italy	1

					Goals		
	P	W	D	L	F	A	Pts
Poland	3	3	0	0	12	3	6
Argentina	3	1	1	1	7	5	3
Italy	3	1	1	1	5	4	3
Haiti	3	0	0	3	2	14	0

Group A

Brazil	1	East Germany	0
Holland	4	Argentina	0
Holland	2	East Germany	0
Brazil	2	Argentina	1
Holland	2	Brazil	0
Argentina	1	East Germany	1

					Goals		
	P	W	D	L	F	A	Pts
Holland	3	3	0	0	8	0	6
Brazil	3	2	0	1	3	3	4
East Germany	3	0	1	2	1	4	1
Argentina	3	0	1	2	2	7	1

Group B

Poland	1	Sweden	0
West Germany	2	Yugoslavia	0
Poland	2	Yugoslavia	1
West Germany	4	Sweden	2
Sweden	2	Yugoslavia	1
West Germany	1	Poland	0

					Goals		
	P	W	D	L	F	A	Pts
West Germany	3	3	0	0	7	2	6
Poland	3	2	0	1	3	2	4
Sweden	3	1	0	2	4	6	2
Yugoslavia	3	0	0	3	2	6	0

Third place play-off

Poland	1	Brazil	0

Final

West Germany	2	Holland	1

West Germany: Maier, Vogts, Schwarzenbeck, Beckenbauer, Breitner, Bonhof, Hoeness, Overath, Grabowski, Muller, Holzenbein

Holland: Jongbloed, Suurbier, Rijsbergen (De Jong), Haan, Krol, Jansen, Neeskens, Van Hanegem, Rep, Cruyff, Resenbrink (Van de Kerkhof)

Scorers: Breitner (pen), Muller for West Germany
        Neeskens (pen) for Holland

1978

One of the world's worst oil pollution disasters occurred in March when the supertanker *Amoco Cadiz* ran on to rocks on the coast of Brittany. The ship was on her way from the Persian Gulf to Rotterdam with around 230,000 tons of crude oil when her steering gear broke in heavy seas. The tanker eventually split in two. Marine pollution experts believed the spill to be the worst in history. Over 100 miles of Brittany coastline were affected. There was unprecedented destruction of marine and bird life. French riot police fired smoke bombs at a crowd of 2,000 students in Brest demonstrating against the pollution.

The body of the former Italian Prime Minister, Aldo Moro, was found in the back of a car in Rome on 9th May. Signor Moro had been kidnapped by members of the Red Brigade on 16th March. His captors, who shot him with a burst from a machine pistol, made a grim political joke. They left the car halfway between the headquarters of his Christian Democrat Party and those of the Italian Communist Party. On the day he was kidnapped, the two parties were to become allies in government.

In what may be the modern world's largest instance of mass suicide, some 913 members of an American religious cult, the People's Temple, were found dead at their commune in Jonestown, Guyana, on 29th November. The cultists, all of whom lived in an agricultural commune, appeared to have been poisoned. Survivors who hid in the jungle claimed that the Reverend Jim Jones forced them all to drink a mixture of soft drink Kool-Aid laced with cyanide. Quite how Jones induced his followers to kill themselves remains a mystery. But rumours from the commune told how the former Methodist preacher, who founded the Temple in 1957 and moved 1,000 of its members to Guyana in 1976, had turned from a philanthropist into a dictator. He apparently often rehearsed the cultists in such acts of self-destruction.

*　　*　　*

On 6th July 1966 in London, FIFA decided that Argentina would host the 1978 World Cup. The choice of Argentina, at first sight, seemed perfectly reasonable. Argentina, historically, had produced high quality football and a galaxy of stars. The capital city of Buenos Aires was equipped with some fine stadia and excellent football clubs, and the country was stable.

But by 1978 Argentina had become a highly controversial venue. In 1976 a military dictatorship seized power. The generals, acting ruthlessly, began to fight a 'dirty war' against their own people. Eleven thousand 'subversives' 'disappeared', were held in camps, and secretly killed. A favourite method was to pump them with sodium amytal and drop them from aeroplanes into the River Plate.

The Argentinian Junta, led by General Videla, had guaranteed a trouble-free tournament, and when left-wing groups also issued statements indicating no violence or kidnappings because 'soccer is a game of the working class', FIFA were prepared to accept pledges of total security. The Junta set up a new body, the Ente Autarquico Mundial (EAM) to ensure that all preparations for the tournament, including the construction of three new stadia and redevelopment of three others, would be completed in time. But the state of some pitches left much to be desired and were well below international standard. The grass at the River Plate stadium was foolishly sprinkled with seawater and died. A new pitch was hurriedly laid, but its bounce was odd.

The EAM started inauspiciously in 1976 when its newly appointed President, General Actis, was assassinated a few hours before his inaugural press conference. But thereafter the left-wing opposition decided that the Finals presented them with an ideal opportunity of stating their case to the world that was simply too good to miss.

Argentina's longing for credibility meant it was prepared to go to extraordinary lengths to polish its image. It is estimated that the final bill for the World Cup was around $700 million. This is a quite staggering figure given that West Germany, a much more affluent nation, spent less than half that amount in staging the Olympic Games. A full-scale government row broke out over the escalating costs with the Treasury Secretary, Juan Alemann, bravely opposing the colossal expense. Worried about Argentina's alarming rate of inflation, once 900 per cent annually and still running as high as 165 per cent annum at the time of the World Cup, Alemann called the cost of staging the Finals 'the most visible and indefensible case of non-priority spending in Argentina today'. Of course, what Alemann overlooked was the fact that the 1978 World Cup Finals had virtually become the Junta's *raison d'être*.

The generals hired an American public relations firm, Burson-Marsteller, to prettify the country. Many inhabitants of slum dwellings in places where World Cup matches were to be staged were transferred to other areas as their homes were razed. On the main road to Rosario, a wall was constructed painted with the façades of nice houses, to conceal the slums from unsuspecting foreigners. The *militares* carried out Operation Barrido. This entailed swooping on the politically suspect and removing them from the proximity of foreign journalists. Some secret camps were relocated and prisoners killed to prevent discovery.

There were 106 entrants registered for the qualifying competition. Sri Lanka became the first country to withdraw when its government refused to grant permission to pay the entrance fee. Further withdrawals included North Korea, United Arab Emirates, Central African Republic, Sudan, Tanzania and Zaire.

Uruguay and England, two previous winners of the tournament, were conspicuous absentees. Don Revie resigned as the

England manager midway through the qualifying tournament. The standard of English football at international level had reached its nadir. Nevertheless, the manner in which Revie departed, induced by the financial rewards of the United Arab Emirates, was thoroughly contemptible. Ron Greenwood revived England's fortunes but Italy won the group with a superior goal difference.

Northern Ireland were unfortunate to be in the same group as Holland, who qualified with consummate ease, dropping only one point in six matches. Johan Cruyff, such an inspiration in 1974, decided to withdraw from the pressures of international football. Van Beveran, the country's leading goalkeeper, Gaels, the centre forward, and Wim Van Hanegem and Hovenkamp were all absent from a much diminished Dutch side.

Wales were eliminated by Scotland in highly controversial circumstances. At Anfield, Liverpool, only twelve minutes remained with the match scoreless. Willie Johnston's long throw into the Welsh box was met by a clash of heads and hands. The French referee, Robert Wurtz, awarded a penalty to Scotland. Archie MacPherson, commentating for BBC Scottish Television, endorsed the decision with his detached and objective reporter's eye, screaming down the microphone, 'a penalty if ever there was one'. Certainly a hand had been used, but it belonged to Scotland's Joe Jordan. Don Masson directed the penalty past Dai Davies and Dalglish sealed a 2-0 victory with an explosive header. For the second consecutive series Scotland was Britain's sole representative and were to provide almost unconfined entertainment and ridicule. Their odds had shortened to an incredulous 8-1 to lift the trophy. This was surely symptomatic of a nation completely immersed in self-delusion. Seldom can an expedition have set out with such high hopes and returned in such disarray. The stage was set by the ludicrous optimism of Ally MacLeod, one time manager of Ayr United and Aberdeen, and now successor to Willie Ormond. As the competition grew nearer, MacLeod's fatuous utterances grew more extreme. 'I'm a winner!' he stated, and the exultant, intoxicated fans were swept along on a wave of outrageous optimism. Scotland had appeared in the World Cup finals three times before, but never succeeded in reaching the latter stages. The rousing send-off before Scotland's departure unwisely chose to ignore the fact that they had failed to win a match in the British Championship.

West Germany, as holders, entered the final stages automatically. Franz Beckenbauer abdicated from the tournament when he accepted a substantial offer to join the American soccer gold rush. In April 1977 he stunned the footballing world by joining New York Cosmos. West Germany had to defend their title without a number of distinguished players, including Paul Breitner, Wolfgang Overath, Uli Hoeness, Gerd Muller and Jurgen Grabowski.

Poland continued where they had left off in West Germany and qualified undefeated, eliminating Portugal in the process. Austria reached their first finals for 20 years, narrowly ousting East Germany. By beating Bulgaria in Paris in their final match, France qualified for the first time since 1966, in a group which included the Republic of Ireland. Sweden progressed to the finals in a group which contained their fierce rivals, Norway. Romania appeared to have an excellent opportunity of qualifying in Group 8, but in their penultimate game in Bucharest lost 6-4 to Yugoslavia. Spain then won in Belgrade to ensure a place in the finals. Hungary finished top of Group 9 and faced a play-off with Bolivia. Bolivia achieved an impressive seven points from their four matches with Uruguay and Venezuela. But in the group final played in Cali, Colombia, Bolivia surrendered a total of 13 goals to Brazil and Peru, who both qualified. Bolivia had to enter the Europe/South America play-off match, which Hungary won 9-2 on aggregate.

Brazil were managed by Claudio Coutinho, a former physical training instructor in the army, in which he held the rank of captain, and a former volleyball player. He was resented from the start because of his military background, which prompted some to believe he had been planted in the job deliberately by Brazil's military government. Coutinho placed great emphasis on fitness, stamina and teamwork. He felt that South American football had fallen behind that of Europe and was convinced his synthesis offered Brazil the only means of regaining the world title they had lost to West Germany. Despite rumblings of discontent, Brazil went to Argentina as favourites.

Cesar Luis Menotti, the Argentinian manager, had enormous difficulty building a side as many of his leading players were based in Spain. Menotti decided to recall only three overseas players, Kempes, Piazza and Wolff, for the championship. Wolff did not feature, as Real Madrid refused to release him at the beginning of April. Menotti radically altered the style and ethos of his team, electing to play skilful, attacking football. That he accomplished this without many of his gifted players was a considerable achievement.

Mexico emerged as the CONCACAF winners following an exacting route to the finals. They won Group 1 with a superior goal difference to the United States but then proceeded to amass 20 goals in five games during the group final, and achieved maximum points. The Group 1 encounter between Canada and the USA made history by being the first World Cup match to be played on an artificial surface. The return at Seattle was the first World Cup match to be played indoors.

Iran were impressive winners of the Asia-Oceania group. They won all four games in Asian Group 3 before advancing to the group final, where they obtained 14 points from eight games and remained unbeaten. Tunisia were the last team to qualify. They narrowly survived a first-round match beating Morocco on penalties. Thereafter, they gained momentum and in the last match of the group final qualified by decisively defeating Egypt in Tunis, 4-1.

The format for these finals was the same as 1974, although group matches were not played at a single venue, or at two venues as in previous finals. Most grounds would stage games from different groups. Two groups shared Buenos Aires and Mar del Plata and, in total, nine of the 16 teams were programmed to play groups in the capital.

On 16th January 1978, in the Cultural Centre of San Martin, Buenos Aires, the 16 national teams were divided into the following groups:

Group 1: Argentina, France, Hungary, Italy

Group 2: Mexico, Poland, Tunisia, West Germany

Group 3: Austria, Brazil, Spain, Sweden

Group 4: Holland, Iran, Peru, Scotland

Group 1 was considered to be one of the most competitive groups since the inception of the World Cup, with all four participants boasting strong sides. Enzo Bearzot, the Italian manager, was less optimistic about his side's chances as a consequence of losing his highly experienced captain and sweeper, Giancino Facchetti. He reshaped a team which comprised of no fewer than eight Juventus players. Scirea succeeded Facchetti and complemented Bellugi at the centre of the defence. Marco Tardelli moved from full-back to midfield and Cabrini took over from Tardelli. Paolo Rossi, an expensive goal-scoring prodigy, was preferred to Graziani in attack.

Sponsorship and an influx of overseas players had greatly revived French football. Platini, Bathenay and Tresor were all high quality players. St Etienne's progress in European club football highlighted the steady progress of the French.

Italy and France kicked off the opening game in the seaside resort of Mar del Plata. France could scarcely have started in more encouraging fashion, with a goal after 31 seconds. A swift interchange of passes in the French half produced a long ball to Didier Six, who raced down the byline. Bernard Lacombe received a perfectly flighted cross and steered the ball wide of Zoff with his head. Italy, thereafter, played uncharacteristically open football which was rewarded with a bizarre equaliser after half an hour. A ball was crossed from the left which Bettega miskicked. Causio headed the ball against the bar before Rossi equalised with a messy goal from the rebound. Shortly after the interval, Zaccarelli, who had replaced Antognoni in midfield, drove a low shot into the net to give Italy a morale boosting victory.

Asked to name the likely winners of the 1978 World Cup

before Hungary's defeat by England at Wembley the week before the World Cup, Lajos Baroti, the Hungarian manager, singled out Holland and West Germany before adding: 'But the host nation always does well traditionally. Everything is in their favour. Even the referees are under the influence of the home crowds...'.

Argentina emerged to a snowstorm of ticker-tape which cascaded down the River Plate stadium. A frenzied, explosive, jingoistic fervour reverberated throughout the majestic stadium. Baroti probably thought his words were prophetic after two of his players were sent off as the game degenerated into violence and recrimination. But a display of ill-temper and pique was promoted by Hungary, who engaged in some quite ruthless tackling. The match itself was highly exciting but refereed weakly by the Portuguese official, Antonio Garrido. Hungary scored after only ten minutes when, following an intricate four-man move, Zombori struck a fierce shot which was parried and Csapo seized onto the rebound. Luque equalised for Argentina five minutes later when Gujdar failed to hold a powerful free kick by Kempes. With 20 minutes remaining, Hungary had an opportunity to restore the lead, but Nagy headed a centre by Martos marginally wide of the post. Ten minutes from time Torocsik, who had earlier been booked, kicked Gallego and was dismissed. Three minutes later the substitute, Bertoni, slid the ball into the net for the winning goal. Hungary were reduced to only nine men one minute from time when Nyilasi, also previously cautioned, harshly tackled Tarantini.

An automatic one-match suspension applied to Torocsik and Nyilasi as a weakened Hungary faced Italy in Mar del Plata. Both Benetti and Bettega gave outstanding performances as Italy quickly imposed their superiority. Rossi gave Italy the lead after 34 minutes when he pounced on a deflected Tardelli shot. Bettega almost immediately doubled the lead, cleverly beating two defenders to score. Benetti, who had matured into an intelligent, skilful and highly influential player, added a third goal after an hour. Toth reduced the arrears with a penalty ten minutes from time. It was a measure of Italy's domination that they also struck the woodwork on three occasions.

Argentina and France could rightfully claim to have participated in one of the greatest ever World Cup matches in Buenos Aires. France were possibly the finest side ever to be eliminated from the first phase of the competition.

A highly entertaining game produced almost unrelenting attacking play at high speed. The Swiss referee, Jean Dubach, gave substance to Lajos Baroti's warning about officials favouring the host nation. France largely outplayed Argentina during the first half, exhibiting delightful one-touch football. With half-time approaching, Luque darted into the penalty area and as Tresor challenged he involuntarily handled the ball. The referee was in close proximity but felt the need to consult with a linesman. A penalty was awarded, which Passarella converted to give an unjust scoreline. After 56 minutes Bertrand-Demanes in the French goal damaged his back against a post after tipping a thunderous volley by Valencia over the bar. He had to be replaced by Baratelli. France finally equalised after an hour when Lacombe lobbed the ball against the bar and Platini converted the rebound. Six then had a golden opportunity to put his side ahead after a splendid run and pass from Platini, but shot wide with Fillol beaten. With 16 minutes remaining, Luque struck a tremendous and unexpected volley which beat Baratelli's belated dive. Five minutes later Six was blatantly pulled down in the penalty area but no action was taken. France had performed quite magnificently and were extremely unfortunate to be eliminated. Tresor, their black player from Marseilles, had excelled.

Italy and Argentina had both qualified for the next phase when they met in Buenos Aires. The winners would remain in the capital. Italy reverted to their counter-attacking style, which seemed eminently sensible given that Argentina's strategy was very much based on all-out attack. The only goal of the game was scored after 67 minutes following a clever, swift, double interchange of passes between Antognoni and Rossi. Bettega moved cunningly into the penalty area to receive a perfect pass from Rossi. He evaded a flying tackle by Olguin and fired an angled shot past Fillol as he advanced off his line. Italy thus won the group, with Argentina finishing second.

Television viewers with black and white sets could not distinguish between the blue of France and the red of Hungary. France were supposed to be playing in their normal colours but, unfortunately, both teams turned up with their change strip of white, causing the match to be delayed for 40 minutes. France emphasised why their exit was so poignant as they played with considerable creativity and panache. Three goals were compressed into a five-minute spell during the first half. Lopez scored with a 25-yard drive midway through the half. Berdoll added a second after 36 minutes when he evaded a series of tackles to score. Zombori struck back for Hungary four minutes later but Rocheteau immediately restored the two-goal advantage.

The inaugural game of the eleventh World Cup was a Group 2 encounter between World Champions West Germany and third-placed Poland. The River Plate stadium witnessed yet another monumental bore of a scoreless draw. Incredibly, there had not been a goal scored in the opening match of a tournament since 1962. Perhaps there was an argument for playing all group games on the opening day, thus relieving the excessive tension following the lavish opening ceremony. West Germany clearly felt the loss of Gerd Muller and Franz Beckenbauer. They looked a beleaguered side, who were under pressure during the second half when Poland attacked strongly.

Tunisia were 1,000-1 outsiders to win the tournament but produced one of the most surprising results in defeating Mexico. They became the first African country to win a game in the World Cup finals. Tunisia dominated the first half, but Mexico were awarded a controversial penalty a minute from half-time. An innocuous shot by de la Torre struck Jebali on the arm and Ayala converted the penalty kick. Ten minutes after the interval Ali Kaabi equalized. During the final ten minutes Gommidh and Dhouieb secured victory for the faster and more purposeful Tunisians.

Tunisia emphasised their World Cup credentials with a skilful performance against Poland in Rosario. Tunisia, indeed, were unfortunate to lose to a solitary goal scored by Lato three minutes from half-time, following a mistake by Labidi. Dhouieb struck the Polish crossbar in the second half as Tunisia imposed themselves for long periods.

Following the disappointing display against Poland, Helmut Schoen, the West Germany manager, recalled Rummenigge and introduced Dieter Muller and Dietz. Mexico were extremely poor and, although they had to replace their goalkeeper, Reyes, after 38 minutes, they were already trailing 3-0. Although West Germany won 6-0 with goals by Rummenigge (2), Flohe (2), H Muller and D. Muller, they failed to impress with the overall quality of their play.

The decline of West Germany as an international force was highlighted as they laboured to a goalless draw against Tunisia. Their impoverished performance might have resulted in defeat had Tunisia not adopted a defensive posture. The North Africans departed from the World Cup with an enhanced reputation, having won the affection of an appreciative audience.

Poland gained an uninspiring victory over Mexico, who introduced five new players after their wretched displays. Boniek started his first full match of the tournament and scored the opening goal three minutes from half-time. Rangel equalised for Mexico six minutes after the interval. Deyna unleashed an excellent long-range shot to restore the lead. Tomaszewski produced good saves from Sanchez, Rangel and Cuellar before Boniek clinched victory six minutes from time. Poland won Group 2, with West Germany remaining in Cordoba as a consequence of finishing second.

Sweden had conceded 16 goals to Brazil in their three previous World Cup defeats. It was something of a relief, therefore, when they gained a 1-1 draw with a workmanlike

166

performance in the opening Group 3 match in Mar del Plata. Sjoberg beat Leao with a right-foot shot after 38 minutes. Reinaldo levelled the match right on half-time following a defensive misunderstanding. The most controversial moment of the match occurred in the dying seconds. Brazil forced a corner on the right, taken by substitute Nelinho. Zico headed the ball into the net but the Welsh referee, Clive Thomas, had already blown the final whistle.

Spain took to the field against Austria in Buenos Aires as one of the tournament's favourites despite an abysmal World Cup record. Schachner, who played in the second division of the Austrian league, scored a remarkable goal very early in the game. In possession of the ball on the half-way line, a sinuous run left defenders in his wake, and as he bore in from the right he fired a fierce, angled shot past Miguel Angel. Spain equalised after 21 minutes when Dani's shot deflected past Koncilia in the Austrian goal. Hans Krankl, Europe's leading goalscorer, gave Austria victory 11 minutes from time with a deflected shot.

Austria maintained their form against Sweden in Buenos Aires. Hans Krankl again scored the decisive goal with a controversial penalty kick. Krankl had pushed the ball past Nordqvist, the Swedish captain, and tumbled to the ground as he pursued the ball.

Rivelino was missing from Brazil's encounter with Spain in Mar del Plata. He was allegedly injured, but a more likely explanation was that he was dropped following open disenchantment with Coutinho. Spain introduced five changes following their defeat by Austria. Cardenosa of Spain had an opportunity to break the deadlock in the second half but shot weakly. After the goalless draw an effigy of Claudio Coutinho was burned in the streets of Rio de Janeiro.

Brazil had to beat Austria in Mar del Plata to ensure qualification for the second round. It is believed that Coutinho's role had been seriously undermined by his side's performances. There was a strong suggestion that a five-man selection committee was overseeing Coutinho's choice of players.

The only goal of the game was scored by Roberto five minutes from the interval. Pezzey misjudged a cross by Toninho which was deflected to Roberto. Both sides seemed content with the scoreline, which ensured their qualification.

Spain and Sweden both needed to win to have any chance of remaining in the tournament. Spain dominated a match they deservedly won with a goal 14 minutes from time. Juanito passed to Asensi, who outpaced Sweden's defenders before driving a left-foot shot into the net. The victory was rendered worthless as Austria and Brazil qualified for the next phase.

Holland approached the opening Group 3 match against Iran in Mendoza a mere shadow of the side which had enraptured the football world in 1974. Without the inspirational Cruyff and Van Hanegem, Rob Resenbrink became the side's central figure. Iran were well organised and steadily improving in international terms. They nearly scored after eight minutes when Faraki's shot deflected off Rijsbergen, but rolled past the post with Jongbloed out of position. Rene Van de Kerkhof was upended by Abdollahi after 39 minutes and Resenbrink converted the penalty. Resenbrink headed a second goal after 62 minutes and completed a hat-trick with a second penalty 11 minutes from time.

The Scottish expedition was ill-planned from the start. Gordon McQueen had been injured against Wales and, though still unfit when the party left, was not replaced. His absence left a glaring hole at the heart of Scotland's defence. The team's hotel and food were reputed to be poor, and there was misunderstanding and bitterness over the bonuses to be paid in the unlikely event of success. The recriminations started early on and hardly helped the atmosphere of the camp.

Scotland, nevertheless, confidently faced Peru in Cordoba despite the fact that they had only ever won one game, against Zaire, in the finals. In the 14th minute Quiroga, the eccentric Peruvian goalkeeper, failed to hold a powerful drive by Bruce Rioch and Jordan scored. Cubillas, the black former winger, who had been a revelation in Mexico, began to show his pedigree as a world class player. Now playing in midfield, aided by Cueto, he began to orchestrate penetrating attacks. A clever exchange of passes between the two climaxed in Cueto equalising two minutes from the interval. In the 64th minute Scotland had an excellent opportunity to regain the lead when Rioch was brought down by Cubillas. Masson's soft effort was comfortably saved by Quiroga. During the final 25 minutes Peru overran Scotland, who must have regretted that Cubillas was dissuaded from retiring before the tournament. In the 70th minute he strode through the Scottish defence unmarked to give his side the lead. Six minutes later he struck a venomous, swerving free kick past a static Alan Rough.

The random dope test which follows every World Cup match had singled out Scotland's Willie Johnston and Kenny Dalglish. In Johnston's case the result proved positive. The West Bromwich Albion winger was found guilty of taking a stimulant, fencamfamin, rated highly dangerous by FIFA. Johnston was subsequently banned from international football and immediately returned home, in disgrace. He claimed it was a practice he had followed in club games for West Bromwich Albion, so forcing the Football Association to intro-duce dope testing in the English league. Johnston's perfor-mance against Peru had been so utterly lethargic that one has to seriously question the efficacy of the drug.

Scotland's morale had taken a veritable battering and MacLeod made six changes for their second match against Iran in Cordoba. The full-back partnership of Kennedy and Buchan was discontinued. Buchan reverted to his role as sweeper. Kennedy and Forsyth were excluded. Gemmill and Macari were preferred to Masson and Rioch, and Robertson replaced Johnston on the left wing. Inconceivable though it might seem, Scotland actually gave an even more inept perfor-mance as the thoroughly demoralised side laboured to a draw. Eskandarian scored an outrageous own goal from 15 yards two minutes from the interval. Danaifar equalised from a pass by Sadeghi during the second half following a series of errors in the Scottish defence. Ghassempour had an opportunity to win the match two minutes later but, on receiving a delightful pass from Faraki, shot straight at Rough.

When Holland and Peru met in Mendoza there appeared to be growing unrest in the Dutch camp. A conflict of approach surfaced between Ernst Happel, the lugubrious and pragmatic Austrian, and Jan Swartkuis, who had managed the team before assisting Happel. Happel elected to drop Rep from the attack and smother his midfield in an attempt to stifle Peru's offensive thrusts. The redeployment into a 3-5-2 system resulted in a tedious goalless draw. Neeskens had to retire midway through the second half with injured ribs.

Peru won Group 4 with an emphatic victory over Iran. Velasquez headed home a Munante header after only two minutes. Thereafter, Cubillas scored three goals, two of which were penalties. Rowshan scored for Iran in a 4-1 defeat.

Ally MacLeod finally relented to pressure to recall Graeme Souness, the Liverpool midfield player, to the side. Scotland required to win by an improbable three clear goals. One Scottish wag commented, 'Where are we going to find three Dutchmen prepared to score own goals?' MacLeod belatedly discovered the right combination of players with the recall of Rioch, Forsyth and Kennedy. The side were unrecognisable from the previous shambles, with Souness ably complementing the craftsmanship of Gemmill. Holland scored first when Kennedy fouled Rep in the penalty area and Resenbrink netted the 1,000th goal in World Cup finals. Neeskens had already retired, injured early in the first half after tackling Gemmill. A minute from half-time Scotland equalised. Souness chipped a ball from the left and Jordan headed it down for Dalglish to volley into the net. A minute after the interval Scotland were awarded a penalty when Souness was fouled and Gemmill beat Jongbloed with considerable ease. Half-way through the second half Archie Gemmill extended Scotland's lead with what *El Grafico*, the Argentinian sports magazine, believed to be the best goal of the tournament. Gemmill embarked on a mazy run from outside the penalty area, eluding three defenders before unleashing a swerving shot into the far corner of the net. Momentarily, Scotland were within sight of the three-goal margin. But four minutes later Rep easily penetrated the Scottish defence before striking a fulminating 25-yard drive past a vulnerable Alan Rough, to ensure Holland reached the next phase.

Scotland were able to claim that they were eliminated, for the second consecutive World Cup, on goal difference. It is unlikely that this was actually the case. Had they finished above Holland with a three-goal victory margin it is almost certain that FIFA would have deducted two points because of Johnston's indiscretion.

The two surviving second round groups comprised of Austria, Holland, Italy and West Germany in Group A and Argentina, Brazil, Peru and Poland in Group B.

An eagerly anticipated clash between Italy and West Germany at the River Plate stadium, Buenos Aires, rapidly turned into a hugely disappointing goalless draw. West Germany adopted a highly defensive strategy. Bettega, uncharacteristically, missed two good opportunities in the first half. Sepp Maier, in the West German goal, played his 16th game in the finals, thus surpassing the record previously held by Carbajal of Mexico. In completing 449 minutes of continuous World Cup football without conceding a goal, he also broke the goalkeeping record previously held by Gordon Banks during the 1966 tournament.

Against Austria, away from the altitude and long grass of the Andean city of Mendoza, Holland's performance paralleled some of those in 1974. Enforced changes as a consequence of injuries to Neeskens, Suurbier and Rijsbergen resulted in appearances by Wildschut, Brandts and Haan. Happel's dissatisfaction with Jongbloed led to his replacement by Schrijvers. Austria had lost only one of their last 14 games – to Holland. Holland simply demolished the Austrians. Brandts headed powerfully past Koncilia after just six minutes. Resenbrink scored his fifth goal of the tournament with a penalty in the 35th minute. A minute later a centre from

Resenbrink was not cleared and Rep lobbed the ball over Koncilia. Rep scored his second goal after 53 minutes before Obermayer netted a consolation goal. Only two minutes later Willy Van de Kerkhof completed a 5-1 rout which established Holland amongst the favourites.

Holland met West Germany in Cordoba, seeking revenge to eradicate the memory of the 1974 Final. West Germany recalled Abramczik and Dieter Muller to the attack. They scored after three minutes when Abramczik dived forward to head home a free kick by Bonhof. Holland then proceeded to play the 'Total Football' associated with 1974. Haan scored a spectacular equaliser after 26 minutes with a rising shot from 30 yards which left Maier motionless as it landed in the top right-hand corner. Rep came desperately close to scoring a further goal immediately afterwards. West Germany re-established their lead in the 70th minute when Dieter Muller headed in a cross from Beer. Rep then unluckily struck the crossbar after beating three defenders. With seven minutes remaining, Rene Van de Kerkhof waltzed through the German defence before drawing Maier off his line and shooting past him. Russmann handled the ball as it entered the net, but the referee allowed the goal to stand. In the final minute Nanninga, who had played for only ten minutes as a substitute, was dismissed. He and Holzenbein were involved in a confrontation. In the ensuing melee the Uruguayan referee was unsure what had happened as Rene Van de Kerkhof walked off the pitch. The winger had only gone to report events to the Dutch bench. Nanninga appeared to be sent off for laughing derisively at the referee. The match was one of the best of the tournament.

Italy and Austria contested a stultifying game in Buenos Aires. The only goal was scored by Rossi after 13 minutes. He back-heeled the ball with a clever flick to Causio, who outpaced Obermayer before returning the ball for an exquisite goal. After the interval Krankl had a goal disallowed and Austria were denied two legitimate penalty claims.

Holland entered their final group match knowing that a

draw would probably enable them to contest a second successive World Cup Final. Italy, on the other hand, required a victory. The game was an ill-tempered affair. Italy attacked briskly and Rossi skimmed the bar with a header while Cabrini squandered a good chance. Italy led after 19 minutes when Brandts scored an own goal. Rossi and Bettega had beaten the offside trap and Brandts' desperate sliding tackle only succeeded in steering the ball into his own net. In doing so, he collided with Schrijvers, who had to be stretchered off and replaced by Jongbloed. Jongbloed immediately distinguished himself with saves from Rossi and Benetti. The game degenerated as Haan kicked the prostrate Zaccarelli in response to being kicked by Benetti. Rep upended Benetti and Benetti, in turn, fouled Resenbrink in response to ill treatment from Rep. The aggression was not sufficiently punished, but Rep and Benetti were cautioned. Benetti, who had been arguably Italy's most influential player, would miss the Final if Italy won. Holland revamped their side at half-time and the tactical acumen of Happel soon became apparent when Brandts equalised five minutes after the resumption. He struck a marvellous right-foot shot which hurtled into the net from 20 yards. Weak refereeing by Angel Martinez of Spain meant that aggressive incidents continued unabated. Haan was booked for tripping Rossi; Rep threw himself at Cuccureddu; Cabrini was cautioned for fouling Haan; Benetti elbowed Neeskens in the face and Tardelli was booked for an indiscretion. During a moment of respite, and completely out of context, Haan scored a quite magnificent goal when, receiving a short free kick, he struck a searing, high velocity shot past Zoff from 35 yards. Holland had been largely outplayed during the first half but they had shown remarkable resilience in reaching their second successive Final.

In order to reach the Final West Germany had required Holland and Italy to draw, whilst they had to beat Austria by five clear goals. In the end, it was a sad exit for Helmut Schoen, the 62-year-old West German manager. He retired having achieved one World Cup win, one second place and one third place in the previous three tournaments.

West Germany started promisingly when Rummenigge opened the scoring after 19 minutes. Bertie Vogts scored an own goal on the hour. Six minutes later Hans Krankl gave another demonstration of his ruthless finishing. Although Holzenbein equalized in the 72nd minute, Krankl scored the winner two minutes from time, dismissively beating Russmann, cutting inside Vogts and steering the ball wide of Maier. Austria had achieved their first victory over West Germany in 47 years.

Whereas Group A had comprised of four European sides, Group B contained three South American teams. Brazil played Peru in Mendoza with Zico, Reinaldo, Edinho and Rivelino still out of favour. Despite the unpopularity of Coutinho, Brazil proceeded to give one of their best performances since the 1970 Final. Munante and La Rosa missed chances for Peru early in the game before Dirceu swerved a 22-yard free kick around the Peruvian wall in the 14th minute. Another long range shot by Dirceu in the 27th minute travelled under Quiroga's body into the net. Roberto was fouled in the penalty area with 20 minutes to go and Zico, a substitute for Gil, converted the spot kick.

Argentina faced Poland in Rosario without Luque, who had a shoulder injury. Mario Kempes returned to his former home, as he had played for Rosario Central before moving to Spain. He celebrated his return with two goals. After 14 minutes his near post header from a high centre by Bertoni was powerfully placed past Tomaszewski. Deyna, playing his 100th game for Poland, missed a penalty in the 39th minute after the ubiquitous Kempes made a spectacular one-handed save. Twenty minutes from the end, Ardiles advanced to the penalty area and passed to Kempes, who fired a low shot past Tomaszewski.

In a one-sided match in Mendoza, Poland beat Peru by a solitary goal when Szarmach headed past Quiroga in the 64th minute. There was a quite extraordinary incident two minutes from the end when the Peruvian goalkeeper, justifiably nicknamed 'El Loco', advanced to the half-way line to intercept a

Polish attack. One minute later he rugby-tackled Lato inside the Polish half and was promptly booked.

There is intense rivalry between Argentina and Brazil and the meeting between the two in Rosario became crucial. Argentina enjoyed the best record of any nation against Brazil in Brazil, but they had failed to defeat the Brazilians in Argentina for 18 years. An astonishing 17 fouls were committed in the first ten minutes of the match. Chicao, Edinho and Zico of Brazil and Villa of Argentina were all booked. A further four players departed from the field injured.

Brazil dominated midfield. Menotti's strategy of playing Kempes in the middle of the park failed. Ortiz missed the best opportunity of the game when from eight yards he fired a low centre from Bertoni wide of the goal. Villa was extremely fortunate to remain on the field when he inflicted a sickeningly brutal tackle on Batista. The goalless scoreline left these two powerful nations uncertain about who would contest the Final. Brazil held a one-goal advantage over Argentina and faced Poland in Mendoza. The hosts, in playing Peru, would know exactly what they had to do to reach the Final as Brazil's match would kick off earlier. Brazil were understandably annoyed about the time lag and the insistence of FIFA on allowing Argentina to continue with their evening kick-off. Brazil were also handicapped by having to make the lengthy journey back to Mendoza while Argentina remained in Rosario.

It was not inconceivable that Poland could reach the Final if they beat Brazil and Argentina faltered against Peru. Brazil attacked ferociously but received a blow after seven minutes when Zico went off injured. Five minutes later Nelinho struck a free kick of exceptional power into the top corner of the net. A minute from the interval Lato equalised, following defensive chaos in the Brazilian penalty area. But for inspired form by Leao, Poland would have been ahead at the interval as he repelled efforts from Maculewicz, Deyna and Lubanski. In the 57th minute Roberto scored for Brazil when he followed up a cross which rebounded off a post. Five minutes later Roberto scored again after the ball had rebounded off the post and crossbar. Brazil, at least temporarily, headed the group, knowing they would contest the Final unless Argentina could score at least four against Peru.

Argentina conveniently knew exactly what they had to do to reach the Final. Many people will remain convinced that the match was fixed and it would be extremely naïve to hold a contrary view. Peru, after all, had not conceded more than three goals in any one game in the tournament. So why did they suddenly meekly capitulate, leaking six goals? Argentina attacked with five forwards from the start but under normal circumstances this would have left them very vulnerable defensively. Munante struck the post early on for Peru and Oblitas shot across goal when clean through. After 21 minutes Kempes scored with a left-foot shot. Luque then struck the post and Ortiz clipped the bar. A Bertoni corner two minutes from half-time resulted in a low header by Tarantini finding the net. A well contrived free kick between Kempes and Luque resulted in a third goal shortly after half-time, when Kempes scored with the return pass. A minute later Luque scored with a diving header. Two minutes after replacing Bertoni, Houseman scored a fifth goal, following a dashing run and cross by Ortiz. Luque added a sixth goal in the 72nd minute after an excellent move initiated by Larrosa, who was deputising for the injured Ardiles. Argentina had reached the World Cup Final for the first time since the initial tournament when they crossed the River Plate and lost to Uruguay in the Final. After the game, Quiroga, the Peruvian goalkeeper who was born in Rosario, Argentina, published an open letter defending himself and his team. It has since been alleged that Admiral Carlos Lacoste, who was responsible for organising the World Cup and also served as Vice President of FIFA, made arrangements for 35,000 tons of free gain to Peru, and probably arms too. At the same time, the Argentine Central Bank unfroze $50 million in credits for Peru.

The third place play-off between Italy and Brazil in Buenos Aires was a surprisingly enjoyable match. Brazil were loudly jeered by Argentinian fans after their claims of drug taking by

Mario Kempes and bribes offered to Peru. One source claimed that Argentinian players had received drug injections under orders from the Junta.

Italy were vastly superior in the first half and deservedly led when Causio scored with a far post header from a Rossi corner. Causio then hit the bar as Brazil's defence looked troubled. Brazil gave a very determined performance after the resumption and won the match with two spectacular goals. Nelinho scored with an outrageous 35-yard shot near the right-wing corner flag. The ball swerved, first one way, then another, as it understandably deceived Zoff. A minute later Rivelino came on as a substitute and, in his final World Cup appearance, contributed to the winning goal. His cross was chested down by Mendonca for Dirceu to unleash another volley into the net from 20 yards. Dino Zoff, with a reputation as one of the world's leading goalkeepers, had conceded four goals in the last two games from long range shots. A degree of petulance crept into the game which Brazil won 2-1, thus enjoying the distinction of being the only unbeaten side in the eleventh World Cup.

Argentina and Holland contested the Final in the River Plate stadium on 25th June. The match, watched by a crowd of 77,260, was beamed to a television audience in 90 countries. The inevitable question being posed was could Holland win without Cruyff? No European team had won the World Cup in South America. But Holland had improved as the tournament progressed and Argentina displayed obvious defensive frailties. It was Holland's second successive appearance in the Final and the Dutch again experienced a delay in the kick-off. On this occasion the reason was less innocent as Argentina decided to engage in psychological warfare. They kept their opponents waiting for a full five minutes then complained about the small plaster cast on Rene Van de Kerkhof's right forearm. The injury had been sustained in Holland's opening game. Rather alarmingly, Sergio Gonella, the Italian referee, upheld the protest. At one point, the Dutch threatened to walk off the field. In the end, Van de Kerkhof was allowed to wear the cast with a soft cover. Gonella was a compromise choice when the FIFA Referees Committee could not agree on the man to officiate the Final. Abraham Klein of Israel was the original choice, but Argentinian officials complained because of Holland's ties with Israel.

Holland were clearly incensed and started the match in an ugly, vengeful mood. Poortvliet committed a crude foul in the first minute. Gonella's refereeing was both weak and disturbingly inconsistent. Twice he allowed Gallego to handle the ball without cautioning him. Ruud Krol was booked for a brutal foul in the 14th minute. Ubaldo Fillol in the Argentinian goal made competent saves from Rep and Resenbrink as Holland penetrated Argentina's suspect offside trap. Holland's man-to-man marking appeared to be effective until the 38th minute. Ardiles orchestrated an attack on the left which found Luque, who delivered a square pass to Kempes. He evaded a protective wall of defenders and rolled the ball under Jongbloed. Fillol made a critical save from Resenbrink on the stroke of half-time and distinguished himself again with an excellent save from Neeskens shortly after the interval. After 59 minutes Nanninga replaced Rep with the intention of troubling Argentina in the air. Seven minutes later Larrosa replaced Ardiles, who was not fully fit. Neeskens was crudely brought down by Galvan, who was cautioned. He then fouled Resenbrink in the penalty area but no action was taken. Brandts joined the Dutch attack to complement Nanninga as Willy Van de Kerkhof retreated.

With eight minutes remaining, Haan delivered a delightful long ball to Rene Van de Kerkhof, who centred for Nanninga to score with a decisive header. Passarella elbowed Neeskens in the face before Rob Resenbrink infiltrated the defence in the very last minute. Argentina were in disarray as Resenbrink flicked at the ball from five yards and struck the left-hand post.

Holland, who were better organised and more efficient, would have been worthy winners. They appeared to have the initiative, latterly dominating the game as an exhausted

Argentina approached extra time. But Menotti roused his team just as Alf Ramsey had done in 1966. Extra time was punctuated by a series of fouls before Kempes gave Argentina the lead a minute from the end of the first period. He received the ball from Bertoni and powered his way through the defence aided by a favourable rebound. Holland, in pursuit of a second equaliser, left alarming gaps in their defence. Argentina exploited the situation with five minutes remaining, when a perfectly executed interchange between Kempes and Bertoni resulted in the winger scoring a third goal. For the third time in four tournaments, the host country triumphed. In becoming the fifth nation to win the World Cup, Argentina could, momentarily at least, forget their political and economic problems.

Results: Argentina 1978

Group 1

Argentina	2	Hungary	1
Italy	2	France	1
Argentina	2	France	1
Italy	3	Hungary	1
Italy	1	Argentina	0
France	3	Hungary	1

	P	W	D	L	F	A	Pts
					Goals		
Italy	3	3	0	0	6	2	6
Argentina	3	2	0	1	4	3	4
France	3	1	0	2	5	5	2
Hungary	3	0	0	3	3	8	0

Group 2

West Germany	0	Poland	0
Tunisia	3	Mexico	1
Poland	1	Tunisia	0
West Germany	6	Mexico	0
West Germany	0	Tunisia	0
Poland	3	Mexico	1

	P	W	D	L	F	A	Pts
					Goals		
Poland	3	2	1	0	4	1	5
West Germany	3	1	2	0	6	0	4
Tunisia	3	1	1	1	3	2	3
Mexico	3	0	0	3	2	12	0

Group 3

Austria	2	Spain	1
Sweden	1	Brazil	1
Austria	1	Sweden	0
Brazil	0	Spain	0
Spain	1	Sweden	0
Brazil	1	Austria	0

				Goals		
	P	W	D	L	F	A	Pts
Austria	3	2	0	1	3	2	4
Brazil	3	1	2	0	2	1	4
Spain	3	1	1	1	2	2	3
Sweden	3	0	1	2	1	3	1

Group 4

Holland	3	Iran	0
Peru	3	Scotland	1
Scotland	1	Iran	1
Holland	0	Peru	0
Peru	4	Iran	1
Scotland	3	Holland	2

				Goals		
	P	W	D	L	F	A	Pts
Peru	3	2	1	0	7	2	5
Holland	3	1	1	1	5	3	3
Scotland	3	1	1	1	5	6	3
Iran	3	0	1	2	2	8	1

Second Round

Group A

West Germany	0	Italy	0
Holland	5	Austria	1
Italy	1	Austria	0
West Germany	2	Holland	2
Holland	2	Italy	1
Austria	3	WestGermany	2

				Goals		
	P	W	D	L	F	A	Pts
Holland	3	2	1	0	9	4	5
Italy	3	1	1	1	2	2	3
West Germany	3	0	2	1	4	5	2
Austria	3	1	0	2	4	8	2

Group B

Argentina	2	Poland	0
Brazil	3	Peru	0
Argentina	0	Brazil	0
Poland	1	Peru	0
Brazil	3	Poland	1
Argentina	6	Peru	0

				Goals		
	P	W	D	L	F	A	Pts
Argentina	3	2	1	0	8	0	5
Brazil	3	2	1	0	6	1	5
Poland	3	1	0	2	2	5	2
Peru	3	0	0	3	0	10	0

Match for third place

Brazil	2	Italy	1

Final

| Argentina | 3 | Holland | 1* |

*(after extra time) 1-1 at 90 minutes

Argentina: Fillol, Olguin, Galvan, Passarella, Tarantini, Ardiles (Larrosa), Gallego, Kempes, Bertoni, Luque, Ortiz (Houseman)

Holland: Jongbloed, Jansen (Suurbier), Brandts, Krol, Poortvliet, Haan, Van de Kerkhof W, Neeskens, Van de Kerkhof R, Rep (Nanninga), Resenbrink

Scorers: Kempes (2), Bertoni for Argentina
        Nanninga for Holland

1982

From April to June the South Atlantic became the focus of world attention as Britain and Argentina went to war over the Falkland Islands. The conflict began on 2nd April when Argentinian forces invaded and captured the islands in support of a long-standing claim to sovereignty. The single company of Royal Marines guarding the islands' capital, Port Stanley, were overwhelmed. On 3rd April cheering crowds gathered outside the Casa Rosada presidential palace in Buenos Aires to celebrate the recapture of islands that the Argentinians called 'Las Malvinas'. General Galtieri, the leader of the ruling junta, said the military leaders had 'only interpreted the sentiment of the Argentine people'. Britain took swift action. A large task force was assembled and set sail for the South Atlantic. During the three weeks it took to cover the 8,000 miles to the Falklands there was intense diplomatic activity by the USA and others to find a peaceful solution to the crisis. On 14th June Argentinian forces surrendered to the British commander of land forces. The hostilities had cost 254 British and 750 Argentinian lives.

During March the Iran-Iraq war, which might already have claimed the lives of as many as 100,000 people, took a decisive turn. Iranian troops recaptured 850 square miles of land which the Iraqis had gained after launching an offensive in 1980. In May, revolutionary forces entered the key border town of Khorramshahr, an important oil port. Over the following months the Iraqis were driven out of Iran almost completely. President Saddam Hussein responded by launching a series of air attacks on Iranian oil installations in the Gulf.

Israel launched a full-scale invasion of Lebanon in early June following months of mounting tension. One day after the Israeli ambassador in London had been shot by Palestinian gunmen, Israel's jets bombed guerrilla targets in reprisal raids. The operation, code-named 'Peace for Galilee', had the declared aim of driving the Palestine Liberation Organisation out of the bases near Israel's northern border. However, the invasion force of some 90,000 troops pushed on to Beirut in house to house fighting, leaving coastal cities in ruins and trapping many PLO fighters including Yasser Arafat in the capital as they surrounded it. The PLO evacuated Beirut following their defeat by the Israelis and dispersed to Syria, Jordan, Sudan, North and South Yemen, Algeria, Iraq and Tunisia.

*   *   *

At the 1964 FIFA Congress in Tokyo, Spain had been chosen to stage the 1982 World Cup. King Carlos signed a decree forming the 1982 World Cup Organisation Committee, with Raimundo Saporta appointed President. On 17th May 1979 in Zurich, FIFA, reacting to pressure from Third World Countries, expanded the finalists from 16 to 24 teams. This produced a record entry of 109 from a FIFA membership of 147 nations. Increased final places had an encouraging effect on Third World participation.

There were worries about security arrangements because of terrorism involving Basque separatists, and the added concern of England possibly meeting Argentina only months after the Falklands conflict, but those fears were never realised.

There would be 52 games instead of the 38 played in Argentina. Spain spent £40 million revamping a record number of stadia used to stage the finals. The increased number of entrants led to a new format. The 24 teams were divided into six groups of four. The top two teams then advanced into four further groups of three with the group winners progressing to a semi-final knock-out stage.

Anyone who witnessed the draw for the World Cup finals held in Madrid on 16th January 1982, would scarcely have believed that Spain had spent £60 million on organisational costs. England courted controversy by being one of the six seeded teams along with Italy, West Germany, Argentina, Brazil and Spain. There was considerable argument provoked by the decision, especially from France and Belgium. They justifiably complained that England had finished second in their qualifying group and struggled to reach the finals. In order that Peru and Chile would avoid the same group as their South American rivals Argentina and Brazil, the miniature footballs containing their names were supposed to be left out of the cage until the first two names drawn out had been placed in Argentina's and Brazil's groups. Someone forgot to remove them, and to compound the confusion, Scotland appeared twice. Initially, Scotland were placed in Argentina's group before it was realised that Belgium should have been in the group. Scotland were then transferred to Brazil's group. The Pythonesque proceedings worsened as the giant cage containing the footballs jammed, splitting one unfortunate nation in half.

The Home Countries had their best representation since 1958. England, somewhat fortunately, qualified for the finals for the first time in 20 years (in 1966 and 1970 the right of entry had been automatic as hosts and holders). Scotland and Northern Ireland both won places from the lowest scoring of all the European groups. But for an unaccountable lapse at home to Iceland, Wales would also have qualified. The Soviet Union won the group, with Czechoslovakia ousting Wales on goal difference. West Germany won all their eight games and were joined by their neighbours Austria, who finished second. The Republic of Ireland narrowly failed to qualify, losing out on an inferior goal difference to France who, together with Belgium, reached Spain.

Yugoslavia and Italy qualified from their group but Italy failed to impress, being held at home by Greece and defeating Luxembourg in Naples by a solitary goal. Poland won all four matches in their group comprising of East Germany and Malta.

Brazil qualified with considerable ease, as did Peru at the expense of Uruguay, who thus became the only former champions not to reach the finals. Chile progressed to Spain without conceding a single goal.

The CONCACAF winners had a familiarly complex journey to the finals. The groups were split into three zones: Northern, Central and Caribbean which, in turn, was divided into two groups. Two nations from each zone competed in a final round of five matches from which El Salvador and Honduras qualified.

Africa's representatives were Cameroon and Algeria. Cameroon defeated Morocco in Yaounde, watched by a crowd of 120,000. Algeria beat Nigeria to share the distinction of reaching the finals for the first time.

The Asia/Oceania group was divided into a series of subgroups which eventually brought together four group finalists, competing for two places. With Kuwait already assured of a place, China appeared certain to join them. New Zealand needed to defeat Saudi Arabia by six clear goals in Riyadh in order to displace China. This seemed an impossible task, given that they could only manage a 2-2 draw in Auckland. Astonishingly they won 5-0, thereby forcing a play-off. New Zealand beat China 2-1 in Singapore. After 15 matches and 55,000 miles of travel, the Kiwis finally qualified. *En route* to the finals, they established a new World Cup record score when beating Fiji 13-0.

In Group 1 Italy faced Poland in the knowledge that they had won their last four opening matches. Poland eliminated Italy during the 1974 World Cup in a game which has since produced claims of attempted bribery. Dino Zoff made his 100th international appearance as Italy's goalkeeper. Paolo Rossi returned to the Italian team after a two-year suspension following a match-fixing scandal. Whilst on loan with Perugia in 1980 he was accused of taking a bribe after scoring both goals in a 2-2 draw with Avellino. Rossi was suspended for three years but continually protested his innocence. The ban was commuted to two years, the suspension ended on 29th April 1982 and Rossi was immediately recalled to international football. It was perhaps not surprising that Rossi was off form. On this occasion, Italy failed to win against a resolute and well organised Polish team, who deservedly earned a goalless draw.

French-speaking Cameroon were managed by Jean Vincent, one of the stars of France during the 1958 tournament. In Thomas N'Kono, Cameroon boasted the greatest African goalkeeper of all time. In 1980 N'Kono won the African Footballer of the Year award. He also scored the winning goal for his club Canon de Yaounde in the African Champions Cup final, with a crisply struck penalty in the dying moments. Roger Milla, a striker, played for the French club Bastia. Cameroon met Peru in their opening match. Peru were managed by the 71-year-old Brazilian-born Tim. They were a huge disappointment and were somewhat relieved to gain a goalless draw.

Italy remained in Vigo for their next encounter against Peru. Conti scored in the 18th minute following a well contrived move involving Cabrini and Antognoni. Italy were lucky to escape unpunished when Gentile tripped Oblitas in the penalty area. An ineffectual Rossi was substituted at half-time by Causio. Diaz deservedly equalised for Peru when his shot was turned into the net by the Italian defender Collovati.

Relations between the press and the Italian camp were steadily worsening. Growing tension arose as a consequence of severe criticism by the media, particularly about bonuses. The Italian team had a public relations officer named Gigi Personace, but he died suddenly in December 1980. Now there was no buffer and relations broke down almost completely. The players refused to talk to the Press except through the veteran goalkeeper Dino Zoff, who was not the most garrulous of players.

Cameroon again acquitted themselves well, in La Coruna, as they gained another goalless draw. Although Poland attacked strongly during the first half, Cameroon could easily have won the game as they stretched the Polish defence with their thrusting counter-attacks.

Given that the opening four games had produced a mere two goals, it was something of a surprise when Poland and Peru shared six. For 55 minutes there was no score, but a vivacious Polish side eventually overwhelmed their feeble opponents. Smolarek scored before Lato achieved his tenth World Cup goal. Boniek, Bruncol and Ciolek added further goals before La Rosa netted a consolation goal for Peru.

The final match of the group between Italy and Cameroon determined who would join Poland in the next round. Conti missed a remarkably easy opportunity in the early minutes. Italy eventually scored on the hour when a Graziani header found the net, aided by N'Kono's stumble. Cameroon equalised one minute later when McBida, looking suspiciously offside, scored. Cameroon's third draw of the tournament enabled Italy to go through on goal difference, joining Poland, who won the group. Cameroon departed undefeated and sounded a warning that African football was becoming a potent force. Italy entered the next phase without registering a single victory, having scored just two goals in three games.

West Germany, under new manager Jupp Derwall, had won the European Championship in 1980 and scored 33 goals in eight World Cup qualifying matches whilst conceding just three. With Horst Hrubesch, Karl-Heinz Rummenigge and newcomer Pierre Littbarski, they were re-emerging as one of the leading football nations. Not surprisingly, seeded West Germany were installed as 3-1 second favourites to win the tournament. Algeria, by contrast, making their World Cup finals debut, were 1,000-1 outsiders. Algeria, masterminded by African Footballer of the Year, Lakhdar Belloumi, provided a shock in Gijon which paralleled victories by the United States over England in 1950 and North Korea over Italy in 1966. Despite German territorial domination, Madjer gave Algeria the lead in the 54th minute after Belloumi's shot rebounded off Schumacher. Karl Heinz Rummenigge equalised in the 68th minute but Lakhdar Belloumi scored the winning goal one minute later. Remarkably, this was Algeria's second successive win over West Germany, whom they previously defeated in a 1964 friendly match.

Austria defeated Chile with relative ease in Oviedo. Schachner headed the only goal from a Krauss centre. Four minutes later Chile had an opportunity to equalise when Caszely was brought down by Krauss in the penalty area, but Caszely missed the spot-kick.

Karl-Heinz Rummenigge, the West German captain, passed a late fitness test and proceeded to score a hat-trick against Chile in Gijon. Reinders added a fourth goal within two minutes of replacing Littbarski. With seconds remaining, Moscoso scored a splendid goal, bringing scant consolation for Chile.

In Oviedo Algeria lost their momentum playing Austria. Schachner opened the scoring in the 56th minute and a left-foot shot by Krankl 11 minutes later ensured a 2-0 victory for Austria.

Belloumi was missing for Algeria's final group match against Chile. Algeria launched a wave of attacks and were rewarded with a 3-0 lead by half-time. Two goals by Assad within the first half hour, and a further strike by Bensaoula, emphasised the dominance of the Africans. A penalty by Niera and an exquisite piece of individualism by Letelier reduced the arrears to 3-2 as Algeria visibly tired.

Despite Algeria achieving a commendable two victories, they were eliminated because of a contrived result between Austria and West Germany in Gijon. A shameful final game which saw the Germans beat their supposedly bitter rivals by a solitary goal became a telling indictment of the system of qualification. After Hrubesch scored in the 11th minute the game deteriorated into farce, with both sides effortlessly settling for the one-goal scoreline which ensured their qualification. Algeria protested to FIFA, claiming the game was fixed, and called for both teams to be disqualified. Unfortunately, their protest was not upheld.

Argentina's defence of their crown began while the conflict

between that nation and Britain over the sovereignty of the Falkland Islands was still casting a heavy shadow. If Argentine troops needed a morale boost from their football team, that responsibility was too heavy a burden for the team which opened the tournament against Belgium.

Argentina continued to be managed by Cesar Menotti. Although they were largely unchanged from the side which triumphed in 1978, they had an emerging world superstar in Diego Maradona. Maradona was, in fact, in the squad of 1978, but as a 17-year-old prodigy was not risked by Menotti. He was enormously quick in thought and movement and was rapidly surfacing as an exceptional talent. Maradona had just transferred from Boca Juniors to Barcelona for £4 million when he made his World Cup debut in the Nou Camp Stadium against Belgium.

The Group 3 inaugural match produced a goal for the first time since 1962. But it was Belgium, returning to the World Cup arena after an absence of 20 years, who triumphed. They defended *en masse*, their cynical tactics successfully denying Argentina. Just after an hour of play, a cross by Vercauteren was met by an unmarked Vandenbergh, who struck a left-foot shot past Fillol. Argentina became the first defending champions to lose their opening match since Italy in 1950.

Hungary created a new World Cup record score in the finals when they met El Salvador in Elche. Perhaps the El Salvadoran players were preoccupied with the horrendous civil war ravaging their country. Hungary routed their opponents 10-1 with Kiss, who appeared as a substitute in the 55th minute, scoring three, Nyilasi two, Fazekas two, and Toth, Poloskei and Szentes one each.

Any notion that Hungary were going to romp through the qualifying stage was rapidly dispelled against Argentina in Alicante. Maradona was irrepressible, displaying his full gamut of skills, scoring two goals and contributing to two. In the 26th minute he headed a Passarella free kick into the path of Bertoni, who scored. Maradona then made his goal-scoring debut two minutes later. An excellent drive by Maradona ten minutes after the interval, and a further goal by Ardiles, secured an emphatic victory before Poloskei reduced the margin of victory to 4-1.

The Belgian goalkeeper, Jean-Marie Pfaff, nearly drowned in a swimming pool accident only hours before his side's match with El Salvador. The Central Americans packed their defence and successfully engaged in a damage-limitation exercise. Only a first-half goal from a free kick by Belgium's Coeck separated the sides.

Hungary needed to win their final group game against Belgium to advance to the next phase. They led through a goal by Varga, but with 14 minutes remaining, Czerniatynski equalised, which resulted in Belgium winning the group.

Another creditable performance by El Salvador, with the emphasis on massed defence, restricted Argentina to a 2-0 victory which nevertheless ensured their qualification. Passarella scored with a highly contentious penalty midway through the first half. Bertoni added a second goal shortly after the resumption.

England qualified for the finals for the first time since 1962. They were deprived of Kevin Keegan and Trevor Brooking through injury for their opening Group 4 match against France in Bilbao. With the temperature exceeding 100°F, England started in extraordinary fashion with Bryan Robson scoring after only 27 seconds. Giresse split the English defence after 25 minutes, enabling Soler to equalise. This was to be the only goal conceded by Peter Shilton in the finals. Bryan Robson headed powerfully into the net after 66 minutes and Mariner added a third goal eight minutes from time.

Kuwait, playing in their first finals, were coached by Carlos Alberto Perreira, who succeeded Zagalo as Kuwait's manager in 1978. Against Czechoslovakia in Valladolid, they unluckily conceded a penalty converted by Panenka midway through the first half. An energetic Kuwaiti side were dominant and deservedly equalised after the interval, when Al Dakhil struck a long-range shot which deceived Hruska.

A particularly poor Czechoslovakian side restricted England to a 2-0 victory in Valladolid. Trevor Francis capitalised on another goalkeeping error after 63 minutes. Three minutes later an own goal by Barmos emphasised England's superiority.

One of the tournament's most astonishing incidents occurred during the France versus Kuwait clash in Valladolid. France established a lead after 30 minutes when Genghini scored with a swerving free kick. Platini added a second goal three minutes from half-time. Shortly after the resumption, a marvellous volley by Six gave France a 3-0 lead. Al Bouloushi reduced the arrears with 15 minutes remaining. The Soviet Union referee, Stupar, then disallowed an apparently legitimate goal by Bossis. This was, by no means, an isolated error by the match official. One minute later an already simmering match exploded when Alain Giresse scored from close range. The Kuwaiti players stood motionless, claiming they had stopped upon hearing a whistle. The Kuwaiti FA President, Prince Fahid, came onto the pitch and protested vehemently. He appeared to beckon his players off the field before the referee inexplicably reversed his decision. France were understandably angry and their manager, Michel Hidalgo, had to be restrained by police during the furore. After an eight-minute delay, play was resumed and Bossis scored a fourth goal in the dying seconds. FIFA imposed an £8000 fine on the Kuwaitis for Prince Fahid's interference.

France required a draw against Czechoslovakia to qualify for the next phase, whereas Czechoslovakia needed to win. Didier Six put France ahead midway through the second half, following a pass from Lacombe. Panenka equalised, converting a penalty in the 84th minute. The closing stages were frantic, with Czechoslovakia vigorously pursuing a second goal. Vizek was sent off for kicking Platini before Nehoda had an effort cleared off the line.

England gained maximum points in defeating Kuwait 1-0, with a first-half goal by Trevor Francis.

The hosts, Spain, must have been confident playing 500-1 outsiders Honduras in their opening Group 5 match in

Valencia. The Central Americans shocked their much fancied opponents with a goal scored by Zelaya after only seven minutes. It took Spain almost an hour to breach an obdurate, highly competent defence. It was perhaps inevitable that a disingenuous Spanish attack would equalise with a penalty converted by Lopez Ufarte.

The following day in Zaragoza, Northern Ireland returned to the World Cup finals after an absence of 24 years. It was perhaps fitting that Billy Bingham, who was a player in the 1958 team, now managed the side. Bingham boldly introduced Norman Whiteside, the Manchester United centre-forward. At 17 years and 41 days, he beat Pele's record by becoming the youngest ever debutant in the World Cup finals. Although Yugoslavia were vastly more talented, the midfield skills of Martin O'Neill and Sammy McIlroy helped Northern Ireland earn a meritorious goalless draw.

Spain gained a controversial victory in their second match against Yugoslavia in Valencia. Gudelj scored first for Yugoslavia. Only minutes later, Spain were awarded a spot-kick when Alonso appeared to be fouled by Zajec outside the penalty area. Lopez Ufarte's woeful effort missed the target. However, the Danish referee, Lund-Sorensen, adjudged that Pantelic had moved. Juanito converted the second attempt. Yugoslavia outplayed their opponents but a defensive error in the second half allowed Saura, a substitute, to score an undeserved winner.

Gerry Armstrong gave Northern Ireland an early lead against Honduras after a McIlroy free kick had struck the bar. Honduras were rewarded for their attacking play, equalising on the hour when substitute Laing scored.

Honduras further enhanced their growing reputation with a diligent, determined performance against Yugoslavia in Zaragoza. Petrovic scored the decisive goal in the 87th minute with a penalty. Yearwood of Honduras was dismissed for his protestations. Yugoslavia's fate rested on the final match.

Northern Ireland required a victory against Spain in Valencia to reach the next phase. They defied logic, a Paraguayan referee who sent off Mal Donaghy for a mild infringement, and a partisan 50,000 crowd, to win by a goal from Gerry Armstrong. Northern Ireland refused to be intimidated in a highly physical match. Two minutes after the interval Billy Hamilton raced up the right and crossed. Arconada, playing diffidently, merely pushed the ball out to Gerry Armstrong, who lashed it into the net. After an hour's play Donaghy was brought down by Camacho and responded by pushing his opponent. Ortiz sent him off. Northern Ireland won the group, with Spain also qualifying on the basis of scoring one more goal than Yugoslavia.

Brazil were now managed by Tele Santana and reverted to the style of play with which they became synonymous in 1970. Tragically, Claudio Coutinho, who managed the side in 1978, died in a drowning accident. Brazil's plethora of talented midfield stars, which included Zico, Socrates, Cezezo and Falcao, was not matched by players of equal stature in attack.

The Soviet Union provided a severe test for Brazil in the opening Group 6 contest in Seville. Perez, the Brazilian goalkeeper, allowed a shot by Bal to slip through his arms in the 33rd minute. The Soviet Union held a one-goal advantage until 15 minutes from time, when Socrates equalised with a thunderous long-range shot. Only two minutes remained when Eder struck a swerving shot past Dasaev to clinch a narrow victory.

New Zealand's marathon trek through an arduous 15 qualifying games was not rewarded against Scotland in Malaga. Scotland were now managed by Jock Stein, who had never fully recovered from a dreadful car crash. Argentina had clearly not served as a learning experience, given that Alan Rough was still in goal. By half-time Scotland had gained a comfortable lead with two goals by Wark and one by Dalglish. A defensive misunderstanding in the 55th minute between Alan Rough and captain Danny McGrain allowed Sumner to score. Ten minutes later Wooddin scored a second as New Zealand threatened to seriously embarrass Scotland. A

Robertson free kick and a strike by Archibald eventually restored the three-goal margin.

A carnival atmosphere greeted Brazil and Scotland in Seville. The temperature was in excess of 90 degrees as Scotland wilted against opposition playing delectable football. David Narey gave Scotland the lead after 18 minutes. The self-effacing, highly underrated Dundee United defender powered a marvellously struck swerving shot, so reminiscent of Brazilian goals, into the roof of the net. Brazil were irresistible, with Socrates, Zico and Cerezo operating in the middle of the park and Eder, wide on the left, punishing Scotland with every attack. Zico equalised with a beautifully flighted free kick from 25 yards. After the interval a near-post header, by Oscar from a Junior corner, gave the Brazilians the lead. The high quality of the goals was brilliantly sustained by Eder in the 64th minute. He deftly chipped the ball over the bewild-ered and sadly exposed Alan Rough. Four minutes from the end Falcao blasted a low shot into the net off an upright to emphasize Brazil's superiority. Scotland had by no means disgraced themselves and departed from the field generously acknowledging the marvellous attributes of an exuberant Brazilian side.

The Soviet Union comfortably defeated New Zealand 3-0 in Malaga. Gavrilov scored midway through the first half when the ball rebounded to him following a Bal shot. Oleg Blokhin doubled the lead shortly after the interval with a left-foot shot and also contributed to the third goal scored by Baltacha.

Scotland had to beat the Soviet Union in order to enter the next phase, because of their inferior goal difference. They recalled Joe Jordan, who scored another important goal for his country in the 15th minute, following an uncharacteristic error by Chivadze. Scotland played well during the first half and retained their lead until Chivadze equalised after an hour. A bizarre defensive mix-up between Hansen and Miller enabled Shengelia to break clear and score with only six minutes remaining. Souness scored an exceptional goal with three minutes left but it was too late for Scotland to salvage the tie.

For the second successive tournament they were eliminated on goal difference.

New Zealand contested the biggest game in their football history against Brazil in Seville. Brazil gave yet another exhilarating display but were never seriously challenged by the Antipodeans. Zico met a Leandro cross with a spectacular bicycle kick to give Brazil the lead. Only two minutes later Zico again scored from a Leandro cross. Further goals from Falcao and Serginho completed a 4-0 victory.

The 12 qualifying teams formed four further groups of three with the group winners progressing to a semi-final knock-out stage. The groups comprised as follows:

Group A: Belgium, Poland, Soviet Union
Group B: England, Spain, West Germany
Group C: Argentina, Brazil, Italy
Group D: Austria, France, Northern Ireland

Belgium had performed particularly well in the 1980 European Nations Cup, narrowly losing to West Germany in the final. But they gave an insipid, supine display against Poland in Barcelona. A magnificent performance by Zbigniew Boniek resulted in a hat-trick. Lato, a survivor of the Polish side who fared so well in the 1974 World Cup, was inspirational in midfield. He created the opening goal after four minutes when he pulled back the ball for Boniek to strike a powerful shot into the roof of the net. By pursuing an equaliser, Belgium left alarming gaps in their defence which were ruthlessly exploited. In the 26th minute a cross from Kupcewicz was directed by Buncol's head to Boniek who, in turn, headed the ball into the net. Seven minutes into the second half Lato beat the offside trap, thus enabling Boniek to score with ease.

Belgium introduced four changes for their next match against the Soviet Union. A much improved performance was not adequately rewarded as Vandenbergh missed two good opportunities in the second half. The decisive goal arrived four minutes after the interval. Gavrilov pulled the ball back from the by-line and Oganesian failed to fully connect with

197

the ball, which nevertheless entered the net for a messy goal to give the Soviet Union victory.

Poland only required a draw against the Soviet Union to reach the semi-finals. The Soviet Union created three good chances during the first half, but Blokhin, Oganesian and Sulakvelidze all failed to capitalise. Poland grew in confidence and their penetrating and incisive counter-attacks could have produced a goal. Boniek foolishly allowed himself to be cautioned for the second time and thus missed Poland's crucial semi-final match.

The England against West Germany Group B clash in the Bernabeu Stadium, Madrid, lacked the drama and excitement of their encounters in 1966 and 1970. The game was a sterile affair between two sides fearful of losing. West Germany almost won the match in the dying moments when Rummenigge's shot crashed against the bar. Without the artistry of Hoddle and Brooking, England never seriously threatened the Germans.

Spain's prospects of winning the World Cup evaporated against West Germany in front of a crowd of 90,000 at the Bernabeu Stadium. West Germany imposed their superiority from the start and only wasteful finishing resulted in a goalless first half. Rummenigge had to retire injured at half-time. But in the 50th minute Arconada, in goal, giving another substandard performance, failed to hold a long-range shot by Dremmler and Littbarski capitalised. Paul Breitner, playing outstandingly well, initiated a further move which led to Littbarski rounding Arconada before passing to Fischer, who shot into the unguarded net.

A Zamora header nine minutes from time came too late to salvage Spain's hopes. Once again, they had been a huge disappointment on the world stage.

England faced Spain needing to win by two clear goals to reach the semi-final. Ironically, Spain did not concede a goal for the first time in the tournament. They had goalscoring chances but both Alonso and Satrustegui missed. With 27 minutes remaining, Brooking and Keegan were finally introduced to the competition. Keegan headed over an open goal in the 70th minute following a cross by Bryan Robson. England departed from the tournament unbeaten, having yielded only one goal in five games. It was Ron Greenwood's sad farewell as he handed over to his successor, Bobby Robson. West Germany, predictably, advanced to the semi-finals.

It was widely anticipated that the Group C clash between Italy and Argentina at the Sarria Stadium, Barcelona, would be an explosive encounter. Sadly, those fears were realised with Claudio Gentile assigned to man-mark Maradona. His thoroughly odious excesses were reminiscent of the maltreatment Pele received in the 1966 tournament. Italy, intent on stifling the opposition, restricted Argentina to a solitary shot by Diaz during the first half. With Maradona overshadowed, Italy became more adventurous after the interval. Conti instigated a movement which led to Antognoni producing a delicate pass for Tardelli to score. Maradona struck a post from a free kick before Rossi broke clear, with Argentina appealing for offside. Although Fillol blocked his shot, the ball ran free and was pulled back for Cabrini to score. Passarella reduced the arrears with a free kick from 25 yards six minutes from time while Italy were still organising their defensive wall.

The all-South American clash between Argentina and Brazil was a surprisingly one-sided affair. The Brazilians, on occasions, surpassed their brilliance of 1970 with exquisite one-touch football. Eder struck a free kick which simultaneously swerved and dipped before striking the underside of the bar, enabling Zico to thump the ball into the net. It was perhaps surprising that Brazil's dominance was not further rewarded until the 67th minute, when Serginho rose to head home a Falcao cross at the near post. Five minutes later Junior scored a stunning goal following an intricate move of collective beauty. With five minutes remaining, Maradona, clearly frustrated by his lack of impact, committed a despicable foul on Batista and was dismissed. A minute from the end, Ramon Diaz scored for Argentina but the World Champions made an undignified exit.

There was a dramatic climax to the final Group C match, which was a pulsating contest. Brazil only needed to draw to reach the semi-finals whereas Italy had to win. Italy attacked from the start and were rewarded after only five minutes with a goal of stunning simplicity. Cabrini crossed from the left and Rossi headed home his first goal of the competition. Brazil were level by the 12th minute. Zico eluded Gentile and delivered an enticing angled pass which allowed Socrates to race through the defence and score. Italy regained the lead after 25 minutes following a dreadful defensive blunder. Cerezo carelessly allowed his pass to Junior to be intercepted by Rossi, who was in irrepressible form. Italy had two good chances to increase their lead, one of which was squandered by Rossi. Brazil appeared to have salvaged the tie with a marvellous goal by Falcao. He wrong-footed the defence and struck a left-footed shot past Zoff midway through the second half. With 15 minutes remaining, Rossi scored the winning goal. Junior headed weakly, only half clearing a corner. Tardelli drove the ball into the goal mouth and Rossi's ruthless opportunism sealed victory. In the dying moments Oscar sent in a thrusting header that the Brazilians claimed was over the line before Zoff, with unbelievable reflexes for a 40-year-old veteran, dived to stop. Brazil had paid dearly for boldly adhering to a philosophy that thrilled millions.

In Group D, played in the Calderon Stadium, Madrid, France were imperious victors over Austria. A clever free-kick by Genghini six minutes from half-time deceived Koncilia in the Austrian goal. Even without the highly influential Michel Platini, France were commanding winners.

Austria introduced five changes for their next match against Northern Ireland, omitting Hans Krankl. Pat Jennings was injured and replaced by Jim Platt, the deputising goalkeeper for Northern Ireland. After 27 minutes Gerry Armstrong advanced down the right, beat two defenders and delivered a perfect cross for Hamilton to head home. Austria equalised five minutes after the interval when Schachner struck the post and Baumeister seized onto the ball to equalise. Six minutes later Schachner netted again, but the goal was adjudged to be offside. Midway through the second half, substitute Hintermaier swept in a free kick pushed to him by Prohaska. Austria's brittle defence succumbed to yet another Hamilton header from a lob by J. Nicholl, thus completing a 2-2 draw.

Northern Ireland needed to defeat France in the final group game in order to reach the semi-finals. Pat Jennings returned to goal but Northern Ireland were completely outclassed by a French side containing some extremely talented individuals. Tresor gave a majestic display as sweeper and, allied to the midfield skills of Platini, Giresse and Genghini, France were a creative joy. Platini manufactured the opening goal after 33 minutes when he raced to the by-line and pulled the ball back for Giresse to score. Two minutes into the second half, Dominique Rocheteau exploited weak defending to double the lead. Rocheteau scored again when he launched a header past Jennings, following a cross by Tigana. With 15 minutes remaining, Norman Whiteside's cross was mishandled by Ettori, which enabled Armstrong to score. Five minutes later France ensured their semi final place when Giresse headed home a Tigana cross. History had repeated itself, as Northern Ireland had been eliminated in their last World Cup appearance in 1958 by a French side who scored four goals against them.

The semi-finals paired Italy with Poland in the Nou Camp, Barcelona, and West Germany with France at the Sanchez Pizjuan Stadium, Seville.

Italy and Poland had previously met in the opening Group 1 match which was a drab, sedate, goalless draw. Italy were without Gentile and Poland Boniek as both players had received two cautions. In the absence of Boniek, Poland carried little menace. Italy, gaining momentum, won comfortably, with Rossi bringing his goal tally to five in two matches. Poland resorted to robust play in an attempt to stifle their opponents. Midway through the first half, Antognoni drove a free kick against a wall of defenders and Rossi agilely deflected the ball past Mlynarczyk. Five minutes later Antognoni had to depart with an injured foot. In the 35th minute Poland came close to equalising when a Kupcewicz free kick grazed the post. Smolarek appeared to have a legitimate penalty claim just before the hour mark. Ten minutes later Graziani was stretchered off. His replacement, Altobelli, initiated the second and decisive goal. He intelligently released Conti on the left. Conti's perceptive far-post cross was delivered with stunning accuracy to Rossi, who ran in from the right to head Italy into the final. Rossi again emerged as the inspiration who had transformed his side's fortunes.

France and West Germany produced the match of the tournament and the first World Cup tie to be decided on penalties. Ettori of France was considered to be an inadequate goalkeeper and it was his failure to hold a shot from Fischer in the 18th minute which led to Littbarski scoring for West Germany. In the 27th minute Michel Platini equalised with a penalty after Rocheteau was held by Bernd Forster. The match appeared to turn on an horrendous incident in the 57th minute. Patrick Battiston, who had replaced Genghini only eight minutes earlier, hurtled through the German defence. Schumacher raced out of goal but, as Battiston beat him, the goalkeeper inflicted an utterly ruthless body check. Battiston lay unconscious for three minutes before being treated, as the Seville police had ludicrously banned the Red Cross from the pitch. Almost unbelievably, the referee, Charles Corver of Holland, took no action. Although Corver obviously did not see the incident, his linesman could scarcely have missed such an outrageous indiscretion.

France inevitably had to reorganise, with Lopez replacing Battiston. No further goals were scored in 90 minutes although both sides had goalscoring opportunities and Stielike made a clearance off the line. Two minutes into extra time, a Giresse free kick was athletically volleyed into the net by Tresor. Six minutes later France appeared to have won the match when Giresse struck a powerful shot in off a post. Jupp Derwall gambled on a half-fit Karl-Heinz Rummenigge replacing Briegel two minutes before France's third goal. Rummenigge gave West Germany greater penetration and, having only been on the field for six minutes, pulled a goal back when he drove home a chip from Littbarski. Six minutes later West Germany demonstrated their remarkable resilience when Forster crossed and Hrubesch nodded the ball to Fischer, who twisted in mid-air to volley an equaliser. There was still time for Amoros to strike the bar before the match entered into a penalty shoot-out. Giresse, Kaltz, Amoros, Breitner and Rocheteau all scored before Stielike's shot was saved by Ettori. Didier Six took the next penalty, which was saved by Schumacher. Littbarski and Platini made the score 4-4. When Maxime Bossis shot, Schumacher saved again. The responsibility of gaining a World Cup Final place rested with Horst Hrubesch, which he coolly achieved. West Germany had reached their fourth World Cup Final.

The third place play-off between Poland and France took place in Alicante. France, embittered by the brutal assault on Battiston and the flaccid refereeing of Charles Corver, were too traumatised to attach much significance to the match. They introduced seven changes, some enforced as a result of injuries. Poland welcomed the return of the irreplaceable Boniek. Girard scored for France in the 13th minute. Soler missed an excellent chance to double their lead one minute later. Poland then proceeded to score two goals within three minutes shortly before half-time. Szarmach scored with a shot which entered the net via a post. An error by Castaneda, who misjudged Kupcewicz's corner, allowed Majewski to put Poland ahead. Castaneda further blundered one minute after the interval when he allowed Kupcewicz to score direct from a free kick. Couriol scored a second French goal from a Tigana pass in the 73rd minute and, although France staged a late rally, Poland held out to emulate their third place of 1974. Zmuda, Lato and Szarmach enjoyed the distinction of playing in both sides.

The Final between Italy and West Germany took place at the Bernabeu Stadium, Madrid, on 11th July and was watched by a crowd of 90,000. Italy had improved beyond recognition as the tournament progressed and were clear favourites to win. There was hostility directed at West Germany following their defeat of a French team who had greater style, grace and charm. The heinous foul committed by Schumacher, the German goalkeeper, scarcely endeared the side to the footballing world. There were also bitter memories of the collusion with Austria during the opening phase of the tournament.

Frantic efforts to get the unlucky Antognoni fit proved to be in vain. Enzo Bearzot gambled on replacing him with the 18-year-old Bergomi. The Germans chose Dremmler in their midfield again, Fischer was preferred to Hrubsech at centre-forward and Hansi Muller was a substitute.

The first half was a wretched affair punctuated by fouls. Italy were marginally better but neither side had shape or cohesion. Some of the tackling was quite shameful. Arnaldo Cesar Coelho from Brazil was selected as the first South American to referee a World Cup Final. Despite the brutal play, he only wielded two yellow cards.

West Germany had a rare goal-scoring opportunity as early as the fourth minute. When Breitner centred and Fischer moved the ball on, Rummenigge, turning on the ball, had perhaps more time than he realised. He rushed his shot and the Italian defence was relieved to see it roll past the post. Three minutes later Graziani was tackled and, in falling, aggravated the shoulder injury which had forced him to retire from the semi-final against Poland. Altobelli came on as a substitute and made a telling contribution in the 25th minute. He crossed the ball, which Conti pursued. Briegel, his direct opponent, dragged him away and a spot kick was rightly awarded. Antognoni would have taken the penalty, but in his absence Cabrini shot feebly wide of the post. In doing so, he wrote his name into the World Cup record books by becoming the first player to miss a penalty in the Final. Bearzot's benign influence ensured that Italy retained their composure.

Eleven minutes into the second half, Italy took the lead. A foul by Rummenigge on Oriali initiated the move. Tardelli prodded the ball to Gentile, who delivered a splendid low cross which bemused the German defence. The ball fell to Rossi, who dashed in from the left, unmarked, to head Italy into the lead. His sixth goal of the tournament brought the extra accolade of top scorer.

Derwall decided to bring on Horst Hrubesch for Dremmler after 62 minutes. In the 68th minute Italy scored a decisive goal. Conti began the movement, Scirea broke out of defence up the right and exchanged passes with Rossi. As the ball came over, Tardelli struck a brilliant left-foot shot from the edge of the penalty area. With only nine minutes remaining, Conti ran more than half the length of the field before crossing from the right. Altobelli nonchalantly beat Schumacher. Paul Breitner pulled a goal back two minutes later with a powerful shot from the edge of the box. Bearzot, sentimentally, sent on Causio to replace Altobelli in order that Causio gained a World Cup medal.

The 40-year-old Dino Zoff collected the World Cup for Italy from King Juan Carlos of Spain. Italy joined Brazil as three-time winners of the World Cup, an achievement which seemed inconceivable during the first phase of the tournament. Their success was a personal triumph for manager Enzo Bearzot, who inculcated positive values and freed the players from the defensive strictures which so pervaded their domestic game.

Results: Spain 1982

Group 1

Italy	0	Poland	0
Peru	0	Cameroon	0
Italy	1	Peru	1
Poland	0	Cameroon	0
Poland	5	Peru	1
Italy	1	Cameroon	1

	P	W	D	L	F	A	Pts
Poland	3	1	2	0	5	1	4
Italy	3	0	3	0	2	2	3
Cameroon	3	0	3	0	1	1	3
Peru	3	0	2	1	2	6	2

Group 2

Algeria	2	West Germany	1
Austria	1	Chile	0
West Germany	4	Chile	1
Algeria	0	Austria	2
Algeria	3	Chile	2
West Germany	1	Austria	0

	P	W	D	L	F	A	Pts
West Germany	3	2	0	1	6	3	4
Austria	3	2	0	1	3	1	4
Algeria	3	2	0	1	5	5	4
Chile	3	0	0	3	3	8	0

Group 3

Argentina	0	Belgium	1				
Hungary	10	El Salvador	1				
Argentina	4	Hungary	1				
Belgium	1	El Salvador	0				
Belgium	1	Hungary	1				
Argentina	2	El Salvador	0				

	P	W	D	L	Goals F	A	Pts
Belgium	3	2	1	0	3	1	5
Argentina	3	2	0	1	6	2	4
Hungary	3	1	1	1	12	6	3
El Salvador	3	0	0	3	1	13	0

Group 4

England	3	France	1
Czechoslovakia	1	Kuwait	1
England	2	Czechoslovakia	0
France	4	Kuwait	1
France	1	Czechoslovakia	1
England	1	Kuwait	0

	P	W	D	L	Goals F	A	Pts
England	3	3	0	0	6	1	6
France	3	1	1	1	6	5	3
Czechoslovakia	3	0	2	1	2	4	2
Kuwait	3	0	1	2	2	6	1

Group 5

Spain	1	Honduras	1
Northern Ireland	0	Yugoslavia	0
Spain	2	Yugoslavia	1
Honduras	1	Northern Ireland	1
Honduras	0	Yugoslavia	1
Northern Ireland	1	Spain	0

	P	W	D	L	Goals F	A	Pts
Northern Ireland	3	1	2	0	2	1	4
Spain	3	1	1	1	3	3	3
Yugoslavia	3	1	1	1	2	2	3
Honduras	3	0	2	1	2	3	2

Group 6

Brazil	2	USSR	1
Scotland	5	New Zealand	2
Brazil	4	Scotland	1
USSR	3	New Zealand	0
Scotland	2	USSR	2
Brazil	4	New Zealand	0

	P	W	D	L	Goals F	A	Pts
Brazil	3	3	0	0	10	2	6
USSR	3	1	1	1	6	4	3
Scotland	3	1	1	1	8	8	3
New Zealand	3	0	0	3	2	12	0

Second Round

Group A

Poland	3	Belgium	0
Belgium	0	USSR	1
Poland	0	USSR	0

			Goals				
	P	W	D	L	F	A	Pts
Poland	2	1	1	0	3	0	3
USSR	2	1	1	0	1	0	3
Belgium	2	0	0	2	0	4	0

Group B

West Germany	0	England	0
Spain	1	West Germany	2
England	0	Spain	0

			Goals				
	P	W	D	L	F	A	Pts
West.Germany	2	1	1	0	2	1	3
England	2	0	2	0	0	0	2
Spain	2	0	1	1	1	2	1

Group C

Italy	2	Argentina	1
Brazil	3	Argentina	1
Italy	3	Brazil	2

			Goals				
	P	W	D	L	F	A	Pts
Italy	2	2	0	0	5	3	4
Brazil	2	1	0	1	5	4	2
Argentina	2	0	0	2	2	5	0

Group D

France	1	Austria	0
Northern Ireland	2	Austria	2
Northern Ireland	1	France	4

	P	W	D	L	F	A	Pts
					Goals		
France	2	2	0	0	5	1	4
Austria	2	0	1	1	2	3	1
Northern Ireland	2	0	1	1	3	6	1

Semi-finals

Italy	2	Poland	0
West Germany	3	France	3*

*(after extra time) 1-1 at 90 minutes
(West Germany won 5-4 on penalties)

Match for third place

Poland	3	France	2

Final

Italy	3	West Germany	1

Italy: Zoff, Cabrini, Scirea, Gentile, Collovati, Oriali, Bergomi, Tardelli, Conti, Rossi, Graziani (Altobelli) (Causio)

West Germany: Schumacher, Kaltz, Stielike, Forster K H, Forster B, Dremmler (Hrubesch), Breitner, Briegel, Littbarski, Fischer, Rummenigge (Muller)

Scorers: Rossi, Tardelli, Altobelli for Italy
          Breitner for West Germany

1986

Tragedy struck the United States space programme on 28th January when the *Challenger* shuttle exploded seconds after take-off from Cape Canaveral. All seven of the crew were killed, including Christa McAuliffe, a schoolteacher selected as the first to fly in the 'citizen in space' programme. Well-wishers and relatives of the crew watched in horrified disbelief as the shuttle burst into flames 72 seconds into its tenth mission. Challenger was travelling at nearly 2,000 mph at a height of ten miles, when it was suddenly enveloped in a red, orange and white fireball as thousand of tons of liquid hydrogen and oxygen fuel exploded. The accident, which was traced to a fault in one of the twin solid fuel booster rockets, led to staff changes at the top of the American space agency, NASA.

Olaf Palme, the Prime Minister of Sweden, was assassinated in Stockholm on 28th February. He was shot dead as he was walking home with his wife after an evening at the cinema in Stockholm. His wife was wounded in the attack. A lone gunman ran off before any attempts could be made to capture him.

The world's worst ever nuclear accident took place in April when a disastrous fire at the Chernobyl nuclear power station in the Ukraine contaminated much of Europe with radioactive fall-out. There was widespread international criticism of the Soviet Union's secrecy and slow reaction to the disaster, which came to light only after high radiation levels were detected in Sweden. Meltdown was avoided by sealing the damaged reactor with concrete, but restrictions were imposed on the sale of animal foodstuffs in many countries as tests showed levels of radioactivity well above normal in grazing animals such as sheep, cows and reindeer. Doctors differed in the estimates of the number of additional cancer deaths likely to be caused by the disaster in later years.

*   *   *

Colombia was the original choice of venue for the 13th World Cup but it could not raise the finance required and FIFA selected Mexico as an alternative. Given the level of instability, the many active guerrilla groups and the growing power and violence of local drug cartels, it was perhaps as well that Colombia was displaced. Mexico undertook a large programme of building for the 1986 Olympic finals. In 1970, when only 16 teams competed, Mexico prepared five stadiums in five different cities. In 1986, with 24 teams involved, a total of twelve stadiums in nine cities were used. Severe earthquakes shook the area in 1985, but the stadiums were not affected. Mexico thus became the first nation to host the World Cup twice.

The organisation of the tournament reverted to a straight knock-out basis after the first round, with the top two from each of the first six first-round groups of four progressing to the second-round, together with the best third-placed teams. In the event of there being a stalemate at the end of any of the knock-out games, provision was made for extra time, followed by a penalty shoot-out as necessary.

England, Scotland and Northern Ireland were all represented, as they had been in 1982. But it was Scotland who entered the finals on a wave of sentiment following their dramatic, traumatic and poignant qualification. As the Scotland supporters who had descended on Ninian Park, Cardiff, on 15th September 1985 got ready to celebrate a laboured draw against Wales, the atmosphere turned to one of collective mourning. Jock Stein who, along with Herbert Chapman, was arguably the greatest manager ever to grace British football,

collapsed on the touchline at the end of the match. Contradic-
tory reports emanated from the dressing room during a
protracted and agonising wait before the awful declaration
that the Big Man was dead. Twenty thousand travelling
supporters rapidly went numb and a nation turned sombre
and doleful. The Scottish Football Association appointed Jock
Stein's assistant, the highly successful Aberdeen manager
Alex Ferguson, as successor. Ferguson would operate on an
interim basis until the conclusion of the World Cup campaign.
By finishing second in their group, Scotland faced a two-
legged play-off against the winners of the Oceania group,
Australia. Scotland eventually qualified for Mexico, unimpressively defeating the Antipodeans 2-0 at Hampden Park before
struggling to a goalless draw in Melbourne.

South America was represented by Argentina, the winners
of Group 1; Uruguay the winners of South America Group 2;
Brazil, the winners of South America Group 3; and Paraguay,
the runners-up of South America Group 3, who proceeded to
eliminate Colombia and Chile in play-offs. Europe included
the holders, Italy, along with Belgium, Bulgaria, Denmark,
England, France, Hungary, Northern Ireland, Poland, Portugal,
Spain, Scotland, the Soviet Union and West Germany. Only
England, of the European nations, were undefeated in qualifying matches, scoring 21 goals in 8 games and conceding just 2.
But England's qualification, along with that of Northern
Ireland, was not without controversy. Romania were managed by Mircea Lucescu, who was their captain in Mexico
in 1970. He complained bitterly when England drew at
Wembley in their decisive match against Northern Ireland,
thus eliminating his side. Suspicions of collusion appeared to
be well-founded, with some England players revealing their
preference for the Ulstermen competing in the finals over the
ideologically unsound Romanians.

Mexico participated as hosts. Algeria narrowly defeated
Angola before impressive wins over Zambia and Tunisia.
Morocco eliminated Sierra Leone, Malawi, Egypt and Libya.
Canada were winners of CONCACAF Group 3. They then

won play-offs involving Costa Rica and Honduras. Iraq won the Asian Group 1, sub-group B, despite a heavy away defeat against Qatar. They then eliminated the United Arab Emirates on away goals before advancing in the Asian play-offs at Syria's expense. Finally, South Korea were winners of Asian Group 3, sub-group A. By beating Indonesia in the Asian second round, they met Japan in the Asian play-offs. They ensured qualification by winning both home and away. The first round groupings were:

Group A: Argentina, Bulgaria, Italy, South Korea
Group B: Belgium, Iraq, Mexico, Paraguay
Group C: Canada, France, Hungary, USSR
Group D: Algeria, Brazil, Northern Ireland, Spain
Group E: Denmark, Scotland, Uruguay, West Germany
Group F: England, Morocco, Poland, Portugal

The competition began on 31st May 1986 in the Azteca stadium when the Champions, Italy, met Bulgaria. The Mexican crowd loudly jeered the President during the opening address. Trainspotting in Iceland would normally generate more excitement than the curtain-raiser to a World Cup. On this occasion, however, the inaugural match was an improvement on previous tournaments. Altobelli scored shortly before half-time, but Sirakov equalised with six minutes remaining.

South Korea have the distinction of being the first Asian nation to qualify for the World Cup finals. Their visit to Switzerland in 1954 was brief, as they leaked 16 goals without reply to the irresistible Hungarians and Turkey. The team manager, Kim-Sung-nam, fashioned a miserly defence which conceded only three goals in eight qualifying games.

South Korea performed aggressively against Argentina, showing considerable stamina. Their rigorous and punishing warm-up schedule prior to the finals was perhaps too demanding, as they capitulated 3-1. The South Americans displayed wonderful artistry, largely orchestrated by an inspired Maradona, who had matured since 1982. He contributed to all three goals, two of which were scored by the graceful Valdano and one by Ruggeri. Park Chang-sun consoled his countrymen with a stunning strike.

Italy and Argentina clashed in Puebla and, once again, Altobelli gave the holders a lead, this time with a sixth-minute penalty. Enzo Bearzot gave his Napoli colleague Salvatore Bagni the unenviable task of marking Maradona. The strategy was by no means foolproof, with Maradona showing sublime skills and equalising after 33 minutes with a mesmerising goal. Unfortunately, the game degenerated into an ill-tempered affair. The final score filled Italy with apprehension. Embedded deep in the Italian psyche was the memory of the team being pelted with tomatoes following its premature return from the World Cup in England.

South Korea earned their first World Cup points against Bulgaria. Getov gave the Eastern Europeans a first-half lead. However, Jung-boo equalised.

The humiliation following defeat by North Korea in 1966 still haunted Italy as they required a win to advance to the second round. Yet again, Altobelli established a lead which should have doubled, but for a penalty miss. Soon-ho, remarkably, equalised at the start of the second half. Altobelli scored a second and Italian anxieties were finally allayed by a Kwang-rae own goal. Jung-moo reduced the arrears in the dying seconds.

Argentina were already assured of qualification prior to their final group game. In the Olympic Stadium they defeated Bulgaria 2-0, with Valdano again scoring, together with Burruchaga. Argentina topped Group A with 5 points, followed by Italy with 4. Bulgaria also advanced to the second round as one of the better third-place teams.

Mexico, the hosts, played Belgium in their Group B encounter at the Azteca Stadium in front of 110,000 spectators. Mexico won 2-1, with goals from Quirarte and Hugo Sanchez, a qualified dentist. Vandenbergh reduced the lead on the stroke of half-time. Belgium's defensive vulnerability and general ineptitude gave little indication of their later success.

Paraguay's run-up to the tournament was disrupted by

their manager, Cayetano Re, frequently threatening to resign. They boasted the South American 'Footballer of the Year' in Julio Romero and had other top strikers in Canete and Cabanas. They met Iraq in their opening match. Iraq were coached by the Brazilian, Jorge Keira. They were an attack-minded side who adhered to a simple, short-passing game. A Romero goal eventually separated the sides; Amaiesh did score for Iraq, but the referee had already blown for half-time.

Mexico played Paraguay in front of a record crowd of 114,600. Flores scored early in the game but Romero, who was hailed as a hero in Brazil, equalised for Paraguay with five minutes remaining. Mexico had the opportunity to win with an 88th minute penalty, but Fernandez turned Sanchez's effort onto the post.

Belgium gained their only group win by beating Iraq 2-1, with the highly adroit Enzo Scifo scoring the opening goal. Mexico then defeated Iraq narrowly with a goal by Quirarte. Belgium drew their final encounter with Paraguay, thus squeezing into third place qualification behind Mexico and Paraguay.

France, the European Championship holders, qualified for the World Cup for an unprecedented third time in a row. However, there was diminution in confidence following 2-0 defeats against Bulgaria in Sofia and East Germany in Leipzig. There appeared to be disquiet concerning tactics following Michel Hidalgo's departure after the European championship. Henri Michel, a former Nantes player, had never coached a side prior to his appointment as national coach. Well established players in the French team, including Platini and Giresse, appeared to clash over his strategy. Nevertheless, France entered the tournament with a vast array of talent.

In the opening Group C fixture in Leon, France played Canada, who were competing in the World Cup finals for the first time. The Canadians acquitted themselves extremely well. Competent defending by Canada and wasteful finishing restricted the French to a solitary goal scored by Papin.

The Soviet Union met Hungary at Irapuato. The USSR gave

lacklustre performances *en route* to Mexico. Eduard Malafeev, the Soviet coach, was dismissed before the finals and replaced by Valeri Lobanovski. Ironically, it was Malafeev who had succeeded Lobanovski following the USSR's failure to qualify for the European Championships in 1984. The Soviet Union's strategy was to fill the side with players from Dynamo Kiev. In Spain, the Soviets arrived the day before they met Brazil, rather unluckily losing 2-1 as weariness set in. On this occasion, they gave the Hungarians a comprehensive mauling. Two goals ahead after only three minutes, the Soviets proceeded to inflict a 6-0 thrashing on a nation more accustomed to emphatic victories.

France and the Soviet Union qualified from their group with consummate ease. In the hot, humid conditions in Leon, Vasily Rats scored arguably the best struck goal of the tournament with a fearsome drive from 30 yards. The French soon equalised with a goal by Fernandez. Although less gifted than the glut of creative Gallic midfield players, Fernandez was named France's player of the year in 1985 and developed into an assiduous and highly influential player.

Brazil entered the tournament with a reputation as the most potent football nation on this planet. But reservations persisted about an over-exuberant side who played with such panache in Spain yet were eliminated by appalling defensive frailties. There were also major concerns regarding an over-representation of veteran players, including Socrates, Falcao, Junior and Zico.

Brazil met Spain in their opening Group D match in Guadalajara. It was here in 1970 that England narrowly succumbed to Brazil in a truly classic World Cup encounter. Bobby Moore and Gordon Banks had their finest hour there and became permanently etched in the annals of sporting history. Spain were troubled by a number of injured players. In Emilio Butragueno, nicknamed El Buitre, 'the Vulture', they had an exceptional talent. He simply glided past defenders, displaying his predatory skills with ruthless efficiency. Although the sides were evenly matched, Brazil were fortunate that a

Michel shot which bounced down off the crossbar over the line was disallowed. Just to compound Spain's sense of injustice, Socrates scored a late winner which was almost certainly offside.

Northern Ireland adopted a relaxed, informal and welcoming approach to their campaign. Billy Bingham, their manager, had masterminded their famous victory in the 1982 World Cup, defeating the hosts, Spain. Northern Ireland boasted a very experienced squad of players but their scoring ratio was quite dismal, averaging slightly less than a goal a game during the last six years. This unenviable record was maintained as they were held to a 1-1 draw by Algeria in an ill-tempered affair. Spain then exacted revenge with a 2-1 victory. Finally, Northern Ireland were simply overwhelmed by a Brazilian side gaining in momentum. Pat Jennings, on his 41st birthday, gave an heroic performance, largely contributing to the avoidance of a landslide defeat as Brazil strolled to a 3-0 win. Brazil gained maximum points, with Spain also qualifying.

Group E was nicknamed 'the group of death' by the Mexican fans. Denmark competed in their first World Cup finals and immediately lit up the tournament with a plethora of highly accomplished players. Michael Laudrup, a fluent Juventus player, complemented the midfield skills of Frank Arnesen and Soren Lerby. Preben Elkjaer scored a messy goal in the opening match against Scotland, which ultimately separated the sides. The loss of Kenny Dalglish inevitably meant that the Scotland attack lost much of its potency.

Although included in the top six seeds for Mexico, West Germany were, unusually, unfancied by most soccer experts. By the end of 1985 they had an uncharacteristically bad run of six matches without a win. During qualification they endured their first ever home defeat in a World Cup tie, losing 1-0 to Portugal. West Germany were making their ninth successive appearance in the Finals since they were readmitted to FIFA following the Second World War. Franz Beckenbauer was appointed coach in 1984. He had made 103 appearances for his country, playing as libero, and had led his team to World Cup success in 1974. However, he did not hold a coaching licence and so West Germany broke with tradition. For nearly half a century, the departing incumbent had always been succeeded by his qualified assistant.

West Germany met Uruguay, the South American champions, in their opening match. A goal by Aizamendi allowed the Uruguayans to lead for most of a game played in oppressively hot conditions. Klaus Allofs' late equaliser nullified Uruguay's advantage.

Scotland again lost narrowly, on this occasion to West Germany in Queretaro. Although Gordon Strachan performed tirelessly and gave Scotland an early lead, West Germany predictably equalised soon afterwards through Voller. Once again, Allofs scored in the second half. Scotland's impotent attack could scarcely have looked less threatening until the belated menace of substitute Davie Cooper began to torment the German defence.

Denmark achieved an astonishing win against Uruguay by six goals to one in their next game. After Preben Elkjaer started the goal feast, Bossio of Uruguay was sent off for a thoroughly odious foul. Only 2-1 ahead at half-time, Denmark humiliated their opponents as artistry triumphed over brutality.

Uruguay's reputation as aggressors was vindicated in their final group match against Scotland. Remarkably, Batista was sent off within the first minute following a foul on Strachan. A disingenuous Scotland side failed to capitalise and were deservedly eliminated following the scoreless draw. Uruguay entered the next stage without winning a single game, whilst at the same time amassing one goal in three games. Their boorish and cynical tactics were an affront to the game. Uruguay's advancement was accompanied by paranoia on the part of their coach, Omar Borras, who had the temerity to accuse FIFA of victimisation.

Denmark convincingly won the group by beating West Germany 2-0 in Queretaro. Their devastating performances were slightly tarnished by Arnesen foolishly allowing himself to be sent off in the last minute when he injudiciously assaulted Matthaus. West Germany deliberately fielded an understrength side, thus evoking memories of 1954 when they lost 8-3 to Hungary in a preliminary round. The teams subsequently met in the final, with West Germany victorious.

Group F was staged in Monterrey, which meant very hot and humid conditions would prevail. As this venue was lower lying, the qualifying nations would be at a not inconsiderable disadvantage, having to acclimatise at a later stage.

Poland entered the World Cup as one of the six seeded teams but were widely regarded as the weakest. Their detractors seemed rather churlish, given that Poland finished third in 1974 and 1982. Their participation was their fourth consecutive appearance. In Zbigniew Boniek they had one of the finest players Poland has ever produced. The AS Roma star was an inspiration to his fellow players. But Anton Piechniczek, the Poland manager, appeared to place too much emphasis on physical prowess at the expense of finely honed skills. He indulged in a scientific approach which included daily monitoring of the players' physiology.

Morocco conceded only one goal in eight qualifying matches. This was largely attributable to Badou Ezaki, who was an outstanding goalkeeper. In the opening match it was perhaps no surprise that Morocco drew 0-0 with Poland.

Reports from within the Portuguese camp hinted at insurrection. Disenchanted with their administrators, the players apparently accused their officials of creaming off sponsorship money and failing to allow adequate preparation for the finals.

None of this was in evidence against an incompetent England side who suffered from a paucity of ideas. After 75 minutes, Carlos Manuel scored following defensive ineptitude, bringing to an abrupt end England's long unbeaten run. Further defensive lapses could have further embarrassed them.

Three days later, England were exceptionally lucky not to

be eliminated from the tournament. A woeful performance against Morocco scarcely merited a scoreless draw. Bryan Robson departed after 40 minutes with a dislocated shoulder. The situation further degenerated when Ray Wilkins uncharacteristically threw the ball at the referee and was ordered off. But Morocco retreated into a defensive shell when they could have thoroughly demoralised England.

In a meandering and highly unpredictable group, Poland, endowed with good fortune, defeated Portugal 1-0 with a goal by Smolarek.

England approached their final game against Poland in a state of crisis. There was reported to be deep dissent amongst a faction of England players, largely directed at the tactics of Bobby Robson, the manager. Robson appeared to relent to player pressure and introduced a midfield of Trevor Steven, Peter Reid and Steve Hodge, with Glenn Hoddle enjoying a creative, roving role. England were transformed, winning 3-0, with Gary Lineker distinguishing himself by scoring the first World Cup hat-trick by an England player since Geoff Hurst in the 1966 final.

Morocco became the first African representative to reach the second round by defeating Portugal 3-1 in Guadalajara. Morocco therefore won the lowest scoring group, which contained many surprises. England finished second and Poland, who accumulated the same number of points, also qualified. Portugal, after a promising start, were eliminated.

The knock-out games in the second round produced the following ties:

Mexico v Bulgaria
USSR v Belgium
Argentina v Uruguay
Brazil v Poland
France v Italy
England v Paraguay
West Germany v Morocco
Denmark v Spain

Mexico easily defeated Bulgaria in front a capacity crowd at the Azteca Stadium. Bulgaria's contribution was feeble as they meekly succumbed to goals from Negrete and Servin.

The tie of the round took place in Leon. Belgium and the Soviet Union, against all expectations, contested an engrossing match of almost unrelenting excitement. Belgium's entry to the second round resulted from a revised format which absurdly enabled two-thirds of the initial field to advance.

Injuries to established stars including Vanderbergh and Vandereycken, together with disappointing form from veteran players, suggested Belgium had little chance. This ominous view seemed to be borne out by the USSR's highly impressive group performances. Belanov gave the Soviet Union the lead in the first half. But the game was very evenly balanced and breathtakingly absorbing. Inspired by Jan Ceulemans in midfield, Scifo equalised after half-time. Igor Belanov, the rapacious Dynamo Kiev striker, scored again, but Ceulemans, looking suspiciously offside, levelled to take the match into extra time. The resilient Belgians added two goals through Demol and Claesen before Belanov reduced the arrears with a penalty, and his third goal, three minutes from time. Belgium had clearly awoken from a very deep slumber and, against all the odds, produced a truly astonishing victory. The USSR, could justifiably feel aggrieved by some dubious refereeing, but this was tempered by their marvellous contribution to one of the most pulsating matches in the entire history of the World Cup.

The Argentina versus Uruguay match in Puebla was their first World Cup encounter since the 1930 Final. A potentially explosive match was never realised, although the second half was punctuated by a violent thunderstorm. Uruguay seemed to be content to engage in a damage limitation exercise. Their highly provocative coach, Omar Borras, was sensibly banished from the bench. The game was played in a restrained manner with an excellent Italian referee, Luigi Agnolin, ensuring discipline was maintained throughout. Pasculli scored the only goal for Argentina shortly before half-time. Maradona produced another scintillating performance as Argentinian superiority failed to yield further goals.

Poland started very promisingly against Brazil in the Jalisco Stadium, with Dziekanowski hitting a post and Karas the bar. But Brazil's flair eventually swamped the artistically challenged Poles. Socrates scored a penalty before half-time and further goals by Josimar, Edinho and a Careca penalty produced a 4-0 margin of victory.

At the Olympic Stadium in Mexico City, France met Italy in what was considered to be the most glamorous tie.

It paired the European Champions with the World Champions. France had not beaten Italy in a major tournament since 1920. The game, however, proved to be something of an anti-climax. Enzo Bearzot adopted highly questionable tactics, deciding to man-mark Platini. This strategy demonstrably failed when the Frenchman scored after only 13 minutes. Stopyra added a second, following creative play. The Italians were strangely languid, tamely relinquishing their title after an insipid performance.

West Germany and Morocco played in stifling heat in Monterrey. A dull game appeared to be heading for extra time, with opportunities proving to be minimal. But to the consternation of Morocco, a free-kick by Matthaus in the final minute breached the defensive wall and the despairing Ezaki, who had been quite splendid.

Astonishingly, Franz Beckenbaeur accused the Moroccans of negative play. Perhaps he was suffering from severe amnesia following the inexcusable and sickening collusion between his own nation and Austria at the expense of Algeria in the 1982 World Cup. Morocco performed quite heroically for a country with less than one 20th of the Gross National Product of West Germany.

England approached their game with Paraguay at the Azteca Stadium in an optimistic vein after their encouraging win over Poland and with a revamped side. A crowd of almost 99,000 watched early defensive blunders by England go unpunished before Lineker opened the scoring. Beardsley complemented

Lineker with his incisive and unselfish play. It was fitting, therefore, that he should add a second goal. At this point, Lineker was receiving attention on the touch line following a brutal assault by Delgado. However, the reliable and popular Everton striker returned and scored a second goal, thus completing a comfortable 3-0 win.

The final second round tie between Denmark and Spain in Queretaro produced a truly remarkable match. Denmark were rapidly becoming favourites to win the World Cup. This view was undiminished when Jesper Olsen gave them a lead with a controversial penalty after half an hour. But the game turned following an aberration by Olsen just before half-time. His inexplicable back-pass across the penalty area was intercepted by Butragueno and Spain had gained parity by the interval. Butragueno destroyed Denmark in the second half with a virtuoso performance. When Spain established a lead, Denmark attacked suicidally, leaving themselves vulnerable to ruthless counter attacking. Butragueno's four goals, together with a Goicoechea penalty, eventually crushed Denmark 5-1.

The quarter finals were contested by Mexico, Belgium, Argentina, Brazil, France, England, West Germany and Spain and produced the following ties:

Brazil v France
Mexico v West Germany
Spain v Belgium
Argentina v England

The first of the quarter finals was an intriguing clash between France and Brazil in Guadalajara, which produced a memorable match. Careca scored for Brazil after 15 minutes. They almost doubled their lead when Muller struck the post. France absorbed a wave of Brazilian attacks before countering with a simple equaliser by Platini shortly before half-time. Brazil had second-half opportunities by Junior but Bats was defiant in the French goal. Branco was tripped by Bats, who conceded a penalty. But he redeemed himself with a relatively easy save from Zico's effort. During extra time France gained the initiative. There was a highly controversial incident with four minutes remaining. Carlos, the Brazilian goalkeeper, cynically fouled Bellone, who advanced on goal unchallenged but was unable to capitalise from the 'advantage' applied by the Romanian referee, Igna. A penalty shoot-out decided the fate of what had been an undulating match embellished with intricate skills and improvisation. Despite a penalty miss by Platini, Socrates' failure to convert the first penalty, together with an excellent save by Bats from Julio Cesar, meant that France reached the semi-finals as in 1982. Brazil had achieved four victories, were previously unbeaten, scored ten goals and conceded only one to Michel Platini.

On the same day in Monterrey, Mexico and West Germany met in difficult conditions. Thick grass, oppressive heat and enervating humidity conspired against the possibility of a good match. A highly partisan crowd had their enthusiasm dampened by a stifling and dour West German side, who had Berthold sent off after 65 minutes. During extra time Aguirre, who had come closest to scoring, was also sent off. The penalty shoot-out was an embarrassment for the host nation, with only Negrete scoring. West Germany won emphatically 4-1.

Belgium and Spain met in Puebla. Belgium were gaining momentum and establishing a reputation for their organisational skills. But on this occasion they struggled to contain Spain and it was something of a surprise when Ceulemans opened the scoring with a diving header. Belgium defended quite magnificently and for once Butragueno was silenced. The Spanish attacks were incessant, but it was substitute Senor who eventually equalised with a venomous 30-yard drive in the dying minutes. Unsurprisingly, extra time yielded no further goals as tiredness drained the players. During the penalty shoot-out, only Eloy of Spain failed to score as the outstanding Pfaff dived to his right and produced an excellent save. Momentarily, at least, the bribe scandal which had rocked Belgian football was forgotten.

The last quarter-final tie matched Argentina with England. Inevitably, memories of 1966 were evoked when Alf Ramsey, incensed by the behaviour of Argentinian players, had branded them 'animals'. But a more immediate back-drop was the confrontation of the Falklands/Malvinas war. If there was any substance to allegations that captured Argentinian prisoners were made to bury their own soldiers, in violation of the Geneva Convention, then Ramsey's little grievance paled into insignificance. The notion that sport and politics are inextricably linked was not a view shared by the Argentinian players, who remained calm and focused in the face of intense media provocation. Perhaps they felt that sufficient damage had already been inflicted by the fervour of jingoistic journalists.

Argentina decided to make tactical changes and, with Garre suspended, introduced Olarticoechea. Pasculli, who had scored against Uruguay, was omitted from the side. Argentina clearly had considerable respect for England, deciding to closely mark Lineker, Beardsley and Hoddle.

A crowd of 114,580 amassed in the Azteca Stadium. During the first half the England attack showed little menace and there was no score at the interval. The game exploded after 50 minutes, with Maradona inevitably at the centre of a controversy which still rages. Maradona penetrated the England defence but lost possession, as did Valdano. Steve Hodge, the recipient of the ball, sliced a back pass intended for Shilton in goal. Maradona, in challenging, used a hand to guide the ball into the net. The inexperienced Tunisian match official allowed the goal to stand. England could legitimately have argued that they were still shell-shocked, but five minutes later Maradona scored again with a highly improbable goal even by his outrageous standards. He received the ball on the half way line and, as he hurtled forward, swerved past Stevens, and embarrassed the statuesque Butcher and Fenwick with his devastating speed and improvisation, before dismissively beating Shilton with nonchalant ease. Argentina thereafter incomprehensibly adopted a defensive stance at a time when their supremacy threatened to humiliate England. Winger John Barnes entered the fray and began to expose a vulnerable

Argentinian defence. With ten minutes remaining, Barnes produced sublime skills which enabled him to beat Giusti and deliver a perfect cross for Lineker to reduce the deficit. Another exquisite cross three minutes from the end nearly brought a Lineker equaliser.

After the match Maradona offered an appalling rationalisation for blatant cheating when he talked about 'the hand of God'. Although England deserve great praise for a spirited comeback, a hard luck story smacked of self-delusion. The chilling reality is that England came perilously close to being completely overrun. Gary Lineker departed from Mexico with the distinction of finishing top striker in the tournament with six goals.

The first semi-final in the Jalisco stadium in Guadalajara between France and West Germany was a re-run of Seville in 1982, when the Germans won. The fate of that match appeared to rest on the horrific incident when Schumacher brutally assaulted Battiston as he converged on goal. Astonishingly, Schumacher had escaped dismissal as Battiston lay unconscious with serious internal injuries. West Germany proceeded to win a penalty shoot-out but were met with the wrath of an outraged footballing public.

Both Battiston and Schumacher played in 1986 shaking hands before the kick-off. Berthold was suspended after his sending-off against Mexico and Rocheteau was injured for France. Beckenbauer decided that Rolff should attempt to stifle Platini and this he did very effectively. France looked exhausted after their exciting match with Brazil, and conceded a goal after only nine minutes. Brehme received a free kick from Magath and struck a shot which was misjudged by Bats, who allowed it to squirm under his body.

France did attempt to attack but carried little conviction, with the exception of a volley by Platini which Schumacher could only beat out. Bossis, a central defender, contrived to miss from six yards. There was always a danger that West Germany would counter attack and score a second goal. In the final minute, substitute Rudi Voller ensured another World

Cup Final for West Germany by lobbing Bats, running past him, and placing the ball in the net. The tie had been hugely disappointing, lacking the excitement and drama of Seville.

Belgium and Argentina contested the second semi-final in the Azteca stadium with 110,420 spectators wondering what to expect next from Maradona. In the 1982 World Cup Belgium had successfully policed Maradona and defeated Argentina 1-0. They must have been less sanguine on this occasion as Maradona looked an unstoppable force. Belgium's massed defence valiantly kept Argentina at bay during the first half, played on a slippery surface. With only six minutes of the second half played, Maradona darted into the penalty area to receive the ball on the blind side, following combined play by Enrique and Burruchaga. Although the Belgian defenders forced Maradona onto his much weaker right foot, he simply swivelled and sent the ball past Pfaff with a flick of his left. Twelve minutes later Maradona felt the need to surpass that goal and gave a graphic illustration of why he is without question the greatest footballer in the world. On the edge of a crowded penalty box, he glided past three bewildered defenders on a solo run before despatching a deft shot past Pfaff. Argentina squandered several other opportunities, but their 2-0 victory gave them the satisfaction of appearing in their second final during the last three World Cups.

The third-place match took place in Puebla between Belgium and France. Although Platini was missing, and Belgium took an early lead through Ceulemans, France proceeded to win the match. Ferrari and Papin gave France a half-time lead. Claesen equalised, but in extra-time Genghini and Amoros completed a 4-2 victory and third place for France. Belgium's fourth place was a quite remarkable achievement. They had reached their nadir in December 1994 when they lost a qualifying match 2-0 to Albania in Tirana. They had to play off with Holland for a place in Mexico and only ensured qualification by scoring a precious away goal in Rotterdam. They were unimpressive in their opening Group B matches and scraped through to the second round. But they somehow galvanised and transmuted into a well-organised, disciplined unit with strong defenders and able attackers. A bribe scandal had rocked the very foundations of Belgian soccer and dealt a psychological blow to the side. Belgium's tenacity and resilience in the face of adversity made them one of the sensations of the 1986 World Cup.

Another was Maradona. Never in World Cup history had one player so pervasively preoccupied the thoughts of the footballing public prior to the final.

Beckenbauer decided to assign Lothar Matthaus to mark Maradona. In 1982, as a 21-year-old, the German had successfully contained Zico and Maradona in international matches. But this strategy was a calculated risk, as Matthaus was a creative, free-running, attacking midfielder. There was a very real danger that West Germany would lose their impetus in sacrificing his midfield talents.

The Azteca Stadium was filled to its capacity of 115,000 and an estimated audience of more than two billion viewed the final world-wide. West Germany looked overawed as Argentina went on the offensive. In 22 minutes Maradona outfoxed Matthaus with a clever backheel. Matthaus felled Maradona and the resultant free-kick was flighted by the highly talented Burruchaga. Schumacher made an uncharacteristic error by misjudging the trajectory of the ball and was ruthlessly punished by Jose-Luis Brown, who headed unmarked into a vacant goal. West Germany's overburdened defence was severely stretched and Maradona could have extended Argentina's lead before half-time. In the 50th minute Jose-Luis Brown injured his shoulder, departed from the field but returned after two minutes. As West Germany attempted to exploit Brown's restricted mobility, they succumbed to a counter-attack. Enrique found Valdano, who advanced on the German right before sidefooting the ball past Schumacher.

Argentina appeared to be strolling to victory. Their players could scarcely believe the freedom of movement they enjoyed as a consequence of German preoccupation with Maradona. But with 17 minutes remaining, substitute Rudi Voller flicked on a Brehme corner with his head and Rummenigge slid in to give the Germans a vestige of hope. Matthaus abandoned his role of man-marking Maradona and began to orchestrate midfield. With only eight minutes remaining, an almost identical corner by Brehme resulted in a nodded flick by Berthold and Voller equalised with a header. West Germany must momentarily, at least, have been thinking the unthinkable. In the 1954 final they had a seemingly impossible task, trailing the Hungarians 2-0 before achieving an improbable victory. As West Germany pursued a winner, it was inevitable that Maradona would destroy their aspirations. With six minutes remaining, he fragmented their defence with an incisive pass, delivered so perfectly for Burruchaga that Schumacher's attempted intervention was too late. Argentina had deservedly won the World Cup for the second time in their history.

The 1986 World Cup was a great success despite reservations about Mexico. The oppressive heat inevitably took its toll on many of the players. The pitches in Monterrey and Mexico City were considered to be unsatisfactory. High altitude venues placed some countries at a distinct disadvantage. The introduction of penalty kicks to determine unresolved games seemed particularly harsh.

But despite these valid criticisms, the 1986 World Cup will be remembered as the best tournament since 1970. It will also be synonymous with Diego Maradona. Maradona is only five feet six inches tall and weighs nearly 12 stone. He has a mesomorphic frame which makes him look ungainly. A bull-like figure, Maradona displayed electrifying pace and power. He simply mesmerised defenders with his seemingly infinite skills. He is undisputedly the best player in the world. Never in World Cup history has one player wielded such a powerful influence on the destiny of the tournament.

Results: Mexico 1986

First Round

Group A

Bulgaria	1	Italy	1
Argentina	3	South Korea	1
Argentina	1	Italy	1
Bulgaria	1	South Korea	1
Italy	3	South Korea	2
Argentina	2	Bulgaria	0

					Goals		
	P	W	D	L	F	A	Pts
Argentina	3	2	1	0	6	2	5
Italy	3	1	2	0	5	4	4
Bulgaria	3	0	2	1	2	4	2
South Korea	3	0	1	2	4	7	1

Group B

Mexico	2	Belgium	1
Paraguay	1	Iraq	0
Mexico	1	Paraguay	1
Belgium	2	Iraq	1
Mexico	1	Iraq	0
Belgium	2	Paraguay	2

					Goals		
	P	W	D	L	F	A	Pts
Mexico	3	2	1	0	4	2	5
Paraguay	3	1	2	0	4	3	4
Belgium	3	1	1	1	5	5	3
Iraq	3	0	0	3	1	4	0

Group C

France	1	Canada	0
USSR	6	Hungary	0
France	1	USSR	1
Hungary	2	Canada	0
France	3	Hungary	0
USSR	2	Canada	0

	P	W	D	L	Goals F	A	Pts
USSR	3	2	1	0	9	1	5
France	3	2	1	0	5	1	5
Hungary	3	1	0	2	2	9	2
Canada	3	0	0	3	0	5	0

Group D

Brazil	1	Spain	0
Algeria	1	Northern Ireland	1
Spain	2	Northern Ireland	1
Brazil	1	Algeria	0
Spain	3	Algeria	0
Brazil	3	Northern Ireland	0

	P	W	D	L	Goals F	A	Pts
Brazil	3	3	0	0	5	0	6
Spain	3	2	0	1	5	2	4
Northern Ireland	3	0	1	2	2	6	1
Algeria	3	0	1	2	1	5	1

Group E

Denmark	1	Scotland	0
Uruguay	1	West Germany	1
West Germany	2	Scotland	1
Denmark	6	Uruguay	1
Scotland	0	Uruguay	0
Denmark	2	West Germany	0

	P	W	D	L	Goals F	A	Pts
Denmark	3	3	0	0	9	1	6
West Germany	3	1	1	1	3	4	3
Uruguay	3	0	2	1	2	7	2
Scotland	3	0	1	2	1	3	1

Group F

Portugal	1	England	0
Morocco	0	Poland	0
Poland	1	Portugal	0
England	0	Morocco	0
Morocco	3	Portugal	1
England	3	Poland	0

	P	W	D	L	Goals F	A	Pts
Morocco	3	1	2	0	3	1	4
England	3	1	1	1	3	1	3
Poland	3	1	1	1	1	3	3
Portugal	3	1	0	2	2	4	2

Second Round

Mexico	2	Bulgaria	0
Belgium	4	USSR	3*
Argentina	1	Uruguay	0
Brazil	4	Poland	0
France	2	Italy	0
West Germany	1	Morocco	0
England	3	Paraguay	0
Spain	5	Denmark	1

*After extra time, 2-2 at 90 minutes

Quarter-finals

France	1	Brazil	1

(after extra time) France win 4-3 on penalties

West Germany	0	Mexico	0

(after extra time) West Germany win 4-1 on penalties

Belgium	1	Spain	1

(after extra time) Belgium win 5-4 on penalties

Argentina	2	England	1

Semi-finals

West Germany	2	France	0
Argentina	2	Belgium	0

Third place match

France	4	Belgium	2*

*(after extra time), 2–2 at 90 minutes

Final

Argentina	3	West Germany	2

Argentina: Pumpido, Cuciuffo, Brown, Ruggeri, Olarticoechea, Batista, Giusti, Enrique, Burruchaga (Trobbiani), Maradona, Valdano

West Germany: Schumacher, Berthold, Jakobs, Forster K H, Briegel, Brehme, Matthaus, Magath (Hoeness), Eder, Rummenigge, Allofs (Voller)

Scorers: Brown, Valdano and Burruchaga for Argentina
Rummenigge and Voller for West Germany

1990

Farzad Bazoft, an Iranian journalist working for the *Observer* newspaper in Britain, was hanged in Baghdad on 15th March. Bazoft, aged 31, had been sentenced to death by a military court which found him guilty of espionage. Iraq's President Saddam Hussein rejected a personal appeal from Margaret Thatcher to spare the reporter's life. Bazoft was arrested when he visited an Iraqi military base to check reports of an explosion in which 700 people were said to have died. After seven weeks in captivity, he 'confessed' on videotape to spying. Daphne Parish, a 52-year-old British nurse who drove him to the site, was sentenced to 15 years' imprisonment.

A huge march and rally in central London on 31st March, in response to the introduction of the poll tax, resulted in hundreds of arrests and widespread violence. The trouble started at the end of a peaceful demonstration when mounted police baton-charged the 300,000-strong crowd in an attempt to clear Trafalgar Square. Tempers rose on both sides, aggravated by small groups of extremist agitators and hooligans who set fire to buildings and cars.

A riot erupted in Manchester's Strangeways prison on 1st April during Sunday morning prayers in the chapel. The prisoners quickly overpowered the guards and took their keys, opening cells throughout the prison and releasing around 1,000 men. Prison staff, overwhelmed by the speed of the riot, urged police to storm the building, but David Waddington, the Home Secretary, preferred a low-key approach. The riot was mainly a protest against the appalling conditions which kept prisoners, including those on remand, locked up three to a cell for 23 hours a day.

A devastating earthquake brought death and destruction to more than 100 square miles of north-west Iran. More than 40,000 people were feared dead and some 100,000 injured. The provinces of Zarjan and Gilan near the Soviet border were the centre of the tremors, which measured 7.7 on the Richter scale.

*   *   *

On 21st July 1978 Dario Borgogno, secretary of the Italian Soccer Federation, officially petitioned FIFA to choose Italy as hosts for the 14th World Cup finals. Five years later, on October 18th 1983, Prime Minister Bettino Craxi gave official support to the project. Greece, Italy, England and the Soviet Union were the final four candidates bidding to stage the event. When FIFA made their choice, only Italy and the Soviet Union remained contenders. On May 19th 1984 Italy was unanimously chosen and became only the second nation, after Mexico, to be selected to host the event on two occasions.

The Italian FA, as was becoming commonplace, was behind schedule with redevelopment programmes. The huge cost of the restructuring was not only counted in millions of lire. Sadly, human lives were sacrificed as workers died in their efforts to convert Italian stadia into some of the finest in the world.

There were 112 entrants registered for the qualifying competition. Bahrain, India, Lesotho, Rwanda, South Yemen and Togo all withdrew from the tournament without kicking a ball. Libya reached the second round after beating Burkina Faso 3-2 on aggregate, despite losing 2-0 in Ouagadougou. But after losing to the Ivory Coast 1-0 they refused to play Algeria and withdrew.

There was a sensation shortly after the qualifying tournament commenced. Mexico, the 1986 hosts and one of the favourites to qualify for the finals, were suspended from all FIFA competitions for two years from 30th June 1988 until

29th June 1990. They had supplied fraudulent details for four players in the World Youth Championship who were over the required age limit.

The match between Brazil and Chile, played in Rio de Janeiro on 3rd September 1989, and watched by a crowd of 141,072, was abandoned. Sixty-nine minutes had elapsed, with Brazil leading 1-0, when a flare was thrown into the Chilean goalmouth. Roberto Rojas, the goalkeeper, fell to the ground, apparently injured. The Chilean team claimed that they were neither mentally nor physically capable of continuing with the match and refused to play on. Subsequent investigation revealed that Rojas had not been hit, no injury had been incurred and he had been acting in an attempt to disqualify Brazil. As a consequence, he received a life ban, as did Chilean FA officials and medical advisers who connived with Rojas. Chile were banned from the 1994 World Cup and fined $100,000. Brazil were awarded the match 2-0.

In Europe, Sweden, England, Holland, West Germany, Yugoslavia and Belgium all qualified without losing a match. Despite finishing only second to Sweden, England did not concede a single goal. Denmark's defeat in Bucharest in the final Group 1 match allowed Romania to advance. The Soviet Union and Austria qualified from Group 3. Yugoslavia were impressive winners of Group 5, with second-placed Scotland qualifying for a fifth successive tournament, a British record. Czechoslovakia finished level on points with Belgium but were runners-up because of an inferior goal difference. Spain and the Republic of Ireland were successful in Group 6, with Ireland qualifying for the first time in their history.

The African qualifying tournament was marred by a terrible tragedy in Lagos. There were some 100,000 spectators crammed into an 80,000 capacity stadium. Seven fans were killed and the 24-year-old Nigerian player, Sam Okwaraji, collapsed and died during the match. Egypt qualified for the finals for the first time since 1934. Cameroon, unbeaten in the 1982 tournament, reached the finals for the second time in three competitions.

Oceania had no representative in the finals. Israel, who topped the group, had to play off against Colombia, winners of the South American Group 2. A solitary goal over two legs enabled Colombia to reach their first finals since 1962. They were joined from their continent by Brazil, who qualified for their 14th finals, and former holders Uruguay.

The United States, after being in the World Cup wilderness for 40 years, qualified despite only scoring 11 goals in 10 games. They defied the odds to defeat the highly-rated Trinidad and Tobago side in Port of Spain. The nation to emerge from the CONCACAF group was Costa Rica, first-time qualifiers.

South Korea won the sprawling Asia zone for the second successive time. The other surprise finalists were the United Arab Emirates. China were four minutes from qualifying. Needing to beat Qatar in their final match, they led 1-0 but conceded two goals late in the game.

For the second successive tournament, all the former champions participated.

The format was the same as 1986, with the 24 finalists divided into six groups. The top two teams in each group, together with the four best third-placed teams, progressed to the knock-out phase.

The 24 national teams were divided into the following groups:

Group A: Austria, Czechoslovakia, Italy, USA
Group B: Argentina, Cameroon, Romania, Soviet Union
Group C: Brazil, Costa Rica, Scotland, Sweden
Group D: Colombia, United Arab Emirates,
    West Germany, Yugoslavia
Group E: Belgium, South Korea, Spain, Uruguay
Group F : Egypt, England, Holland, Republic of Ireland

Over 73,000 people packed the Stadio Guiseppe Meazza in Milan for the opening ceremony, which was beamed to more than 500 million people in 100 countries. They saw a parade of women dressed in national costumes and were then treated to excerpts from Verdi's opera *Nabucco*, which was shown live on giant TV screens from La Scala. By the time the 14th World Cup ended, Italian tenor Luciano Pavarotti was as well-known to soccer fans as the leading players.

The hosts opened their Group A campaign in the Olympic Stadium, Rome, against Austria. Thankfully, Italy was rid of the Fascist ideology which had propagandised their staging of the 1934 tournament. Italy played with considerable vitality and ingenuity. Vialli, Ancelloti and Carnevale missed opportunities before the decisive goal arrived with 12 minutes remaining. Salvatore Schillaci, a young striker playing with Juventus, replaced Carnevale and had only been on the field for four minutes when he headed home a perfect Vialli cross.

When the United States last appeared in the World Cup finals in 1950, they humbled the mighty England. Their opponents on this occasion, Czechoslovakia, were managed by Josef Venglos, a doctor of philosophy, who embraced the notion that football must provide pleasure. In Florence, the central Europeans romped to a 5-1 victory. The United States paid dearly for their defensive naïvety. Their problems were compounded by the dismissal of Wynalda.

An anticipated avalanche of goals never materialised in Italy's next game against the United States. Vialli cleverly dummied a long ball from Carnevale, allowing Giannini to score after only 11 minutes. Thereafter, Italy's pedestrian, unimaginative play never seriously troubled a well-organised United States side. Vialli missed a penalty in the first half, striking an upright.

Czechoslovakia ensured qualification to the next phase with victory by a solitary goal over a robust Austrian side. Klaus Lindenberger, the Austrian goalkeeper who had performed so well against Italy, callously brought down Chovanec, who had to be stretchered off. Bilek, Czechoslovakia's 1989 Footballer of the Year, converted the penalty. Austria's physical approach led to five of their players being booked.

The Italian manager, Vicini, prompted by an injury to Vialli, recalled Roberto Baggio, the £7.7 million former Fiorentina idol. He played alongside Schillaci, whom he would partner at Juventus. Italy had not beaten Czechoslovakia for 37 years. They took the lead after only nine minutes when a corner by Donadoni was struck into the box by Giannini. Schillaci headed the ball into the net between the defender and goalkeeper. Midway through the second half, Griga of Czechoslovakia had a perfectly legitimate goal disallowed for offside. In the 77th minute Baggio scored a goal of outstanding individual brilliance. An exchange of passes with Giannini on the half-way line preceded a mesmeric run through the Czech defence, which climaxed in a superlative goal. Schillaci and Baggio had successfully complemented each other and formed a potent strike force.

The Austria versus United States match was an ill-tempered affair, with nine players booked and Artner of Austria sent-off for a violent tackle on Vermes in the 34th minute. Austria won the match 2-1.

Carlos Bilardo, the manager of Argentina, was publicly criticised by his country's President, Carlos Menem. The reason was that Bilardo had excluded Raymond Diaz, the centre-forward who had won a championship medal with Inter Milan, from the squad. There was widespread speculation that Diaz had criticised Maradona, and the former friends became irreconcilable.

Their opponents in the inaugural match, Cameroon, were now managed by Valeri Nepomniaschi, a Siberian. Relations appeared to be strained within the camp and were not helped by the manager's inability to converse directly with his players. Nepomniaschi came from the Soviet second division, spoke no French and communicated to his players via the driver at the Soviet embassy. The 'interpreter' allegedly infused the messages with his own ideas. The outstanding goalkeeper, Thomas N'kono had been replaced by Bell, who made disparaging remarks about the organisation of the team, and so N'kono was recalled. Roger Milla's return to the World Cup fold was remarkable given that the 38-year-old striker had 'retired' to play Indian Ocean football on the island of Réunion.

It was widely anticipated that the World Cup holders, with Maradona still a potent force, would overwhelm the Africans in Group B. Cameroon resorted to some quite brutal play which clearly unnerved their opponents. The French referee, Michel Vautrot, dismissed Kana Biyik after an hour when Caniggia appeared to make contact with Biyik rather than the reverse. Six minutes later Kana Biyik's brother, Omam, leapt to head a cross which Pumpido allowed to slip under his body. In the final minute Caniggia, a second-half substitute, was the victim of a crude tackle by Massing, whose sending-off reduced Cameroon to nine players. Their 1-0 victory, whilst a surprise, hardly compared with the biggest shocks given that they departed from the 1982 tournament undefeated.

The futuristic setting of Bari, in the capital of Apulia, was the setting for the confrontation between the Soviet Union and Romania. The Soviet Union, managed by Lobanovski, had performed well in the 1988 European Championship, finishing runners-up to Holland. Romania lacked Hagi, their highly influential midfield star. Marius Lacatus, the Romanian outside-right, displayed incandescent skills. It was appropriate that he should score after 41 minutes, with a powerful shot from the outside of his right foot. Lacatus converted a penalty after 54 minutes to complete a 2-0 victory.

Argentina met the Soviet Union in Naples, Maradona's home ground. With only ten minutes played, Argentina's goalkeeper Pumpido was involved in a sickening collision with his team-mate Olarticoechea, which resulted in a double fracture of the leg. Goycochea deputised as the stricken goalkeeper was stretchered off the field. Only minutes later Kuznetsov had a goal-bound header stopped by Maradona's right hand. The referee, Erik Fredriksson of Sweden, in close proximity to the incident, took no action. He was subsequently criticised and departed from the tournament prematurely. Argentina scored after 28 minutes when Troglio headed home a centre from Olarticoechea. Bessonov was sent off three minutes after the interval for an infringement on Caniggia. With ten minutes left, a faulty back-pass by

Kuznetsov was intercepted by Burruchaga to give Argentina a 2-0 win.

Cameroon made history by becoming the first Black African nation to qualify for the second round. Roger Milla, at 38, enjoyed the distinction of becoming the oldest player to score in World Cup finals. He appeared as a substitute in the 59th minute against Romania and netted twice in a ten-minute period, helping his side to a 2-1 win.

Argentina and Romania were conscious that a draw would ensure their qualification. Completely against the run of play, Argentina took the lead in 62 minutes when a Maradona corner was headed into the net by Monzon, positioned at the near post. Balint gained a deserved equaliser with a header five minutes later. Romania had progressed beyond the opening phase for the first time in their history.

Against Cameroon in Bari, the Soviet Union finally produced a forceful performance which gave some indication of their true potential. Protasov, Zygmantovich, Zavarov and Dobrovolsky each scored in a 4-0 rout. Despite the victory, the Soviet Union were eliminated at the initial stage for the first time in their history.

Brazil were now managed by Sebastiao Lazaroni, whose cautious approach did not embrace his nation's familiar philosophy based on artistry and panache. The preoccupation with the past was cynically abandoned and a brand of football contaminated by the strictures of crude pragmatism was introduced. There was reported to be deep dissent within the Brazilian camp. Both Careca and Dunga were keen to be seen as the protagonist.

Against Sweden in Turin, Careca, who played alongside Maradona at Napoli, was in sparkling form. A defence-splitting pass from Branco enabled Careca to score after 40 minutes. He scored a simple second goal after 63 minutes before Tomas Brolin, the young Swedish centre-forward, beat his marker Mozer with considerable dexterity to reduce the arrears.

Scotland were now managed by Andy Roxburgh, a former

headmaster, who was a well-qualified coach. Unlike Ally McLeod, Roxburgh was a man of substance, intelligent and level-headed. Scotland's first match pitted them against Costa Rica in Genoa. Costa Rica were managed by Velibor Milutinovic, who was in charge of the host nation, Mexico, in 1986. Astonishingly, Miltuninovic was Costa Rica's fifth manager since the start of their 1990 campaign. The Costa Rican FA had also appointed three different presidents during the same period. Against a backdrop of such instability, it was hardly surprising that the Central American side were 1,000-1 outsiders to win the World Cup. Four minutes after the interval Scotland's World Cup aspirations, once again, lay in ruins. Jara back-headed the ball into the path of Juan Arnaldo Cayasso, who shot past Jim Leighton in goal. Cayasso, who carries an unshakeable belief in God and immense pride in his Negro culture, learned to play football, like Pele, in the street with balls made from rags.

Against Sweden in Genoa, Scotland lacked Richard Gough, who had retired from the tournament with a hip injury. Once again, from a position of adversity, Scotland gave a remarkably resilient performance. Stuart McColl made his international goalscoring debut after ten minutes. In the closing stages, Aitken was tripped in the penalty area by Nilsson and Mo Johnston converted the spot kick. Stromberg, a substitute, scored with four minutes remaining, but Scotland held out for victory.

Brazil's lack of creativity and defensive profile was highlighted by their deployment of a sweeper against Costa Rica. Even the only goal of the game lacked the style and grace associated with a Brazilian side. In the 33rd minute Muller's shot deflected off the arm of Montero before finding the net.

Costa Rica, in beating Sweden 2-1, achieved the remarkable feat of qualifying for the next stage. Ekstrom put Sweden ahead when a Schwarz free kick was parried by Conejo. In the 62nd minute Medford, the speedy striker, was introduced and swung the balance of the game in Costa Rica's favour. With 15 minutes remaining, he won a free kick taken by Gonzalez which allowed the unmarked Flores to head home. Three minutes from time, during a counter-attack, Medford strode through a casual defence and deceived Ravelli to score a memorable goal. In San Jose, the Costa Rican capital, a statue was to be erected to the glory of Gabelo Conejo for his goalkeeping exploits.

The Scotland against Brazil match appeared to be reaching a goalless conclusion when, with seven minutes remaining, Alemao struck a shot which Leighton failed to hold. Muller pounced to place the ball in the net from a tight angle. Had Scotland attacked more boldly, and not treated Brazil with exaggerated respect, they would almost certainly have qualified for the next phase.

West Germany, still managed by Franz Beckenbauer, had blossoming midfield players in Andy Moeller and Tomas Hassler. Lothar Matthaus, the captain, was by now one of the outstanding talents within the game. Against Yugoslavia in Milan, he scored two goals, one a fulminating shot from 25 yards. A well-organised, balanced side comfortably dominated Yugoslavia, winning 4-1, and underlined the Germans as serious contenders.

The United Arab Emirates were making their first appearance in the World Cup finals. They were managed by the Brazilian Carlos Alberto Perreira, successor to Mario Zagalo, who was dismissed for disparaging his side's prospects. Colombia returned to the finals after an absence of 28 years. Jose Rene Higuita, a former striker, served as their extrovert, flamboyant goalkeeper. His antics were remarkably similar to those of Quiroga, the maverick Peruvian goalkeeper, as he frequently imperilled his team-mates, sacrificing collective responsibility for self-indulgence. Colombia were never seriously tested in Bologna, scoring in the 52nd minute when Redin headed home a cross from Alvarez. Carlos Valderrama, Colombia's captain who played for Montpellier of France, completed a solo run climaxing in a second goal three minutes from time. The inducement of a Ferrari Testarossa for qualification to the second phase now seemed a forlorn hope for the Arab players.

In an insipid match, Yugoslavia beat Colombia with a splendidly controlled half volley by Jozic in the 73rd minute. Although endowed with players of high artistic merit in Valderrama, Rincon and Redin, Colombia lacked any sense of cohesion.

West Germany gave another display of ruthless efficiency against the United Arab Emirates. They attacked unremittingly in torrential rain. Voller and Klinsmann scored during the first half. Two minutes after the restart, Khalid Mubarak netted to earn a Rolls-Royce, which was given by the President of the Federation of the Emirates to every goalscorer. Further goals by Matthaus, Bein and Voller completed a 5-1 rout.

Yugoslavia guaranteed themselves a place in the next phase with a comfortable 4-1 win over the United Arab Emirates. Susic, making his 50th international appearance, scored after only four minutes. Pancev (2) and Prosinecki completed the scoring, with Ali Thani Jumaa heading a goal for the United Arab Emirates. Khaleel Ghanim Mubarak was sent off for retaliation in the 77th minute. He became the 50th player to be dismissed during World Cup finals.

Colombia required a point from their clash with West Germany to avoid elimination. When Littbarski scored in the 88th minute, Colombia appeared to be heading home. But sensationally, in injury time, Valderrama delivered a defence-splitting pass to Rincon, who shot through Illgner's legs to secure a second round place.

South Korea arrived at the finals having played eleven qualifying games, during which they scored 30 goals and conceded just one. Their opponents in Group E, Belgium, surprised many people with their fourth place in the 1986 tournament. On a saturated pitch in Verona, Degryse scored for Belgium in the 53rd minute with a 30-yard lob as Choi In-young raced from his goal. De Wolf scored a second goal with an excellent shot from 25 yards.

Uruguay had abandoned their defensiveness and brutality but, even adorned with the skills of Sosa, Francescoli and Paz, they never looked a potent force against Spain in Udine.

Ruben Sosa should have won the match in the 72nd minute but fired a penalty over Zubizarreta's bar. The tournament had produced its first goalless score.

Belgium scored two goals during a seven-minute period of the first half against Uruguay. Clijsters headed powerfully into the net after 15 minutes. Scifo then unleashed a coruscating shot from 30 yards. Gerets, already cautioned, was unluckily sent off just before the interval when a tackle on Sosa resulted in a theatrical dive. Ceulemans added a third goal in the 47th minute when he strode through a porous defence. Bengoechea scored a goal of little consequence for Uruguay after 73 minutes.

The Real Madrid midfielder, Michel, became the first player to score three goals in the tournament against South Korea. Hwang Bo-kwan netted for a combative South Korean side that refused to be overawed by a Spanish team who remained unconvincing, despite a 3-1 victory.

Spain and Belgium were already assured of qualification prior to their meeting. Spain triumphed 2-1 to head the group.

The final Group E match between Uruguay and South Korea was a thoroughly wretched affair. Francescoli struck the post after 33 seconds but, thereafter, little excitement was generated. Yoon Deuk-yeo was sent off after 71 minutes for time wasting. In injury time Uruguay were awarded a free kick. The ball was directed into a packed penalty area from where Fonseca, a substitute, rose to head the ball wide of a despairing Choi In-young. Uruguay had won their first World Cup finals match since 1970. They reached the second phase, thus depriving Scotland as one of the best third-placed teams.

England participated in the Sardinian-Sicilian Group F alongside Holland, the Republic of Ireland and Egypt. England had, of course, been paired with the Republic of Ireland in the 1988 European Championship, when they lost all three matches. England embarked on their campaign beset by difficulties. The popular press had exposed lurid revelations about manager Bobby Robson's private life. The Football Association appeared to view his position as untenable, as his contract would not be renewed regardless of what happened during the World Cup. Robson had reached an agreement to coach PSV Eindhoven at the conclusion of the World Cup finals. Unfortunately, the release of the news that he would be returning to club football was mishandled and his action was condemned by a scurrilous and unforgiving press. England were compelled to play in Sardinia and Sicily because of the potential for crowd violence. Extremely draconian anti-hooligan measures were taken by the Italian authorities, who over-reacted with an extraordinary police presence accompanied by a ballet of helicopters.

The Republic of Ireland, competing in their first ever World Cup finals, were managed by Jack Charlton, who had played at centre-half for England during the 1966 World Cup. Charlton was something of a pragmatist, content to employ long ball tactics which were anathema to the artistically-inclined. The dubious nationality of a number of the players hardly endeared the side to the soccer purist.

England had been humiliated by the Republic of Ireland in the European Championship of 1988, losing 1-0. After eight minutes of this game they took the lead when Waddle's pass allowed Lineker to gather the ball on his chest before shooting past Bonner. Fifteen minutes from time McMahon, who had just appeared as a substitute, was dispossessed by Sheedy who unleashed a forceful left-foot shot to equalise. A parody of a football match had embarrassingly highlighted the gulf between those two nations and the leading countries of the world.

Holland had produced devastating form to win the European Championship in 1988, with dazzling performers in Van Basten, Gullit and Rijkaard. But Rinus Michels had retired as the manager. Leo Beenhakker, highly successful in Spain, was now in charge. There were rumours of discord within the Dutch camp, with Beenhakker clearly not commanding a high level of respect amongst players and journalists.

Holland's opening match pitted them against Egypt, who made their first finals appearance since 1934. Egypt largely dominated the match, quickly disabusing Holland of their arrogant disdain for a Third World nation who were superior in their technique and enterprise. In the 59th minute Rijkaard dummied a cross which allowed Kieft to score, completely against the run of play. With eight minutes remaining, Koeman held back Hossam Hassan. The initial foul appeared to be committed outside the area, but a penalty was awarded which Abdelghani converted to gain a deserved draw.

England deployed Mark Wright as a sweeper for their next match against Holland in Cagliari. Paul Gascoigne enhanced his status with a dynamic performance which was the only highlight of an abysmal game. Bryan Robson limped off injured in the 64th minute and took no further part in the tournament. Peter Shilton achieved a record-breaking 120th full international appearance.

In Palermo, against the Republic of Ireland, Egypt were unrecognisable from the side which had played so attractively against Holland. Although the Republic of Ireland dominated the game, they lacked the guile or inventiveness to broach the Egyptian defence. A dull, sterile affair fittingly ended in a goalless draw.

In Cagliari, England faced Egypt with all four nations having an equal number of points after four draws. Mark Wright scored the only goal of the game when he rose above the Egyptian defence to glance a header past Ahmed Shobeir from Gascoigne's free kick in the 59th minute. Egypt claimed a penalty when the ball made contact with Wright's arm, but England held out for an undistinguished victory to head a hugely disappointing group.

Holland started promisingly against the Republic of Ireland with Gullit scoring, after ten minutes. He exchanged passes with Kieft before striking a powerful angled shot past Bonner. The Republic of Ireland performed tenaciously and were rewarded in 71 minutes. Bonner cleared the ball upfield, Van Aerle's rushed back-pass was not held by Van Breukelen and centre-forward Niall Quinn seized on the chance to equalise. Both teams ended with identical records and drew lots to determine their fate in the second round matches. The Irish won second spot, pairing them against Romania. Holland faced West Germany.

The knock-out games in the second round produced the following ties:

Cameroon v Colombia
Costa Rica v Czechoslovakia
Argentina v Brazil
Holland v West Germany
Republic of Ireland v Romania
Italy v Uruguay
Spain v Yugoslavia
England v Belgium

Few people could have prophesied the meeting between Cameroon and Colombia in the knock-out stage. A soporific match ought to have been won by Colombia inside 90 minutes. Rincon struck the crossbar with a free kick during the first half, and Fajardo squandered a good chance. An inspired substitution altered the course of the match. Roger Milla replaced M'Fede in the 54th minute. At the start of the second period of extra time, he received a delightful angled pass from Omam Biyik, raced past Perea and evaded Escobar, to strike the ball wide of Higuita. Three minutes later Higuita was dispossessed by Roger Milla well outside his own penalty area. Milla simply advanced to score into an unguarded goal. Redin, a substitute, scored in the 116th minute but it was too late to save Colombia. Tullio Lanese, the Italian official, booked Kana Biyik, Akem N'Dip, M'Bouh and Onana, all of whom would miss their quarter-final tie as they had been previously cautioned.

Facing Czechoslovakia in Bari, Costa Rica felt the loss of their outstanding goalkeeper, Cabelo Conejo, who had an injured ankle. Thomas Skuhravy, the 6'4" Sparta Prague striker, scored three goals in a game which was evenly balanced until the latter stages. Four of the five goals scored, in a 4-1 victory for Czechoslovakia, were headers. Costa Rica had acquitted themselves well against a confident and assiduous Czech side, and departed from the tournament with great pride and honour.

Brazil dominated their fierce rivals, Argentina, in Turin, yet still somehow contrived to lose. They struck the woodwork on no fewer than three occasions. As they assailed the Argentinian goal, Goycochea was absolutely inspirational. He made important saves from Dunga and Alemao and somehow pushed an angled shot from Careca onto the post. An act of larceny was completed in the 80th minute when Maradona, nursing an injury, released Caniggia with a brilliant defence-shattering pass. Caniggia rounded Taffarel with his right foot and scored nonchalantly with his left. Argentina had beaten Brazil for the first time ever in the tournament.

In Milan, West Germany and Holland produced one of the best games of the tournament. Holland started at lightning pace and Winter had two opportunities before the game exploded in the 21st minute. Rijkaard fouled Voller, who responded by diving. The referee, Juan Carlos Loustau of Argentina, cautioned Rijkaard, which meant that he would be suspended for the next game. Rijkaard spat at Voller who, in turn, was shown the yellow card for complaining that the Dutchman had spat at him. Seconds later, the two players became further embroiled in a heated exchange after Voller pursued a ball which Van Breukelen reached first. Following a seemingly innocuous challenge, first Voller, then Rijkaard, were ordered off. As they departed from the field, Rijkaard again spat at Voller. In the 50th minute the deadlock was broken by Klinsmann, who was in irrepressible form. In meeting a Buchwald cross from the left, he steered his header across Van Breukelen and into the far corner of the net. Klinsmann almost doubled the lead with a magnificent shot which struck the post. In pursuing an equaliser, Holland were exposed defensively in the 84th minute. Van Breukelen pulled off a great save from Littbarski but only seconds later Brehme chipped the goalkeeper. A highly contentious penalty was awarded in the 88th minute when Van Basten appeared to dive. Koeman converted the spot-kick, but it was too late to rescue the Dutch from a formidable German side.

Romania felt the loss of the suspended Lacatus for their clash with the Republic of Ireland in Genoa. There were few opportunities throughout the 90 minutes. During extra time Romania looked the stronger side, but Ireland held out and the match was decided on penalties. Hagi, Lupu, Rotariu and Lupescu all converted their spot kicks, as did Sheedy, Houghton, Townsend and Cascarino. Bonner then saved Romania's fifth penalty from Timofte. David O'Leary had replaced Staunton as a substitute in the 94th minute. The fate of the match rested with the veteran's penalty kick. He calmly beat Lung and Ireland had reached the last eight in their first World Cup finals, without winning a game.

Uruguay reverted to a defensive strategy against the favourites, Italy, in the Olympic Stadium, Rome. They omitted Ruben Sosa and Ruben Paz. Vialli sat on the bench for Italy. Schillaci had captured the imagination of the Italian people with his energy and vitality. He could conceivably have scored in the first minute when he volleyed a cross by Baggio past the post. Serena, brought on in the 52nd minute, turned into an inspired substitute. After 65 minutes he delivered a pass for Schillaci, who struck an explosive shot past Alvez. Perdomo had a couple of chances to equalise before Serena headed a second goal seven minutes from time.

An oppressive heat in Verona did nothing to ease the gruelling tactical battle between Spain and Yugoslavia. Spain had territorial dominance but lacked the artistry of Dragan Stojkovic, who largely determined the fate of the match. A dull, lethargic game was enlivened in the final 13 minutes. Spain had struck the post on two occasions from efforts by Vazquez and Butragueno. Vujovic crossed, Stojkovic controlled the ball, bemused a defender with a body feint and shot past Zubizarreta for a goal which could scarcely be surpassed for its sheer grace and beauty. With seven minutes left, Vazquez's cross-shot was prodded into the net by Salinas. After two minutes of extra time, Stojkovic struck a splendid, curling free kick round a brittle defensive wall inside the right-hand post of Zubizarreta to clinch victory.

England displayed remarkable arrogance by booking their flight for a quarter-final match in Naples in advance of their tie with Belgium in Bologna. As both sides appeared to be resigned to a penalty shoot-out, England dramatically won with 30 seconds of extra time remaining. Belgium had dominated the first half playing imaginative football. Ceulemens struck the post with Shilton beaten. John Barnes had an excellent goal disallowed for a dubious offside. Scifo struck the post with a magnificent shot in the second-half with Shilton again helpless. Only seconds remained as Gascoigne curled a free kick to the far post. Platt, who had come on as a substitute, swivelled in mid-air and struck a coruscating volley past a disconsolate Preud'homme for an exceptionally lucky victory.

The quarter finals were contested by Cameroon, Czechoslovakia, Argentina, West Germany, Republic of Ireland, Italy, Yugoslavia and England and produced the following ties:

Argentina v Yugoslavia
Italy v Republic of Ireland
Czechoslovakia v West Germany
Cameroon v England

Yugoslavia and Argentina failed to score after two hours of football in Florence. Stojkovic, together with Prosinecki, orchestrated much of the play and largely overshadowed Maradona, on whom Argentina were too reliant. Yugoslavia were disadvantaged when Sabanadzovic was ordered off after 31 minutes, having received two cautions in as many minutes. Despite being reduced to ten men, they attacked more than their opponents and Jozic and Savicevic had opportunities to win the match. Maradona missed a spot-kick in the penalty shoot-out, as did Troglio. But Stojkovic, Brnovic and Hadzibegic all failed to convert their shots. Argentina winning 3-2 on penalties was a travesty.

Salvatore Schillaci scored his fourth goal of the tournament, which enabled Italy to triumph over the Republic of Ireland

and advance to the semi-finals. In the 37th minute a powerful shot by Donadoni was parried by Bonner. Schillaci pounced to place the ball inside the right-hand post. He also struck a venomous free kick against the underside of the bar during the second half. Ireland contributed to an entertaining game and had their brightest spell early on in the match when a Quinn header was well saved by Zenga.

West Germany reached a record ninth semi-final by defeating Czechoslovakia 1-0 in Milan. They launched a series of penetrating attacks which resulted in Buchwald producing an excellent save from Stejskal, and Hasek clearing off the line. In the 25th minute Klinsmann was brought down by Straka as he dashed into the penalty area. Matthaus scored from the penalty. Hasek again cleared the ball off the line as half-time approached. Bilek produced the third goal-line clearance just after the interval. Czech hopes receded in the 70th minute when Moravcik was sent off.

A seriously depleted Cameroon side were involved in a thoroughly pulsating match with England in Naples. Cameroon nearly scored when Makanaky crossed and Omam Biyik elicited a fine save from Shilton. In the 26th minute Platt scored from a Pearce cross to lull England into a false sense of security. Libiih had a great chance to equalise but missed with a simple header. Roger Milla replaced Maboang a minute after the resumption and galvanised Cameroon. In the 61st minute Milla was upended by Gascoigne and Kunde equalised with the resultant penalty. Four minutes later Ekeke, a substitute who had only been on the field for a couple of minutes, exchanged passes with Milla before striding through the English defence to put his side ahead. Cameroon's improvisation was reminiscent of Brazil as they continued to exploit a defence in disarray. England weathered the storm and were awarded a penalty with eight minutes remaining when Lineker was brought down by Ebwelle. Lineker composed himself and calmly scored. In the final minute of the first period of extra time, Gascoigne's meticulous pass to Lineker led to N'kono felling the striker. Once again, Lineker converted a penalty and England had reached the last four. Cameroon had delighted the football world with a strange mix of delicate skills together with robustness bordering on thuggery. The departure of Cameroon was too much to endure for a Bangladeshi woman who hanged herself. 'The elimination of Cameroon also means the end of my life,' said her suicide note.

In the semi-finals Argentina faced Italy in Naples, and England played West Germany in Turin.

Before Argentina met Italy, Maradona implored Neapolitans to support his side, arguing that southerners were unjustly treated by the people of the north. Maradona clearly underestimated the unifying force of national pride and was to later regret his appeal.

Argentina gave their best performance of the championship against the tournament favourites. Vicini selected Vialli in preference to Baggio, who had complemented Schillaci so well. A goal in the 17th minute by Schillaci appeared to augur well for the Italians. Schillaci instigated a move which led to Giannini delivering a back-header to Vialli, whose shot was blocked by Goycochea. Schillaci seized on the rebound to give his side the lead. Argentina began to assert themselves as Italy became increasingly nervous and uncomfortable defending their lead. Olarticoechea crossed from the left and Caniggia headed home the equaliser in the 67th minute. Zenga had finally conceded a goal after 517 minutes of World Cup football, beating Peter Shilton's previous record by 18 minutes. At the end of the first period of extra time, Giusti was sent off for an off-the-ball incident involving Baggio, a substitute for Giannini. Play was held up for three minutes whilst Maradona attempted to persuade the referee, Michel Vautrot of France, to reverse his decision. The first period of extra time, punctuated by a series of fouls, lasted 24 minutes. In the penalty shoot-out both sides converted the first three spot-kicks. Goycochea then saved Donadoni's effort. Maradona scored before Goycochea saved from Serena. The goalkeeper was second choice, but following Pumpido's injury had emerged as a national hero. Argentina had reached their second successive World Cup Final having scored only five goals in six games, which was an all-time low for the competition.

The second semi-final, played in Turin, was a classic encounter between two sides who clearly respected each other. For the first time in World Cup history, both semi-finals were decided by a penalty shoot-out at the end of 120 minutes play. West Germany had unquestionably emerged as the most potent nation in the tournament, but on this occasion they were looking weary. England played intelligently without carrying a real sense of menace in front of goal. They were certainly the equal of their opponents, but fell behind to a lucky goal scored in the 59th minute. A free-kick by Brehme was wickedly deflected off Paul Parker and looped over Peter Shilton's head. England deservedly equalised with ten minutes remaining. Parker crossed from the right and uncharacteristically slack defending by the Germans allowed Gary Lineker to strike an accurate left-footed shot into the far corner of the net. Gascoigne was reduced to tears in the sixth minute of extra time when he was booked. If England reached the Final he would be suspended, having already been cautioned. Although extra time yielded no goals, both Waddle and Buchwald struck the post. The penalty shoot-out resulted in Lineker, Beardsley and Platt, and Brehme, Matthaus and Riedle, all scoring. Pearce then blasted his kick, which was blocked by Illgner's leg. Thon put West Germany ahead, which meant that the responsibility of keeping England in the tournament rested with Waddle. He fired his kick over the bar. West Germany had reached a World Cup Final for a record sixth time. They also became the first nation to compete in three consecutive World Cup finals. For the second successive tournament, their opponents were Argentina.

The third-place match between Italy and England was a pleasant affair, with both sides committed to attack. Shilton was playing his 125th match for England before retiring. It was most unfortunate that in his final game he erred, allowing

Baggio to dispossess him and score after 70 minutes. A cross from Dorigo enabled Platt to equalise with an excellent header ten minutes from the end. Four minutes later, Schillaci was brought down by Paul Parker and promptly scored with the spot-kick. His sixth goal established him as the leading scorer of the tournament. A Berti goal in injury time was adjudged to be offside, and the score remained 2-1 to Italy. England won the Fair Play Award and were met by a warm reception upon their arrival home.

The Olympic Stadium in Rome, scene of many sporting triumphs in the past, accommodated the worst World Cup Final in history. It was almost inevitable that the 76,603 spectators who had paid a world record £4 million in gate receipts were going to witness, for the first time ever, a Final which yielded fewer than three goals. Argentina had scarcely endeared themselves to the soccer cognoscenti with their negative, cynical tactics. They had four players suspended, including Caniggia, and concentrated on defence from the start. They attempted to exploit the rules of a tournament which made it possible for them to compete in a World Cup Final having won one game and totalled five goals. Maradona was jeered throughout the match by a crowd enraged by his utterances in Naples. Voller had a number of chances, all of which were missed, during the first half. West Germany attacked strongly after the resumption. Augenthaler appeared to be tripped by Goycochea, but no action was taken. The substitute, Monzon, was ordered off the field after 64 minutes when Klinsmann made a meal of a foul tackle. He became the first player to suffer the indignity of a dismissal during a World Cup Final. Both sides were guilty of appalling games-manship. With 15 minutes remaining, Calderon appeared to be tripped in the penalty box and Argentina were unfortunate not to be awarded a spot-kick. A highly dubious penalty was given five minutes from time when Voller was brought down by Sensini. Argentina protested vehemently before Brehme con-verted the spot-kick. Two minutes later Dezotti aggressively challenged Kohler, who was time-wasting, and followed

Monzon to the dressing-room. The Mexican referee, Edgardo Codesal Mendez, was jostled by several Argentinian players, any one of whom could have joined their two disgraced colleagues. It was a sad end to a World Cup tournament which did nothing to promote a positive image of football.

Results: Italy 1990

Group A

Italy	1	Austria	0
Czechoslovakia	5	USA	1
Italy	1	USA	0
Czechoslovakia	1	Austria	0
Italy	2	Czechoslovakia	0
Austria	2	USA	1

	P	W	D	L	Goals F	A	Pts
Italy	3	3	0	0	4	0	6
Czechoslovakia	3	2	0	1	6	3	4
Austria	3	1	0	2	2	3	2
USA	3	0	0	3	2	8	0

Group B

Cameroon	1	Argentina	0
Romania	2	Soviet Union	0
Argentina	2	Soviet Union	0
Cameroon	2	Romania	1
Argentina	1	Romania	1
Soviet Union	4	Cameroon	0

	P	W	D	L	Goals F	A	Pts
Cameroon	3	2	0	1	3	5	4
Romania	3	1	1	1	4	3	3
Argentina	3	1	1	1	3	2	3
Soviet Union	3	1	0	2	4	4	2

Group C

Brazil	2	Sweden	1
Costa Rica	1	Scotland	0
Scotland	2	Sweden	1
Brazil	1	Costa Rica	0
Costa Rica	2	Sweden	1
Brazil	1	Scotland	0

	P	W	D	L	Goals F	Goals A	Pts
Brazil	3	3	0	0	4	1	6
Costa Rica	3	2	0	1	3	2	4
Scotland	3	1	0	2	2	3	2
Sweden	3	0	0	3	3	6	0

Group D

West Germany	4	Yugoslavia	1
Colombia	2	Utd Arab Emirates	0
Yugoslavia	1	Colombia	0
West Germany	5	Utd Arab Emirates	1
Yugoslavia	4	Utd Arab Emirates	1
Colombia	1	West Germany	1

	P	W	D	L	Goals F	Goals A	Pts
West Germany	3	2	1	0	10	3	5
Yugoslavia	3	2	0	1	6	5	4
Colombia	3	1	1	1	3	2	3
Utd Arab Emirates	3	0	0	3	2	11	0

Group E

Belgium	2	South Korea	0
Spain	0	Uruguay	0
Belgium	3	Uruguay	1
Spain	3	South Korea	1
Spain	2	Belgium	1
Uruguay	1	South Korea	0

	P	W	D	L	Goals		Pts
					F	A	
Spain	3	2	1	0	5	2	5
Belgium	3	2	0	1	6	3	4
Uruguay	3	1	1	1	2	3	3
South Korea	3	0	0	3	1	6	0

Group F

England	1	Ireland	1
Egypt	1	Holland	1
England	0	Holland	0
Egypt	0	Ireland	0
England	1	Egypt	0
Ireland	1	Holland	1

	P	W	D	L	Goals		Pts
					F	A	
England	3	1	2	0	2	1	4
Ireland	3	0	3	0	2	2	3
Holland	3	0	3	0	2	2	3
Egypt	3	0	2	1	1	2	2

Second Round

Cameroon	2	Colombia	1*
Czechoslovakia	4	Costa Rica	1
Argentina	1	Brazil	0
West Germany	2	Holland	1
Ireland	0	Romania	0**
Italy	2	Uruguay	0
Yugoslavia	2	Spain	1†
England	1	Belgium	0

*(after extra time, 0-0 at 90 minutes)

**(after extra time, Ireland won 5-4 on penalties)†(after extra time, 1-1 at 90 minutes)

Quarter finals

Argentina	0	Yugoslavia	0*
Italy	1	Ireland	0
West Germany	1	Czechoslovakia	0
England	3	Cameroon	2**

*(after extra time, Argentina won 3-2 on penalties)
**(after extra time, 2-2 at 90 minutes)

Semi-finals

Argentina	1	Italy	1

(after extra time, 1-1 at 90 minutes. Argentina won 4-3 on penalties)

West Germany	1	England	1

(after extra time, 1-1 at 90 minutes. West Germany won 4-3 on penalties)

Third Place Match

Italy	2	England	1

Final

West Germany	1	Argentina	0

West Germany: Illgner, Brehme, Kohler, Augenthaler, Buchwald, Berthold (Reuter), Matthaus, Hassler, Littbarski, Voller, Klinsmann

Argentina: Goycochea, Lorenzo, Sensini, Serrizuela, Ruggeri (Monzon), Simon, Basualdo, Burruchaga (Calderon), Maradona, Troglio, Dezotti
Scorer: Brehme (penalty) for West Germany

1994

An earthquake measuring 6.6 on the Richter scale killed 34 people when it shook Los Angeles before dawn on 17th January. With its epicentre in the commuter belt of San Fernando Valley, at the city's northern limits, it crumbled motorways and destroyed bridges; water mains burst and broken gas pipes spread flames through the area. The death toll would have been much higher if it had struck a few hours later, during the rush hour. Property damage was estimated to exceed $7 billion.

There was carnage at Sarajevo's central market on 5th February when a single mortar bomb slaughtered 68 people and wounded nearly 200 others. The deadly attack came without warning, and the 120mm shell landed in the centre of the market, crowded with weekend shoppers. The effect was devastating, with shrapnel slicing through the stalls. General Sir Michael Rose, who commanded the UN peace-keepers in Bosnia, said it was impossible to say where the shell had come from, but the people of Sarajevo were in no doubt it was the Serbs, their former neighbours, who controlled the hills above the city. World leaders were swift to condemn the massacre.

The stench of death pervaded Kigali, the capital of Rwanda. Decomposing bodies were all around; the living had fled. On 22nd April the Red Cross estimated that more than 100,000 people had been killed in two weeks of tribal slaughter between Hutus and Tutsis following the death of President Habyarimana when his plane crashed – believed to be shot down. Nobody knew the real extent of the killing, which saturated the lush and verdant land with blood. It was feared that starvation and disease would sweep through the makeshift refugee camps.

Ayrton Senna, the Brazilian Formula One driver, winner of 41 Grand Prix, died on 1st May when he spun off a curve during the San Marino Grand Prix at Imola. The 34-year-old idol crashed into a concrete wall. Brazil went into mourning for its national hero, whose death shattered the racing world.

*   *   *

There were four candidates who initially expressed an interest in the staging of the 15th World Cup – Brazil, Chile, Morocco and the United States. The candidature of the United States scarcely seemed appropriate in a country indifferent to the fortunes of world soccer. The game has failed to impact upon the traditional sporting loves of the average American and throughout its history has been an extremely poor relation to gridiron football, baseball and ice hockey.

Association football has had a chequered history and the United States has never been able to establish a professional soccer league of any durability. Probably the best known league was the NASL (North American Soccer League), in which several world superstars such as Pele, Franz Beckenbauer and Johan Cruyff played before large audiences in the major US cities. The NASL eventually collapsed in 1985.

However, the 1984 Los Angeles Olympics soccer tournament was a great success, with close to $1^1/_2$ million paying spectators attending the 32 matches. This emphasised the viability of the 1994 World Cup competition taking place in the United States and in late February 1987 the United States Soccer Federation (USSF) notified FIFA of its interest. With the full backing of the Senate, the then President, Ronald Reagan, signed the official proposal to FIFA, pledging the full assistance of the US Government to the 1994 FIFA World Cup cause.

Chile quickly withdrew its candidature, leaving only Morocco and Brazil as serious challengers to the United States bid. Morocco, with just two stadia at Rabat and Casablanca, lacked the necessary facilities to stage such a major event spanning a period of one month. Brazil was in administrative chaos, suffering hyperinflation; its stadia had become obsolete and Rio de Janeiro had a disturbingly high murder rate. Fittingly, on US Independence Day, 4th July 1988, FIFA Senior Vice-President Harry Cavan announced the selection of the United States as the host country for 1994. The US received 10 votes, with rivals Morocco and Brazil receiving 7 and 2 respectively. Many people felt shocked and, indeed, downright indignant that the world's greatest football event should be given to probably the one nation on earth which does not regard soccer as a major sport.

There was a marathon entry to the 1994 World Cup, with a record 141 nations registered for the qualifying competition. The redefining of the world map, particularly in Europe, led to the highest-ever total of 582 matches preceding the finals.

Only 22 nations would emerge to challenge the defending champions, Germany, and the host nation, the United States.

The qualifying campaign started on 21st March 1992 with Mark Lugris, a New York restaurant manager, scoring the opening goal for Puerto Rico, who achieved their first ever World Cup victory, against the Dominican Republic. There were many dramatic moments during the qualifying competition and none sadder than the plane crash involving Zambia. At midnight on 27th April 1993, the Zambian team were travelling on a military plane from Mauritius to Senegal to compete in a qualifying match. Shortly after taking off from Libreville, their plane crashed into the ocean off Gabon. Eighteen of the nation's finest footballers perished at a time when Zambia had been emerging as a powerful force within African football, with aspirations of reaching the finals. The tragedy united the nation and Zambia continued its participation in deference to the memory of the dead. In the face of overwhelming adversity, they came desperately close to qualifying. Requiring a draw in their final match, they lost 1-0 to Morocco in highly contentious circumstances.

Eight of the 12 available European qualifying places were not determined until the final round of matches held on 17th November 1993. For the first time since all the Home Countries became eligible to compete for the World Cup, none qualified. Scotland, with five successive finals behind them, finished a poor fourth in Group 1, with Italy and Switzerland qualifying. The defeat in Italy in their penultimate match heralded the resignation of manager Andy Roxburgh. Craig Brown, his assistant, took temporary charge before being appointed as Roxburgh's successor. England gained only two points from four matches against the qualifiers, Norway and Holland.

The pressure intensified on manager Graham Taylor, who resigned a week after England's exit. The Republic of Ireland reached their second successive finals in dramatic circumstances. They required a draw against Northern Ireland in Belfast. When they conceded a 73rd-minute goal their prospects looked grim. But substitute Alan McLoughlin equalised, enabling them to join Spain, at the expense of European champions Denmark, on goal difference. Wales needed to defeat Romania in their final match at Cardiff Arms Park in order to qualify. They led 1-0, but eventually lost 2-1, missing a penalty at a critical stage. The match was marred by the tragic death of an elderly spectator who was struck by a flare fired from the stands.

Together with Belgium, Romania progressed to the finals, with Florin Raducioiu scoring nine goals during the qualifying stage. Greece remained undefeated, beating Russia, the other qualifiers, in their final match. They were coached by Alketas Panagoulias, who was in charge when they reached the 1980 European Championship finals. Hungary demonstrated that they had reached the abyss by losing at home to Iceland. In an undemanding group, they amassed a mere five points from eight games. Sweden had already qualified when France faced Bulgaria in Paris, needing only a draw to secure a place in the United States. They gained a first half lead through Eric Cantona. But a second-half fightback led to Emil Kostadinov scoring twice for the visitors, his winner in injury time. Bulgaria's qualification was a remarkable achievement given that their campaign had been troubled by conflict between the Federation and leading club Levski Sofia. Relations between the coach, Dimitar Penev, and the media were so strained that there was almost a total press blackout following a win over Finland.

Colombia were the most impressive of the nations to qualify from South America. In Group A they ended Argentina's long unbeaten run of 31 internationals with a 2-1 victory in Bogota. During the riotous post-match celebrations, 28 deaths were attributed to the aftermath. However, their initial victory was surpassed by one of the most incredible feats in World Cup history, when they defeated Argentina 5-0 in Buenos Aires. A further 78 deaths in Colombia followed the post-match hysteria. Diego Maradona emerged from retirement in a desperate attempt to revive his nation's flagging hopes. He had previously served a 15-month international ban after testing positive for cocaine whilst in Italy. Argentina unconvincingly beat the Oceania winners, Australia, 2-1 on aggregate to advance to the finals. Brazil and Bolivia qualified from Group B. But Carlos Alberto Parreira suffered the indignity of being the first coach to preside over a Brazilian defeat in the qualifying stages when his side lost 2-0 to Bolivia in La Paz.

In Africa, Nigeria, undefeated at home since 1980, won their group with a superior goal difference to the Ivory Coast. Their striker, Rashidi Yekini, scored eight goals during the qualifying phase. A controversial 1-0 victory over Zambia in their last match, played in Casablanca, enabled Morocco to clinch a place in the finals. The Zambians protested to FIFA about the standard of officiating by the Gabonese referee, Jean Diramba. They claimed they should have been awarded a penalty late in the game and implored FIFA to replay the match, but their complaint was not upheld. By defeating Zimbabwe 3-1 in Yaounde, Cameroon qualified for their third finals in four tournaments. Zimbabwe's recruitment of a witch doctor could not prevent the Indomitable Lions reaching the United States. It was a remarkable achievement considering the strife, internal politics and alleged corruption which had affected their qualifying campaign. The coach, Jules Nyongha, was dismissed and replaced by a quartet of ex-international players who worked in conjunction with a 15-strong selection committee, on an interim basis, before Jean-Pierre Sadi was appointed as the new coach.

Mexico, who were banned from the 1990 tournament for forging birth certificates during a FIFA youth tournament, qualified comfortably as CONCACAF group winners. During one of their qualifying ties they defeated St Vincent 11-0, which was the largest World Cup victory since New Zealand's 13-0 victory over Fiji in 1981. The CONCACAF qualifying tournament was marred by a terrible tragedy. Around 60,000 people congregated inside the 45,000 capacity Mateo Flores stadium for Guatemala's match against Costa Rica. A crush against a perimeter fence led to the asphyxiation of 84 spectators. Asia's 29 entries were divided into six groups of either four or five nations, which participated in round-robin tournaments. The six group winners advanced to Qatar, where the top two nations from the final group would earn a place in the United States. There was a highly dramatic conclusion to the event when Iraq equalised against Japan with only ten seconds remaining, resulting in South Korea qualifying at Japan's expense. Saudi Arabia won the group despite having their Brazilian coach, Jose Candido dismissed for ignoring an order from a Royal Prince to substitute the goalkeeper, who had conceded a first-minute goal to Iraq.

The format of the 15th World Cup remained the same as 1990, with 24 countries organised into six groups of four. The top two teams in each group automatically qualified for the sudden-death second round, together with the four best third-placed nations. Thereafter, the teams continued to proceed on a knock-out basis, with penalty shoot-outs to determine the tie in the event of a draw after extra time.

Twenty-six American communities filed formal bids to serve as hosts for the finals, and in mid-March 1992, nine cities were announced at a news conference in New York City. The venues chosen were Boston, Chicago, Dallas, Detroit, Los Angeles, New York/New Jersey, Orlando, San Francisco and Washington. The Detroit 'Silverdome' served as the first ever indoors venue for the tournament. Chicago's Soldier Field Stadium would host the inauguration ceremony on 17th June while the Rose Bowl, Pasadena, would stage the Final one month later.

The draw for the World Cup was held in Las Vegas on 16th December 1993 and produced the following groupings:

Group A: Colombia, United States, Romania, Switzerland
Group B: Brazil, Cameroon, Russia, Sweden
Group C: Bolivia, Germany, Spain, South Korea
Group D: Argentina, Bulgaria, Greece, Nigeria
Group E: Ireland, Italy, Mexico, Norway
Group F: Belgium, Holland, Morocco, Saudi Arabia

Los Angeles, San Francisco and Detroit were hosts to Groups A and B; Chicago, Boston and Dallas to Groups C and D; while New York, Orlando and Washington hosted Groups E and F.

The hosts opened their Group A campaign against Switzerland at the Detroit Pontiac Silverdome. The United States were coached by the wily Yugoslavian Bora Milutinovic, who had made a considerable impact with Costa Rica during the previous World Cup. Switzerland's first appearance in the finals since 1966 was largely attributable to the managerial skills of an Englishman, Roy Hodgson. He succeeded Uli Stielike, the former West German player, in January 1992. The temperature inside the stadium, packed to its capacity of 73,425, was 100°F. Perhaps understandably, the match was played at a sedate pace. Switzerland took the lead six minutes from half-time when Bregy scored from a free kick. With half-time approaching, Sforza fouled Harkes and the resultant free kick by Wynalda curled out of Pascolo's reach to earn a 1-1 draw.

On the same day at the Rose Bowl, Pasadena, 91,865 spectators watched the clash between Colombia and Romania. Expectations were high for a Colombian side renowned for the intricate ingenuity of their passing movements. It was, in fact, Romania who raised the pulse of the opening round with the quality of their attacking play. Florin Raducioiu, a prolific striker, beat the defenders in the 16th minute before shooting low past Cordoba. Hagi, enjoying a free rein, doubled the lead when he exploited eccentric goalkeeping with a dipped shot. A headed goal by Valencia shortly before half-time gave Colombia a vestige of hope. Raducioiu's second goal in the closing stages completed an unexpected 3-1 victory.

Switzerland's attack was fortified by the return of Adrian Knup for their next match against Romania in the Pontiac Silverdome. A resounding 4-1 victory by Switzerland rapidly dispelled the aura emanating from Romania's impressive win over much fancied Colombia. In the 15th minute a Belodedici cross from the right was fired home by Chapuisat. Hagi equalised in the 36th minute with an excellent shot which nestled into the bottom right-hand corner of the net. Switzerland restored the lead after 53 minutes when Chapuisat scored a messy goal. Romania responded with subtle, imaginative attacks which were unrewarded. A brace by Knup in the 65th and 72nd minutes brought Switzerland a 4-1 victory on the 40th anniversary of their last finals win, when they had hosted the tournament.

Colombia started their game against the United States without Gabriel Gomez. An unidentified terrorist group had threatened to bomb his family's house if he played in the match. The United States took the lead after 33 minutes when a cross from Harkes on the left was intercepted by Escobar, who steered the ball into his own net. Six minutes after the interval the United States extended their lead when Ramos played the ball forward to Stewart, who raced ahead of Perea and Cordoba to place the ball in the net. Valencia forced the ball past Meola in the final minute, but the United States won with a performance of dash and vitality.

The United States remained unchanged for their final group match against Romania. The Eastern Europeans played cautiously, and comfortably contained the hosts, who were subdued in comparison to their previous performances. Petrescu scored the only goal of the game in the 17th minute. John Harkes received his second caution of the tournament for encroaching at a Romanian free kick, which meant he would miss the first match of the knock-out stage.

Colombia defeated Switzerland 2-0 in their final game with goals by Gaviria and Lozano. For all their intricate movements and deft touches, Colombia were a deeply flawed side and exited from the tournament having singularly failed to fulfil their promise. Francisco Maturana resigned, after eight years in charge of the team. Tragically the defender Andres Escobar, was shot dead on his return to Colombia. It is speculated that his own goal in the 2-1 defeat by the United States cost the drug barons of Medellin a fortune in gambling losses. Romania, Switzerland and the United States all qualified for the next round.

Cameroon and Sweden contested the opening Group B match at the Rose Bowl, Pasadena. Bell, the Cameroon goalkeeper, misjudged Thern's free kick to present Ljung, unmarked, with a free header in the eighth minute. Cameroon equalised after half an hour when Foe intercepted Andersson's clearance and passed to Embe, who scored. Shortly after the resumption, Omam Biyik dashed between Andersson and Ravelli to give his side the lead. In the 74th minute Larsson struck a thunderous shot against the bar and Dahlin converted the rebound to complete a 2-2 draw.

A seriously depleted Russian side faced Brazil at Palo Alto. A pre-tournament rebellion against the Russian manager, Pavel Sadyrin, resulted in the loss of six key players. Brazil were never extended and took the lead after 27 minutes. An inswinging corner by Bebeto was met by Romario's foot for a simple goal. In the 53rd minute Ternavsky clumsily challenged Romario and Rai scored from the spot kick.

Brazil became the first team to reach the second stage when, three days later, they defeated Cameroon at the Stanford Stadium, San Francisco. Seven minutes from the interval, Romario controlled a pass from Dunga, accelerated past two defenders and placed the ball beyond Bell. Cameroon were reduced to ten men in the 64th minute when the full-back Rigobert Song, at 17, became the youngest ever player to be dismissed from the World Cup finals. He brought down Bebeto, who had slipped past him. Cameroon introduced Roger Milla, who at 42 became the oldest player to appear in the finals. Brazil almost immediately doubled their lead when Jorghino's cross found Santos unmarked in front of goal. Bebeto completed a 3-0 victory with a low shot from a narrow angle in the 74th minute.

Later the same day, in the humidity of the Pontiac Silverdome, Sweden conceded a fourth-minute penalty against Russia. Oleg Salenko coolly sent Ravelli the wrong way. Brolin equalised with the second penalty of the match, in the 37th minute. Gorlukovich was dismissed in the 49th minute for a tackle from behind on Martin Dahlin. Dahlin, the first black footballer to represent Sweden, scored with two spectacular diving headers to secure a 3-1 win.

In Palo Alto, Oleg Salenko, the Valencia striker who replaced the out of favour Sergei Yuran, became the first player to score five goals in the World Cup finals, during Russia's 6-1 victory over Cameroon. A reshuffled Cameroon defence, with Songo'o replacing the disenchanted Bell, could do little to contain the rampant Russians. Salenko completed a first-half hat-trick with simple goals in the 15th and 41st minutes and a penalty on the stroke of half-time. Shortly after the interval, Roger Milla became the oldest player to score in the World Cup finals, but two further strikes by Salenko and a goal by Radchenko completed the rout.

The final group game between Brazil and Sweden produced a 1-1 draw which satisfied both sides. Kennet Andersson gave Sweden a lead mid-way through the first-half. A long crossfield pass by Brolin was chested down by Andersson and the ball flicked beyond Taffarel's reach. Two minutes after the resumption, Romario equalised with a shot into the far corner of the net. Brazil topped the group, with Sweden also qualifying.

The inaugural Group C match between Bolivia and West Germany at the Soldier Field Stadium, Chicago, was preceded by an opening ceremony which provided rich entertainment. The singer Diana Ross was meant to strike the ball into an empty net, but somehow contrived to miss from two yards. The chat show star Oprah Winfrey then fell flat on her face as she left the stage – and it was completely unrehearsed.

In sweltering heat, a cautious game was decided by a Klinsmann goal after an hour's play. Matthaus delivered a pass to Hassler on the left and, with the Bolivian defence attempting an offside ploy, Hassler slipped the ball to Klinsmann, who sauntered through to score. Marco Etcheverry was dismissed in the 82nd minute. Bolivia's leading player, who came on as a substitute, had been inactive since the previous November with a knee injury. His contribution had lasted just three minutes. He was subsequently banned for his country's next two matches.

The following day, Spain met South Korea in Dallas. Spain started inauspiciously when their captain, Miguel Nadal, was sent off for fouling Ko Jeong-woon. Only solid goalkeeping by Canizares prevented South Korea from taking a first-half lead. Spain introduced their substitute, Guerrero, after the resumption, revamped their midfield and scored twice through Salinas and Goikoetxea. But Spain toiled in the oppressive heat and in the final five minutes South Korea staged a remarkable fightback, with goals by Hong Myung-bo and Seo Jung-won, to earn a 2-2 draw.

Spain gave a much more convincing performance against Germany and might have felt that their artistry should have triumphed over Germany's graft. Goikoetxea scored an extraordinary goal in the 14th minute. From the right he delivered a cross to the far post, but the ball dipped and entered the net off the inside of the far post. Two minutes after the interval Hassler's free kick was headed into the net by Klinsmann to gain a 1-1 draw.

Bolivia and South Korea participated in the first goalless draw of the tournament. Hwang Sun-hong squandered a number of good opportunities during the first half. Bolivia were reduced to ten men for the second successive match when Cristaldo departed in the 81st minute following a reckless tackle.

In Chicago, Ramallo of Bolivia struck the left-hand angle of Spain's goal in the second minute. Spain, however, took the lead after 19 minutes when Felipe was fouled and Guardiola converted the penalty. A speedy run by Sergi in the 65th minute led to an exquisite pass to Caminero, who casually slipped the ball past Trucco. A minute later Sanchez of Bolivia unleashed a 25-yard shot which deflected off Voro into the net. Caminero scored an excellent third goal to complete a 3-1 victory. Spain qualified for the second round, but would be without Caminero, who received his second caution of the tournament in stoppage time.

Two goals from Klinsmann and a strike by Riedle gave Germany an emphatic 3-0 lead against South Korea at half-time. But a spirited challenge after the resumption led to Hwang Sun-hong chipping the ball over Illgner in the 51st minute. Ten minutes later a fulminating 35-yard drive by Hong Myong-bo made it 3-2. Germany, in complete disarray, clung to victory aided by Illgner's valiant saves.

Diego Maradona completed his international rehabilitation by playing for Argentina in their opening Group D match against Greece in Boston. His influence in Mexico '86 had been inestimable and despite being injured, he had dragged his side to the 1990 Final. Since then, however, he had been banned for cocaine abuse, lost his fitness and regularly courted controversy, recently attacking journalists with an air-gun. If he were to play in three games he would break the record for World Cup appearances.

The Argentinian coach, Alfio Basile, heavily criticised for defensive tactics, adopted an unfettered approach to the game. With morale clearly raised by Maradona's presence, Argentina played some quite irresistible football. Batistuta scored after only 70 seconds, easily penetrating an inept Greek defence. Seconds before the interval, Chamot surged through two tackles and passed to Batistuta, who drove the ball beyond Minou. Fittingly, Maradona scored with a sublime, curling shot with his favoured left foot in the 59th minute. Batistuta converted a penalty in the dying seconds to notch a third goal in a 4-0 triumph.

Nigeria, generally regarded as the best side in Africa, reinforced that view with a convincing 3-0 victory over Bulgaria in the Cotton Bowl, Dallas. Nigeria established the lead midway through the first half. Predictably, the goal was scored with a header by Rashidi Yekini, a goalscoring phenomenon. Stoichkov thought he had equalised in the 38th minute with a searing shot from 35 yards, but the free kick awarded had been indirect. Four minutes later Yekini crossed for Amokachi to score. Amunike scored the third with a diving header in the 81st minute.

In their next game at the Foxboro Stadium, Boston, Nigeria took an eighth-minute lead against Argentina. Siasi collected a pass from Yekini, sent Ruggeri the wrong way, spotted Islas leaving his goal-line and lobbed to perfection. Claudio Caniggia replied with two goals in a seven-minute period midway through the first half, to defeat a robust Nigerian side coached by the Dutchman Clemens Westerhof. There was a dramatic sequel to the game with Maradona sensationally testing positive. He had taken a 'cocktail' of five banned drugs, all belonging to the ephedrine family. Ephedrine is regarded as a nasal decongestant which also acts as a stimulant. Maradona had almost certainly been using forbidden drugs to lose weight at an unnatural rate. He became only the third player since the inception of the finals 64 years ago to have been expelled for drug use. Maradona was immediately banned by both FIFA and the Argentinian FA. The tainted genius returned to Buenos Aires in disgrace, in advance of Argentina's match with Bulgaria.

Bulgaria claimed their first World Cup finals win in 18 attempts, against a Greek side who were surely the weakest in the tournament. Hristo Stoichkov scored twice with penalties and further goals by Lechkov and Borimorov completed an embarrassingly easy victory.

In a 32-year span of competing in finals, Bulgaria had not achieved a solitary victory. Yet in the space of four days they won two matches. In Dallas, Argentina, without Maradona, looked demoralised and uninspired. After a featureless first-half, Stoichkov penetrated a flat defence to score on the hour. Sirakov added a highly significant goal in injury time which enabled Bulgaria to clinch second place ahead of Argentina.

Greece offered more obdurate resistance in their final match against Nigeria. They held out until the final minute of the first-half, when George scored. Amokachi added a dramatic second goal in injury time which enabled Nigeria to win the group.

The Giants Stadium, New York, was the setting for Ireland's opening Group E match against Italy. Ireland had the backing of possibly as many as 50,000 spectators in the crowd of 73,511. They were intent on revenge after being eliminated by Italy in the 1990 quarter-finals. The only goal of the game arrived after only 12 minutes. The experienced Baresi headed the ball lethargically away from the penalty area. Houghton controlled the ball with his chest, advanced, and sighting Pagliuca well off his line, looped the ball over him with a well struck shot. Although Italy enjoyed much territorial possession thereafter, they rarely seriously tested Ireland.

Norway made their first appearance in the finals since 1938. They largely dominated their encounter with Mexico in the RFK Stadium, Washington. Mexico produced neat and intricate football with considerable imagination, but were unimposing facing a physically superior side. The match was decided by a goal six minutes from the end. Fjortoft was fouled, but commendable refereeing by Puhl of Hungary allowed the advantage. Rekdal raced on to the loose ball and shot past Campos.

The Italian press reacted angrily to Italy's defeat by Ireland. Arturo Sacchi, the coach, received stinging criticism in relation to the rigidity of his side's tactics. The hysteria was not eased midway through the first half of their match with Norway, when they were reduced to ten men. Mykland delivered a through pass to Leonhardsen which exposed the Italian defence. As Leonhardsen bore in on goal, Pagliuca, outside the penalty area, brushed the ball away from his feet with a hand. Pagliuca became the first goalkeeper to be sent off in the World Cup finals. Sacchi withdrew Roberto Baggio, replacing him with Marchegiani, his standby goalkeeper. In the 68th minute Signori swung a free kick from the right which was met by a firm header from Dino Baggio. Italy had triumphed in the face of considerable adversity.

Ireland played Mexico in the Citrus Bowl, Florida, with the temperature approaching 120°F. Short, quick passing and aggressive running again characterised the Mexican style of play. The Mexican coach, Miguel Baron, elected to replace Hugo Sanchez with the taller and more mobile Hermosillo. Just before half-time, Garcia struck a powerful, low drive past Bonner. In the 65th minute Garcia fired another excellent drive into the net.

A petulant Jack Charlton, frustrated in his attempts to field Aldridge as a substitute, had an angry confrontation with FIFA officials. Mexico could easily have extended their lead before Aldridge headed a goal from McAteer's cross with seven minutes remaining. The result meant that all four participants in Group E had an equal number of points prior to their final game.

The final two games were played simultaneously, with Ireland facing Norway in New York and Italy meeting Mexico in Washington.

Ireland and Norway produced a goalless stalemate and some of the worst football in the competition. Ireland dominated the first half with Norway rarely venturing across the half-way line. Norway were slightly more enterprising after the interval but the match provided few goal-scoring opportunities.

The confrontation between Italy and Mexico was also a

thoroughly drab affair. The first half was barren and almost devoid of incident. But the much vilified Sacchi appeared to have worked a master-stroke with the introduction of Daniele Massaro after the interval. Milan's leading scorer controlled Albertini's through-ball on his chest before planting a low shot beneath Campos. Mexico were facing elimination, but ten minutes later they were level with an accurate shot by Bernal. The 1-1 draw confirmed Mexico as group winners ahead of Ireland on goal difference who, in turn, were runners-up by dint of having beaten Italy. Norway were unluckily eliminated on the basis of scoring fewer goals.

The opening Group F match took place at the Citrus Bowl Stadium, Orlando. Belgium and Morocco had to endure oppressive humidity and a 100°F temperature. Belgium scored the only goal in the 11th minute from a Marc Degryse header. Khalil Azmi, the Moroccan goalkeeper, advanced from his goal too late, allowing Degryse, unchallenged, to score. Morocco surprised their opponents with their strong display and were unlucky when Mohamed Chaouch struck the crossbar on two occasions.

Saudi Arabia's players received £100,000 each plus a Mercedes for qualifying. They played uninhibited and imaginative football against a Dutch side who were extremely sluggish in defence. A free kick by Al Bishi found Amin darting behind static defenders to head past De Goey. Five minutes after the interval, Jonk received a pass from Roy and unleashed a 30-yard shot which found the net. With only three minutes remaining, Al Deayea, the Saudi goalkeeper, failed to intercept a centre from Frank de Boer and Gaston Taument headed into an unguarded net to give the wobbly Dutch a narrow win.

The keen rivalry between Low Country neighbours Belgium and Holland produced a match of high entertainment at the Citrus Bowl, Orlando. Holland enjoyed the bulk of the possession and there was a familiarity about their controlled passing. But their wasteful finishing was a source of embarrassment. Preud'homme, the Belgian goalkeeper, gave a flawless performance as he consistently repelled a series of menacing Dutch attacks. Holland were to rue their missed opportunities when in the 66th minute Rijkaard failed to head clear a corner and Albert shot through the legs of Wouters into the net.

On the same day, the first-ever all-Arab finals clash took place between Morocco and Saudi Arabia. Al-jaber converted a penalty to give Saudi Arabia the lead after seven minutes. Mohamed Chaouch equalised after 26 minutes. Saudi Arabia re-established their advantage as half-time approached. A 30-yard shot by Fuad Amin was diverted by the goalkeeper, Khalil Azmi, into his own net for an embarrassing winner. Morocco had dominated the game but Mohamed Chaouch squandered a number of chances.

Dennis Bergkamp scored just before half-time to give Holland the lead against Morocco. Bergkamp, with an outrageous piece of skill, nipped between two defenders, took the ball on his right foot, transferred it to his left and lifted it over the goalkeeper. Two minutes after the interval, substitute Hadji crossed for Nader to score a simple goal. Daoud almost gave Morocco the lead when he struck a wicked free kick from 35 yards. De Goey changed direction in mid-air to combat the swerve and produced a marvellous save. Roy replaced Van Vossen as a substitute and scored a critical goal with 12 minutes remaining. Bergkamp exploited a miskicked clearance and passed to Roy, unmarked, who shot low into the right-hand corner of the net.

Belgium yielded their first goal of the tournament to Saudi Arabia in Washington. Only five minutes had elapsed when Saeed Owairan, in his own half, hurtled past Medved, swerved wide of De Wolf, left Smidts in his wake and fired a searing right-foot shot past Preud'homme. Although Belgium attacked forcefully thereafter, Saudi Arabia defended aggressively and looked dangerous when they mounted penetrating counter-attacks. The 1-0 victory enabled Saudi Arabia to finish second to Holland. Belgium qualified as one of the best third-placed teams.

Romania, Switzerland, United States, Brazil, Sweden, Germany, Spain, Nigeria, Bulgaria, Argentina, Mexico, Ireland, Italy, Holland, Saudi Arabia and Belgium progressed to the second round and produced the following ties:

Germany v Belgium
Spain v Switzerland
Saudi Arabia v Sweden
Romania v Argentina
Holland v Ireland
Brazil v United States
Nigeria v Italy
Mexico v Bulgaria

Less oppressive weather, in the form of wind and rain, greeted Belgium and Germany in Chicago. Germany started brightly, with Matthaus surging forward in the fifth minute and passing to Voller, who promptly scored. Two minutes later an ill-judged header by Voller allowed Grun to equalise. Within three minutes Voller passed to Klinsmann, who completed a remarkable scoring spree in the first ten minutes.

The restoration of Voller appeared to be a masterstroke by the coach Bertie Vogts, as Voller enjoyed a ruthless partnership with Klinsmann. It came as no surprise when Voller gave the Germans a 3-1 lead in the 39th minute. A better balanced German midfield dominated the match. Klinsmann had a couple of outstanding efforts thwarted by Preud'homme during the second half.

Belgium should have been awarded a penalty midway through the second half when Helmer blatantly pulled down Weber, but referee Rothlisberger of Switzerland missed the incident. A late goal by Albert flattered Belgium, who were comprehensively beaten.

Sutter had to withdraw with a broken toe immediately before Switzerland's match with Spain in Washington. Switzerland felt somewhat aggrieved by the loss of their first goal after 15 minutes. Chapuisat was harshly fouled by Nadal and, as the Swiss appealed, Hierro burst through their defence to score. As the Swiss pursued an equaliser, Spain were able to launch penetrating counter-attacks. In the 74th minute Sergi created an opening for Luis Enrique to score. With only four minutes remaining, Pascolo upended Ferrer and Berguiristain converted the penalty to complete a 3-0 victory.

In Dallas, Sweden quickly established a lead over Saudi Arabia. After five minutes Andersson delivered a deep centre which Al Khlaui failed to clear. Dahlin exploited the situation to head the ball into the net. Sweden were dominant, but their second goal did not arrive until the 51st minute, when Andersson beat Al Deayea with a low shot into the right-hand corner. With five minutes remaining, Al Ghesheyan scored a spectacular goal when he twisted inside Ljung and struck a marvellous shot into the roof of the net. Two minutes later Andersson scored his second goal. Sweden had reached the quarter-finals for the first time since they hosted the World Cup in 1958.

Argentina and Romania contested the most outstanding match of the tournament at the Rose Bowl, Pasadena. Maradona was not the only notable absentee. Claudio Caniggia was supposedly injured and Florin Raducioiu suspended. Half the crowd rose in excited animation before the game in response to the presence of Maradona in the broadcasting box. Argentina began at a frightening pace. Simeone penetrated the Romanian defence with a mazy run reminiscent of Maradona. He passed to Balbo who, in hesitating, missed a glorious chance. Completely against the run of play, Romania scored in the 11th minute. From a free kick 35 yards from goal, Dumitrescu swung the ball into the far corner of the net. Four minutes later Argentina were level. Batistuta tore through the defence before being fouled by Prodan. Batistuta composed himself to score with the spot-kick. Romania restored their lead within two minutes. Dumitrescu, deep in defence, dispersed the ball to Hagi on the right touchline. Hagi advanced 50 yards before directing an exquisite, uncannily precise pass to Dumitrescu, who flicked the ball past Islas. The pace of the match continued unabated, with both sides committed to attack. Popescu had two efforts thwarted by Islas and Dumitrescu's goalbound shot was cleared off the line. In the 56th minute

Dumitrescu pounced on a loose ball and sprinted forward. With Selymes screaming for the ball, Dumitrescu nonchalantly awaited Hagi's arrival. The 'Maradona of the Carpathians' fired the ball into the net. With 15 minutes remaining, Caceres shot from 40 yards. Prunea failed to hold the ball and Balbo seized onto it to reduce the arrears. An exhilarating match ended with Romania deservedly reaching the quarter-finals for the first time in their history.

In Orlando, two defensive errors by Ireland led to their elimination by Holland. In the 11th minute Phelan attempted a headed back-pass which lacked pace and fell to Overmars. Overmars crossed and Bergkamp shot low past Bonner. Holland dominated the game with possession play and the match was effectively ended in the 41st minute. Jonk produced a right-foot drive from 30 yards. Bonner half-stopped the ball, which spun from his hands and looped over his shoulder into the net.

In Palo Alto the United States faced Brazil on Independence Day. An anticipated Brazilian landslide never materialised as the aspiring champions produced a wholly unconvincing performance. The first opportunity of the game fell to the United States in the 12th minute. Ramos evaded his marker and swiftly released the ball to Dooley, who narrowly missed from an acute angle. Two minutes from the interval, Leonardo committed an ugly foul, elbowing Ramos on the touchline. Ramos departed with a minor fracture of the skull, Leonardo with a deep sense of shame. In the 74th minute the deadlock was finally broken when Romario conjured a goal for Bebeto. With only minutes remaining, the United States were also reduced to ten men when Clavijo committed a second bookable offence.

In the Foxboro Stadium, Boston, Nigeria attempted to emulate Cameroon in 1990, by reaching the quarter-finals. Their opponents, Italy, conceded a goal after 26 minutes. A corner by George ricocheted off Maldini and Amunlike scored. Dino Baggio appeared for the second-half and almost scored immediately with a shot which struck the post. In the 75th minute

Zola upended himself following a lunge from Nwanu. On being denied a penalty, he harshly challenged the Nigerian defender and was dismissed. With only two minutes left, Mussi advanced and passed to Roberto Baggio, who found space to beat Rufai low to his left. The match was decided in the 12th minute of extra time when Eguavoen fouled Benarrivo and Roberto Baggio scored with the resultant penalty.

The final second-round tie between Bulgaria and Mexico was the victim of some erratic and inconsistent refereeing by Al Sharif of Syria. Stoichkov gave Bulgaria the lead after only six minutes. Aspe equalised with a contentious penalty ten minutes later. The game was punctuated with fouls and degenerated into a thoroughly wretched affair. The battle of attrition was finally decided on penalties, after extra time had failed to yield a goal. Inept penalty taking by Mexico allowed Bulgaria to win the shoot-out 3-1.

The quarter-finals produced the following ties:

Italy v Spain
Brazil v Holland
Bulgaria v Germany
Romania v Sweden

Seven of the eight quarter-finalists were European nations, a feat not equalled since 1958, when Brazil proceeded to win the World Cup.

Italy's precarious existence continued as they rode their luck against Spain in the Foxboro Stadium, Boston. Dino Baggio gave Italy the lead after 26 minutes with a coruscating drive from 30 yards. Spain equalised in the 58th minute when a shot by Caminero deflected off Benarrivo and looped over the head of Pagliuca. Spain attacked in pursuit of a winning goal. In a second half largely dominated by Spain, Salinas had an opportunity to win the match. He outwitted the Italian defence but, with only Pagliuca to beat, he hesitated and allowed his shot to be deflected by the goalkeeper's out-stretched leg. It proved to be a very costly miss as, with only two minutes remaining, Roberto Baggio pounced on a lob by Signori and adeptly shot past Zubizarreta from a tight angle.

In Dallas, Brazil and Holland contested a largely uneventful first half. The match came alive in the 52nd minute when a brilliant pass from Dunga released Bebeto on the left. His cross was met perfectly by Romario, who half-volleyed into the net. Bebeto controversially doubled the lead ten minutes later with Romario in an offside position. The goal signalled a spirited fightback by the Dutch. Bergkamp scored two minutes later. With only 14 minutes left, a corner by Overmars should have been claimed by Taffarel, but Winter raced in to meet the cross. Brazil calmly re-asserted themselves and Branco scored the decisive goal in the 81st minute when he struck a venomous free kick from 30 yards.

The Giants Stadium, New York, was the setting for the confrontation between World Cup holders Germany and Bulgaria. In the 12th minute Sirakov had a cross-shot palmed clear by Illgner. Stoichkov then side-stepped Wagner's lunge and hooked the ball back to Balakov, whose low drive struck the post. Klinsmann almost scored with a diving header midway through the first half. The ball ricocheted off Mikhailov, who only just managed to prevent it entering the net. Three minutes after the interval, Letchkov was adjudged to have fouled Klinsmann in the penalty area. Matthaus, making his record-equalling 21st finals appearance, scored from the spot-kick. Moller almost doubled the lead, striking a post. In the 75th minute Moller fouled Stoichkov. Stoichkov's left foot curled the ball over the defensive wall as a helpless Illgner watched it nestle in the net. Three minutes later Yankov delivered a ball into the goalmouth and Letchkov spectacularly hurled himself to score with an improbable header into the top left-hand corner. Bulgaria's inventive and imaginative football had out-manoeuvred a powerful but rigid German side.

The final quarter-final tie between Romania and Sweden at Palo Alto was the only one to extend to extra time. Sweden almost scored in the fourth minute when Dahlin headed a cross by Ingesson against the post. Hagi was well marshalled by the Swedish defence. The match degenerated into a dreary midfield struggle. Only in the final 11 minutes was the torpor relieved. A free kick by Mild anticipated Brolin's clever run behind the Romanian defensive wall. Brolin struck a shot high into the roof of the net from a tight angle. Only seconds remained when the Swedish defence failed to clear a Hagi free kick and Raducioiu equalised from close range. In the 11th minute of extra time, Raducioiu scored a second goal. Sweden's hopes appeared to recede when Schwarz was dismissed for a second bookable offence shortly afterwards. But with five minutes left, Kennet Andersson headed a goal, thus forcing a dramatic penalty shoot-out which Sweden won 5-4.

The semi-finals paired Bulgaria with Italy in the Giants Stadium, New York, and Brazil met Sweden at the Rose Bowl Stadium, Los Angeles.

Italy rapidly established complete control over Bulgaria. Roberto Baggio scored two goals in the space of five minutes midway through the first half to destroy Bulgaria's dream of becoming the first Balkan country to contest a World Cup Final. In the 21st minute Baggio created an opening when he collected a throw-in, stealthily strode past two players and curled a perfect shot inside the post. Albertini then provided a finely weighted through-pass for Baggio to double the lead. Bulgaria had to endure an onslaught of inspired, attacking football. Albertini struck a post from 25 yards and Mikhailov made an outstanding save. Stoichkov gave Bulgaria a modicum of hope when he converted a penalty a minute from the interval. The second half was an anti-climax largely devoid of incident. Italy had reached their fifth World Cup Final. Already comparisons were being made between Baggio, who had scored five times in the tournament, and Rossi, whose six goals made such an impact in 1982 when Italy won the World Cup.

Brazil completely dominated their opponents in the Rose Bowl. Sweden appeared to be affected by the heavy toll of their gruelling two-hour quarter-final encounter with Romania. Romario, Zinho and Mazinho peppered the Swedish goal during the first half-hour but Brazil had difficulty translating their supremacy into goals. Ravelli, the eccentric goalkeeper, helped give the illusion of a close game with an excellent display. Sweden's cause was not assisted by the dismissal of Thern in the 63rd minute. Brazil eventually scored with a powerful and precise header from Romario in the 81st minute.

Sweden produced their best football of the tournament against Bulgaria in the third place play-off at the Rose Bowl Stadium. They ran amok during the first half, scoring four goals. Brolin started the romp in eight minutes. He then created a second goal for Mild after half an hour. Brolin was also instrumental in the third goal, initiating the move which led to Larsson scoring. Andersson headed a fourth goal two minutes later. Unfancied Sweden had finished a creditable third. Bulgaria departed satisfied that they had caused the biggest surprise in the tournament with their defeat of Germany.

The World Cup Final at the Rose Bowl, Pasadena, was a rematch of the 1970 competition's wonderful conclusion. The likelihood of the 1994 Final resembling the exquisite feast of football served up by Pele, Jairzinho, Tostao, Gerson and Rivelino was thought to be slim, given that the current Brazilian side were much more prosaic and pragmatic. Nevertheless, an intriguing match was anticipated. Brazil possessed Bebeto and Romario, both of whom were prolific goalscorers. Roberto Baggio, like Romario, had scored five times in the tournament. In Maldini, Italy had the one defender capable of suppressing the ruthless skills of Romario. When Milan outplayed Barcelona in the European Cup Final, it was Maldini who blunted the Brazilian 'assassin'.

A crowd of 94,194 watched Brazil set the pace and provide most of the attacking movements. In the 16th minute Romario advanced and passed precisely to Bebeto, who drove the ball towards the near post. The perceptive Maldini blocked the shot. Two minutes later a defence-splitting pass by Baresi was seized on by Massaro, who was thwarted by Taffarel. A Branco free kick was then scrambled clear by Pagliuca. The second half was largely uneventful until the 75th minute.

Mauro Silva struck a cross-shot from 30 yards which slipped through Pagliuca's hands, bounced onto the left-hand post and sprang back to the grateful goalkeeper. He responded by kissing the post. The match remained goalless at the end of 90 minutes. In the third minute of extra time, Pagliuca misjudged a Cafu cross, presenting Bebeto with an open goal which he contrived to miss. Three minutes later Taffarel was slow to react to a 25-yard drive by Roberto Baggio, but recovered to tip the ball over the bar.

The lottery of penalties would decide the fate of the 15th World Cup. Baresi, who had received treatment for cramp only a few minutes earlier, lifted the first over the bar. Pagliuca then saved from Marcio Santos. Albertini, Romario, Evani and Branco all scored, to give a 2-2 aggregate. Massaro's over-deliberate penalty was saved by Taffarel. Dunga converted to give Brazil a 3-2 advantage. The responsibility to keep Italy alive rested with Roberto Baggio. His shot sailed over the bar, a tired response from someone who had been carrying a hamstring injury throughout the game. Brazil had become champions for a record fourth time, and the first time since 1970. The historic shoot-out was a wretched way to decide what had been one of the better tournaments, watched by a record-breaking average attendance of 68,604.

Results: USA 1994

Group A

Switzerland	1	United States	1
Romania	3	Colombia	1
Switzerland	4	Romania	1
United States	2	Colombia	1
Romania	1	United States	0
Colombia	2	Switzerland	0

	P	W	D	L	F	A	Pts
					Goals		
Romania	3	2	0	1	5	5	6
Switzerland	3	1	1	1	6	4	4
United States	3	1	1	1	3	3	4
Colombia	3	1	0	2	4	6	3

Group B

Cameroon	2	Sweden	2
Brazil	2	Russia	0
Brazil	3	Cameroon	0
Sweden	3	Russia	1
Russia	6	Cameroon	1
Brazil	1	Sweden	1

	P	W	D	L	F	A	Pts
					Goals		
Brazil	3	2	1	0	6	1	7
Sweden	3	1	2	0	6	4	5
Russia	3	1	0	2	7	6	3
Cameroon	3	0	1	2	3	11	1

Group C

Germany	1	Bolivia	0
South Korea	2	Spain	2
Germany	1	Spain	1
Bolivia	0	South Korea	0
Spain	3	Bolivia	1
Germany	3	South Korea	2

	P	W	D	L	Goals F	A	Pts
Germany	3	2	1	0	5	3	7
Spain	3	1	2	0	6	4	5
South Korea	3	0	2	1	4	5	2
Bolivia	3	0	1	2	1	4	1

Group D

Argentina	4	Greece	0
Nigeria	3	Bulgaria	0
Argentina	2	Nigeria	1
Bulgaria	4	Greece	0
Bulgaria	2	Argentina	0
Nigeria	2	Greece	0

	P	W	D	L	Goals F	A	Pts
Nigeria	3	2	0	1	6	2	6
Bulgaria	3	2	0	1	6	3	6
Argentina	3	2	0	1	6	3	6
Greece	3	0	0	3	0	10	0

Group E

Ireland	1	Italy	0
Norway	1	Mexico	0
Italy	1	Norway	0
Mexico	2	Ireland	1
Ireland	0	Norway	0
Italy	1	Mexico	1

	P	W	D	L	Goals F	A	Pts
Mexico	3	1	1	1	3	3	4
Ireland	3	1	1	1	2	2	4
Italy	3	1	1	1	2	2	4
Norway	3	1	1	1	1	1	4

Group F

Belgium	1	Morocco	0
Holland	2	Saudi Arabia	1
Belgium	1	Holland	0
Saudi Arabia	2	Morocco	1
Holland	2	Morocco	1
Saudi Arabia	1	Belgium	0

	P	W	D	L	Goals F	A	Pts
Holland	3	2	0	1	4	3	6
Saudi Arabia	3	2	0	1	4	3	6
Belgium	3	2	0	1	2	1	6
Morocco	3	0	0	3	2	5	0

Second Round

Germany	3	Belgium	2
Spain	3	Switzerland	0
Sweden	3	Saudi Arabia	1
Romania	3	Argentina	2
Holland	2	Ireland	0
Brazil	1	United States	0
Italy	2	Nigeria	1*
Bulgaria	1	Mexico	1**

 *(after extra time, 1-1 at 90 minutes)
**(after extra time, 1-1 at 90 minutes)
Bulgaria won 3-1 on penalties

Quarter-finals

Italy	2	Spain	1
Brazil	3	Holland	2
Bulgaria	2	Germany	1
Sweden	2	Romania	2*

*(After extra time, 1-1 at 90 minutes)
Sweden won 5-4 on penalties

Semi-finals

Italy	2	Bulgaria	1
Brazil	1	Sweden	0

Third-place match

Sweden	4	Bulgaria	0

Final

Brazil	0	Italy	0

(after extra time) Brazil won 3-2 on penalties

Brazil: Taffarel, Jorginho (Cafu), Aldair, Marcio Santos, Branco, Mazinho (Viola), Dunga, Mauro Silva, Zinho, Romario, Bebeto

Italy: Pagliuca, Mussi (Apolloni), Maldini, Baresi, Benarrivo, Berti, Albertini, D. Baggio (Evani), Donadoni, R. Baggio, Massaro

ENGLAND
WINNERS OF THE 1966 WORLD CUP

SCOTLAND
WORLD CUP 1998

Line up:
Back row: 8 Craig Burley (Celtic), 4 Colin Calderwood
(Tottenham Hotspur), 9 Gordon Durie (Rangers),
22 Christian Dailly (Derby County), 1 Jim Leighton (Aberdeen),
5 Colin Hendry (Blackburn Rovers).
Front row: 10 Darren Jackson (Celtic), 7 Kevin Gallacher
(Blackburn Rovers), 3 Tom Boyd (Celtic),
11 John Collins (Monaco), 14 Paul Lambert (Celtic)

ENGLAND
WORLD CUP 1998

Line up:
Back row: 4 Paul Ince (Liverpool), 2 Sol Campbell (Tottenham Hotspur), 5 Tony Adams (Arsenal), 14 Darren Anderton (Tottenham Hotspur), 1 David Seaman (Arsenal), 6 Gareth Southgate (Aston Villa).
Front row: 10 Teddy Sheringham (Manchester United), 8 David Batty (Newcastle United), 3 Graeme Le Saux (Chelsea), 16 Paul Scholes (Manchester United), 9 Alan Shearer (Newcastle United)

ITALY
WORLD CUP 1998

Line up:

Back row: 3 Paolo Maldini, 21 Christian Vieri, 2 Giuseppe Bergomi,
12 Gianluca Pagliuca, 11 Dino Baggio.
Front row: 10 Alessandro Del Piero, 4 Fabio Cannavaro,
14 Luigi Di Biagio, 17 Francesco Moriero, 9 Demetrio Albertini,
5 Alessandro Costacurta.

HOLLAND
WORLD CUP 1998

Line up:

Back row: 1 Edwin Van der Sar, 8 Dennis Bergkamp, 3 Jaap Stam,
6 Wim Jonk, 11 Philip Cocu, 9 Patrick Kluivert.
Front row: 16 Edgar Davids, 2 Michael Reiziger, 4 Frank de Boer,
12 Boudewijn Zenden, 7 Ronald de Boer

BRAZIL
WORLD CUP 1998

Line up:

Back row: 1 Taffarel, 5 Cesar Sampaio, 10 Rivaldo, 3 Aldair, 4 Junior Baiano, 2 Cafu.
Front row: 9 Ronaldo, 6 Roberto Carlos, 18 Leonardo, 20 Bebeto, 8 Dunga.

CROATIA
WORLD CUP 1998

FRANCE V BRAZIL - THE FINAL
WORLD CUP 1998
French star Zinedine Zidane heading
home against Brazil.

FRANCE

WORLD CUP 1998 WINNERS

including Chelsea players Frank Leboeuf (front left)
and Marcel Desailly (front right).

WORLD CUP WINNING SQUAD:

Goalkeepers: 16 Fabien Barthez, 1 Bernard Lama,
22 Lionel Charbonnier.
Defenders: 5 Laurent Blanc, 2 Vincent Candela,
8 Marcel Desailly, 18 Frank Leboeuf,
3 Bixente Lizarazu, 15 Lilian Thuram.
Midfielders: 14 Alain Boghossian, 7 Didier Deschamps,
17 Emmanuel Petit, 13 Bernard Diomede, 6 Youri Djorkaeff,
19 Christian Karembeu, 11 Robert Pires,
4 Patrick Vieira, 10 Zinedine Zidane.
Forwards: 12 Thierry Henry, 21 Christophe Dugarry,
9 Stephane Guivarc'h, 20 David Trezeguet.

1998

The World Cup of 1998 in France was the largest ever, being the first time that 32 nations participated; as in 1982, when the number of teams was increased from 16 to 24, people asked whether this would be too many. In practice this was not a problem; the tournament was one of the closest ever and popularity increased again. The total television audience for the tournament was estimated to be 37 billion viewers (an average of 578 million viewers per game); the final was watched live by 2 billion people. The matches were spread out throughout France in ten stadia; the opening game and the final were held in the fabulous new Stade de France, north of Paris. Europe provided 15 finalists, Africa 5, South Amerca 5, Asia 4 and North and Central America 3. The eight four-team groups were spread geographically and all but one of them contained two Europeans, one from the Americas and one from Africa or Asia.

In Group A, Norway managed to beat Brazil in their last match so they qualified for the next round (as did Brazil); this was the first time Brazil had been defeated in a first round match for 32 years. In Group B Italy and Chile went through. Group C contained host nation France, who won all their games and easily outclassed the rest of their group (Denmark also went through). In Group D, Spain was unable to reach the second round, despite a 6-1 win over Bulgaria: Nigeria and Paraguay qualified for the next round. Group E included South Korea, who were again unable to win a World Cup match; Holland and Mexico went through ahead of Belgium, who was undefeated. The German and Yugoslav teams went through in Group F; the USA having lost all its games. In Group G Romania won its match against England 2-1; both teams qualified. In Group H Argentina and Croatia qualified; Argentina won all the games they played without yielding a goal.

In the second round, 10 of the 16 nations who had qualified were Europeans. A goal by Christian Vieri allowed Italy to beat Norway 1-0. Ronaldo scored two goals in Brazil's match against Chile, which they won 4-1. The Chilean goal was scored by star Marcelo Salas, his 4th goal of the World Cup. When France played Paraguay, Laurent Blanc played the winning golden goal in the 113th minute. Denmark, Germany, Holland and Croatia all went through to the third round. In the last match of the second round there were two goals on each side when Argentina played England at Saint-Etienne: the match went to penalties. There was a penalty for each team in the first ten minutes. Michael Owen's goal for England, possibly the best of the tournament, gave them the lead until Javier Zanetti scored just before half-time to equalise. In the second half there were dramatic scenes when David Beckham was sent off for kicking Diego Simeone and Sol Campbell's goal was disallowed; Carlos Roa saved England's final spot kick from David Batty, and allowed Argentina through to the final. This match was commonly agreed to be one of the best World Cup matches of all time.

In the third round there were only two non-European teams. France won their game against Italy on penalties (it was the third World Cup running in which Italy had gone out on penalties). Brazil scored 3-2 over Denmark and

Holland 2-1 over Argentina, with a stunning goal by Bergkamp in the last minute. Seconds earlier there was a miserable ending for Ortega, who was sent off for head-butting the Dutch goal keeper van der Sar. The Croatian team - playing in the World Cup for the first time - proved a force to be reckoned with when they beat Germany 3-0.

In the semi-finals, Ronaldo gave Brazil a lead in their match against Holland, but Kluivert equalised just three minutes before the end. The match went to penalties: Ronald de Boer missed the decisive penalty for Holland so Brazil went through to the final again. In the other semi-final, between France and Croatia, France was trailing 0-1 when Thuram scored twice and France was in to its first ever World Cup final. Thuram had never scored for France before. In the Third Place match between Holland and Croatia, Davor Suker scored his sixth goal of the tournament, winning the match for Romania and making Suker the top goal scorer of the 1998 World Cup.

Before the final, the first ever between a defending champion and the host nation, people asked whether the untried enthusiams of the French team, spurred on by their home audience, could prevail over the confidence and experience of the Brazilian team. This was Brazil's sixth World Cup final and they had been champions in four of the last ten World Cups; they had lost only once, in 1950, when Uruguay ousted them. They had, however, lost to Norway (1-2) in their final group game of 1998 so were not looking quite as invincible as they might have liked. However, they were not likely to be phased by facing an overwhelmingly partisan crowd when it came to the big match. "At this moment," defender Roberto Carlos said two days before the final, "our team has no weaknesses." Zagallo was confident too: "France only has

Zidane; Brazil has several like him."

In contrast, France was in the final for the first time after 68 years and many thought it was national fervour that had got them there. Although they had good results in their first round matches (they scored more goals than any other country in the first round), these were in matches against Saudi Arabia and South Africa, hardly forces to be reckoned with. There hadn't been many goals in their matches after that (three goals from the second round through to the semi-finals, against Brazil's eight) and it was the previously goal-less Lilian Thuram who had hit the two that had taken them past Croatia in the semi-final.

The final was held at the Stade de France on 12 July. Before the match there had been a lot of media coverage of Ronaldo, reported to be suffering from convulsions and rushed to hospital within hours of the final. Zagallo was later criticised for allowing Ronaldo to play. It was Zinedine Zidane who became star of the match, scoring with a header in the 27th minute, and then another in the last minute of the first half, from a rightwing corner from Youri Djorkaeff. In the second half, when Brazil was under extreme pressure to pull back the match, Ronaldo had a chance to take a goal at the 56th minute, but his close-range shot was held by Barthez. A little later the Brazilian team had another chance when Barthez left the goal wide open for a shot from Bebeto. Bebeto took a direct aim but Desailly saved it. France replaced Christian Karembeu with Alain Boghossian and Guivarc'h with Christophe Dugarry. In the 68th minute Marcel Desailly cut down Cafu and was expelled for his second yellow card (his first had come early in the second half of the match, for dissent). Although the French team played on with ten men, Emmanuel Petit managed a third goal in the last minute. When the referee, the Moroccan Belqola - the first African ever to officiate at a World Cup final - blew the final whistle the crowd erupted and later that night the Champs Elysées and Arc de Triomphe were at the centre of the widespread celebrations, which went on all night. Fans held tricolour flags chanting "Allez Les Bleus", fireworks flared in the sky and there was a fabulous light show at the Arc de Triomphe.

After the match it was widely agreed that the French had won because they were the best team players; they may not have had the individual talents of the Brazilian team, but they played team football based on defence, managing perfectly to prevent Bebeto, Denilson, Ronaldo and the others who tried from making a run at the goal. The French team's back line, the "four musketeers" - Laurent Blanc, Marcel Desailly, Bixente Lizarazu and Lilian Thuram - had only given away two goals in over seven matches in the run up to the final. "We won the final because we wanted it the most," Jacquet said. "It was the result of hard work. We really worked as a team. There was good will and friendship between all of us. "We played better and better because we had confidence and we proved we had great players."

The last three World Cup wins - France 1998, Brazil 1994 and West Germany in 1990 - have all had the qualities of team playing, the winning teams constantly working to prevent their opponents get into the match. Even when the French team's main defender Desailly went off the French players maintained their defence, kept their cool, and pushed Brazil to the outer lanes, which they then cut off at the corners, preventing the Brazilians making any clear shots at the goal. The Brazil coach Mario Zagallo, closely involved in his team's previous four world title wins, said after the match: "Brazil lost the final in the first half. In the second half we did everything we could but we were not able to make up the difference." Brazil has never experienced a 0-3 score before in a world championship.

Zinedine Zidane - known as Zizou - is the son of Algerian immigrants who grew up in a rough area of Marseilles. He was one of several players in the French team who were born in or whose family came from Algeria, Armenia, Ghana, Guadeloupe or New Caledonia. In 1996 Jean-Marie Le Pen, France's right-wing National Front party leader, argued that it was "artificial to bring players from abroad and call it the French team," even though every member of the World Cup side had been a French citizen for years. However, as the French team progressed through the World Cup the French became more and more proud of the racial and cultural mix of their team. Although Zidane had been acclaimed as one of the best players for the French since 1995, he had never performed well in the big games. Even in this World Cup he had been thrown out of France's second game for raking his cleats when a Saudi Arabia player fell. He was suspended for two games, then returned to play in his team's third round match against Italy. He played unexceptionally until the final: "It's true that I wanted to score a goal, but two you can hardly imagine," Zidane said after the win over Brazil.

Lilian Thuram, Les Bleus' right back and native of Guadeloupe, became a national hero in the match against Croatia when he scored both the team's goals. There had been no doubt about his skill as a defender, but he had never scored in the 36 previous games when playing for France. Known as a keen reader of philosophy, after his second goal in that semi-final he took up the pose of Rodin's The Thinker on the turf of the stadium. "You write and write about me and Ronaldo," Zidane said in the week after the final, "but you don't even see that the greatest footballer of all is right in front of you: Lilian Thuram."

Some statistics:

Number of games	64
Total goals scored	171
Average per game	2.67
Sendings off	22
Own goals	4
Total attendance	2,775,400
Average attendance	43,366

Top scorers:

Davor Suker (CRO)	6 goals
Gabriel Batistuta (ARG)	5 goals
Christian Vieri (ITA)	5 goals
Marcelo Salas (CHI)	4 goals
Ronaldo (BRA)	4 goals
Luis Hernandez (MEX)	4 goals

Results: France 1998

Group A

Brazil	2			Scotland	1
Morocco	2			Norway	2
Scotland	1			Norway	1
Brazil	3			Morocco	0
Brazil	1			Norway	2
Scotland	0			Morocco	3

	P	W	D	L	F	A	Pts
Brazil	3	2	0	1	6	3	6
Norway	3	1	2	0	5	4	5
Morocco	3	1	1	1	5	5	4
Scotland	3	0	1	2	2	6	1

Group B

Italy	2			Chile	2
Cameroon	1			Austria	1
Chile	1			Austria	1
Italy	3			Cameroon	0
Chile	1			Cameroon	1
Italy	2			Austria	1

	P	W	D	L	F	A	Pts
Italy	3	2	1	0	7	3	7
Chile	3	0	3	0	4	4	3
Austria	3	0	2	1	3	4	2
Cameroon	3	0	2	1	2	5	2

Group C

Saudi Arabia	0		Denmark	1
France	3		South Africa	0
South Africa	1		Denmark	1
France	4		Saudi Arabia	0
France	2		Denmark	1
South Africa	2		Saudi Arabia	2

	P	W	D	L	Goals F	A	Pts
France	3	3	0	0	9	1	9
Denmark	3	1	1	1	3	3	4
South Africa	3	0	2	1	3	6	2
Saudi Arabia	3	0	1	2	2	7	1

Group D

Paraguay	0		Bulgaria	0
Spain	2		Nigeria	3
Nigeria	1		Bulgaria	0
Spain	0		Paraguay	0
Nigeria	1		Paraguay	3
Spain	6		Bulgaria	1

	P	W	D	L	Goals F	A	Pts
Nigeria	3	2	0	1	5	5	6
Paraguay	3	1	2	0	3	1	5
Spain	3	1	1	1	8	4	4
Bulgaria	3	0	1	2	1	7	1

Group E

South Korea	1	Mexico	3
Holland	0	Belgium	0
Belgium	2	Mexico	2
Holland	5	South Korea	0
Belgium	1	South Korea	1
Holland	2	Mexico	2

	P	W	D	L	Goals F	A	Pts
Holland	3	1	2	0	7	2	5
Mexico	3	1	2	0	7	5	5
Belgium	3	0	3	0	3	3	3
South Korea	3	0	1	2	2	9	1

Group F

Yugoslavia	1	Iran	0
Germany	2	USA	0
Germany	2	Yugoslavia	2
USA	1	Iran	2
Germany	2	Iran	0
USA	0	Yugoslavia	1

	P	W	D	L	Goals F	A	Pts
Germany	3	2	1	0	6	2	7
Yugoslavia	3	2	1	0	4	2	7
Iran	3	1	0	2	2	4	3
USA	3	0	0	3	1	5	0

Group G

England	2	Tunisia	0
Romania	1	Colombia	0
Colombia	1	Tunisia	0
Romania	2	England	1
Colombia	0	England	2
Romania	1	Tunisia	1

	P	W	D	L	Goals F	A	Pts
Romania	3	2	1	0	4	2	7
England	3	2	0	1	5	2	6
Colombia	3	1	0	2	1	3	3
Tunisia	3	0	1	2	1	4	1

Group H

Argentina	1	Japan	0
Jamaica	1	Croatia	3
Japan	0	Croatia	1
Argentina	5	Jamaica	0
Argentina	1	Croatia	0
Japan	1	Jamaica	2

	P	W	D	L	Goals F	A	Pts
Argentina	3	3	0	0	7	0	9
Croatia	3	2	0	1	4	2	6
Jamaica	3	1	0	2	3	9	3
Japan	3	0	0	3	1	4	0

Second round

Italy	1	Norway	0
Brazil	4	Chile	1
France	1	Paraguay	0
Nigeria	1	Denmark	4
Germany	2	Mexico	1
Holland	2	Yugoslavia	1
Romania	0	Croatia	1
Argentina	2	England	2

Quarter-finals

Italy	0	France	0
Brazil	3	Denmark	2
Holland	2	Argentina	1
Germany	0	Croatia	3

Semi-finals

Brazil	1	Holland	1
France	2	Croatia	1

Third place match

Holland	1	Croatia	2

Final

Brazil	0	France	3

WORLD CUP -
SOUTH KOREA AND JAPAN 2002

South Korea and Japan are the joint hosts of the 17th World Cups. There are 32 finalists competing (the same number as 1998's record), of which Europe provides 15 places, Africa 5, South America 5, Asia 4 and North and Central America 3.

This is the first time that the tournament has taken place in Asia. A total of 20 stadiums will be used, 10 in Japan and 10 in South Korea. The first round gets under way on 31 May when France begins their defence with a match against Senegal in the South Korean capital Seoul. The final will take place at Japan's Yokohama stadium on 30 June.

This year payments to the World Cup champions will be 70 per cent higher than in 1998, with the winners receiving $7.59 million. Each of the 32 finalists will receive $612,000, a 51 per cent increase on 1998. The President of the organising committee is Joseph S. Blatter.

BASIC INFORMATION

Visitors from Western Europe or Canada can visit South Korea for up to 90 days without a visa. People from elsewhere must renew their visa after 30 days and extensions usually last for 90 days. Most EU residents, US passport holders and visitors from Australia do not require a visa if staying in Japan less than 90 days.

The national currency in South Korea is the won (W). The won comes in coin denominations of W1, 5, 10, 50, 100 and 500 and banknotes of W1,000, 5,000 and 10,000. There are about 1,850 won to £1. The national currency in Japan is the yen (¥). The yen comes in coin denominations of ¥1, 5*, 10, 50*, 100, 500 (*have holes punched in the middle) and banknotes of ¥1,000, 5,000 and 10,000. There are about 190 yen to £1. In general, carrying large amounts of cash is not advisable. It is sensible to take travellers' cheques and use internationally accepted credit cards. Be aware that the majority of cash machines in South Korea and Japan do not accept foreign-issued credit cards.

To call South Korea from abroad, call 00 82 then the area code and local numberr. To call Japan from abroad, call 00 81, then the area code and local number. Both countries are 9 hours ahead of GMT.

South Korea's main cities all have air links, but as the distances are small it may not be worth the extra cost to travel by air. The train service is efficient and trains frequent. Buses go to a wider number of cities than trains; there are two classes of bus - kosok (express) and chikheng (ordinary) - and seats are unreserved. Long-distance share taxis, known as bullet taxis, go between big cities.

Flying is an efficient way to travel from the main islands to any of the small islands in Japan, and is often not much more expensive than going by rail. However, the trains are fast, frequent, clean, comfortable and often very expensive. Services range from small local lines to the shinkansen super-expresses ('bullet trains'), which have become a symbol of modern Japan. It may be worth buying a Rail Pass, which must be pre-purchased overseas and is valid for almost all Japan Rail services. Intercity buses are slower than trains, but cheaper.

In South Korea expect to spend £2 to£5 for a budget meal, £5 to £12 for a mid-range meal and more than £12 for a top-price meal. Accommodation is around £5 to £7 (budget), £7 to £40 (mid-range) and more than £40 for the top-price hotels. In Japan expect to spend £4 to £7 for a budget meal; £7 to £15 for a mid-range meal and more than £15 for a top-price meal. Accommodation is around £15 to £25 (budget), £25 to £50 (mid-range) and more than £50 for the top-price hotels.

Popular South Korean dishes are rice (cooked in many different ways); noodles; dumplings and rice cakes (such as Naeng Myun - cold noodle with beef broth, or Gook Soo Jang Gook - hot noodle and soup) and soups (such as Yook Gye Jang - spicy beef and vegetable, Sam Gye Tang - chicken and ginsang soup, or Saeng Sun Chi' Gae - hot and spicy fish stew).

In Japan popular dishes are rice (eaten for breakfast, lunch and supper and prepared in many forms); sashimi (raw fish); sushi (the most famous and most popular Japanese dish); noodles (many different sorts); tempura (seafood, vegetables, and other things deep fried in Tempura batter); gyoza (Japanese dumplings of Chinese origin) and sukiyaki (beef, tofu and vegetables cooked in a pot and then dipped in raw egg).

THE VENUES

SOUTH KOREA

BUSAN
CAPACITY 55,982
MATCHES Three

DAEGU
CAPACITY 70,140
MATCHES Four

DAEJEON
CAPACITY 42,176
MATCHES Three

GWANGJU
CAPACITY 42,880
MATCHES Three

INCHEON
CAPACITY 51,180
MATCHES Three

JEONJU
CAPACITY 42,477
MATCHES Three

SEOUL
CAPACITY 63,930
MATCHES Three

SOGWIPO
CAPACITY 42,256
MATCHES Three

SUWON
CAPACITY 44,047
MATCHES Four

ULSAN
CAPACITY 43,003
MATCHES Three

JAPAN

IBARAKI
CAPACITY 49,133
MATCHES Three

MIYAGI
CAPACITY 41,800
MATCHES Three

OITA
CAPACITY 50,000
MATCHES Three

SAITAMA
CAPACITY 63,700
MATCHES Four

SHIZUOKA
CAPACITY 51,349
MATCHES Three

KOBE
CAPACITY 42,000
MATCHES Three

NIIGATA
CAPACITY 42,700
MATCHES Three

OSAKA
CAPACITY 50,000
MATCHES Three

SAPPORO
CAPACITY 42,122
MATCHES Three

YOKOHAMA
CAPACITY 70,564
MATCHES Four

HOW THEY LINE UP

GROUP A
FRANCE
SENEGAL
URUGUAY
DENMARK

GROUP B
SPAIN
SLOVENIA
PARAGUAY
SOUTH AFRICA

GROUP C
BRAZIL
TURKEY
CHINA
COSTA RICA

GROUP D
SOUTH KOREA
POLAND
USA
PORTUGAL

GROUP E
GERMANY
SAUDI ARABIA
REP. OF IRELAND
CAMEROON

GROUP F
ARGENTINA
NIGERIA
ENGLAND
SWEDEN

GROUP G
ITALY
ECUADOR
CROATIA
MEXICO

GROUP H
JAPAN
BELGIUM
RUSSIA
TUNISIA

HOW THE TEAMS PROGRESS

GROUP STAGE
The top two teams in ech of the eight groups win a place in the knockout stages.

POINTS SYSTEM
Three points are awarded for a win, one for a draw. If teams are level on points, the winner is determined by goal difference, then goals scored, then by the result against the competing team.

DRAWS
If matches in the knockout stage are level after 90 minutes, a golden goal decides the outcome in 30 minutes of extra time. If there is no goal, the match goes to a penalty shoot-out.

WHO PLAYS WHOM, WHEN AND WHERE

GROUP A

31 MAY	FRANCE v SENEGAL	Seoul
1 JUNE	URUGUAY v DENMARK	Ulsan
6 JUNE	FRANCE v URUGUAY	Busan
6 JUNE	DENMARK v SENEGAL	Daegu
11 JUNE	DENMARK v FRANCE	Incheon
11 JUNE	SENEGAL v URUGUAY	Suwon

GROUP B

2 JUNE	PARAGUAY v SOUTH AFRICA	Busan
2 JUNE	SPAIN v SLOVENIA	Gwangju
7 JUNE	SPAIN v PARAGUAY	Jeonju
8 JUNE	SOUTH AFRICA v SLOVENIA	Daegu
12 JUNE	SOUTH AFRICA v SPAIN	Daejeon
12 JUNE	SLOVENIA v PARAGUAY	Seogwipo

GROUP C

3 JUNE	BRAZIL v TURKEY	Ulsan
4 JUNE	CHINA v COSTA RICA	Gwangju
8 JUNE	BRAZIL v CHINA	Seogwipo
9 JUNE	COSTA RICA v TURKEY	Incheon
13 JUNE	COSTA RICA v BRAZIL	Suwon
13 JUNE	TURKEY v CHINA	Seoul

GROUP D

4 JUNE	SOUTH KOREA v POLAND	Busan
5 JUNE	USA v PORTUGAL	Suwon
10 JUNE	SOUTH KOREA v USA	Daegu
10 JUNE	PORTUGAL v POLAND	Jeonju
14 JUNE	PORTUGAL v SOUTH KOREA	Incheon
14 JUNE	POLAND v USA	Daejeon

GROUP E

1 JUNE	IRELAND v CAMEROON	Niigata
1 JUNE	GERMANY v SAUDI ARABIA	Sapporo
5 JUNE	GERMANY v IRELAND	Ibaraki
6 JUNE	CAMEROON v SAUDI ARABIA	Saitama
11 JUNE	CAMEROON v GERMANY	Shizuoka
11 JUNE	SAUDI ARABIA v IRELAND	Yokohama

GROUP F

2 JUNE	ENGLAND v SWEDEN	Saitama
2 JUNE	ARGENTINA v NIGERIA	Ibaraki
7 JUNE	SWEDEN v NIGERIA	Kobe
7 JUNE	ARGENTINA v ENGLAND	Sapporo
12 JUNE	SWEDEN v ARGENTINA	Miyagi
12 JUNE	NIGERIA v ENGLAND	Osaka

GROUP G

3 JUNE	CROATIA v MEXICO	Niigata
3 JUNE	ITALY v ECUADOR	Sapporo
8 JUNE	ITALY v CROATIA	Ibaraki
9 JUNE	MEXICO v ECUADOR	Miyagi
13 JUNE	MEXICO v ITALY	Oita
13 JUNE	ECUADOR v CROATIA	Yokohama

GROUP H

4 JUNE	JAPAN v BELGIUM	Saitama
5 JUNE	RUSSIA v TUNISIA	Kobe
9 JUNE	JAPAN v RUSSIA	Yokohama
10 JUNE	TUNISIA v BELGIUM	Oita
14 JUNE	TUNISIA v JAPAN	Osaka
14 JUNE	BELGIUM v RUSSIA	Shizuoka

SECOND ROUND

SATURDAY 15 JUNE
MATCH 49	WINNER GROUP E v	
	RUNNER-UP GROUP B	Seogwipo
MATCH 50	WINNER GROUP A v	
	RUNNER-UP GROUP F	Niigata

SUNDAY 16 JUNE
MATCH 51	WINNER GROUP F v	
	RUNNER-UP GROUP A	Oita
MATCH 52	WINNER GROUP B v	
	RUNNER-UP GROUP E	Suwon

MONDAY 17 JUNE
MATCH 53	WINNER GROUP G v	
	RUNNER-UP GROUP D	Jeonju
MATCH 54	WINNER GROUP C v	
	RUNNER-UP GROUP H	Kobe

TUESDAY 18 JUNE
MATCH 55	WINNER GROUP H v	
	RUNNER-UP GROUP C	Miyagi
MATCH 56	WINNER GROUP D v	
	RUNNER-UP GROUP G	Daejeon

QUARTER FINALS

FRIDAY 21 JUNE
MATCH 57   WINNER MATCH 50 v
             WINNER MATCH 54   Shizuoka
MATCH 58   WINNER MATCH 49 v
             WINNER MATCH 53   Ulsan

SATURDAY 22 JUNE
MATCH 59   WINNER MATCH 52 v
             WINNER MATCH 56   Gwangju
MATCH 60   WINNER MATCH 51 v
             WINNER MATCH 55   Osaka

SEMI-FINALS

TUESDAY 25 JUNE
MATCH 61   WINNER MATCH 58 v
             WINNER MATCH 59   Seoul

WEDNESDAY 26 JUNE
MATCH 62   WINNER MATCH 57 v
             WINNER MATCH 60   Saitama

THIRD-PLACE PLAY-OFF

SATURDAY 29 JUNE
MATCH 63   LOSER MATCH 61 v
             LOSER MATCH 62   Daegu

FINAL

SUNDAY 30 JUNE
MATCH 64   WINNER MATCH 61 v
           WINNER MATCH 62   Yokohama

ARGENTINA

This is Argentina's 13th World Cup finals and coach Marcelo Bielsa will have many star players to choose from: Ayala (Valencia), Batistuta (Roma), Crespo (Lazio), Gallardo (Monaco, France), Gonzalez (Valencia), Ortega (River Plate), Samuel (Roma), Sorin (Cruzeiro, Brazil), Veron (Manchester United) and Zanetti (Inter Milan). Other players may be less well known but are probably no less able. This team is one of the favourites to go far in the 2002 tournament.

Ranking: 2

Achievements: Winners 1978, 1986; runners-up 1930, 1990

BELGIUM

This is Belgium's sixth consecutive World Cup final and their team is comprised of players who usually play elsewhere, especially in France, Germany and the Netherlands. Domestic players come from Anderlecht (Walter Baseggio, Glen de Boeck, Marc Hendrikx and Yves Vanderhaeghe), Club Brugge (Timmy Simons and Gert Verheyen) , Racing Genk (Wesley Sonck) and Standard Liege (Eric van Meir). "Mr 1,000 Volts" is the nickname given to the team's star player Marc Wilmots (Schalke 04), renowned for his speed, quality of tackling and long-range scoring.

Ranking: 20

Achievements: 4th 1986

BRAZIL

Brazil narrowly avoided being eliminated in the qualifiers for the 2002 World Cup, which would have been unthinkable - theirs is the only team that has played in every previous tournament, winning four of them and runners up in 1998. There are some fundamental problems in the team's game, which will have to be addressed if they are to get beyond the first round. The team includes many strong players: Cafú, Roberto Carlos (Real Madrid), Denilson (Real Betis), Edilson (Flamengo), Emerson (AS Roma), Roque Júnior (AC Milan), Lúcio (Bayern Leverkusen), Marcos (Palmeiras), Rivaldo (FC Barcelona), Romario (Vasco da Gama), Ronaldo (FC Internazionale Milan) and Vampeta (Flamengo).

Ranking: 3

Achievements: Winners 1958, 1962, 1970, 1994; runners-up 1950, 1998

CAMEROON

This is the fifth time Cameroon will compete in the World Cup, a record for an African country. They are the reigning African champions and have an array of talented players. Their recently appointed current coach is the German-born coach Winfried Schäfer, formerly with Bundesliga clubs VfB Stuttgart and Karlsruhe, who took over just seven months before the start of the tournament.

Ranking: 37

Achievements: Quarter-finalists 1990

CHINA

This is the first time China has made it to the final of the World Cup after playing increasingly well in Asian tournaments in recent years. Key players are Qu Bo, Sun Jihai and Li Tie; the coach is Milutinovic. They will need confidence to do well.
Ranking: 55

COSTA RICA

This is the second time Costa Rica has qualified for the World Cup (the first was in 1990). Key players are Rolando Fonseca, Hernan Medford and Paulo Wanchope.
Ranking: 30

CROATIA

Since their triumph at the World Cup in 1998, when they finished in third place, Croatia's fortunes have not been so good. However, they have been comparatively successful under their new coach Mirko Jozic. The team now contains a mix of experienced and younger players: old hands are Golden Boot winner Davor Suker (currently without a club), Robert Jarni (Las Palmas), Robert Prosinecki (Portsmouth), Dario Simic (Inter Milan), Zvonimir Soldo (Stuttgart), Mario Stanic (Chelsea), Igor Stimac (Hajduk Split) and Igor Tudor (Juventus); younger players include striker Bosko Balaban (Aston Villa), attacker Alen Boksic (Middlesbrough), and the brothers Robert and Niko Kovac (Bayern Munich).
Ranking: 19
Achievements: 3rd 1998

DENMARK

Denmark qualified for the finals by beating Iceland 6-0 in their qualifier. Their team includes Thomas Graveson (Everton); Jesper Gronkjaer (Chelsea); Thomas Helveg (AC Milan) and Martin Jorgensen (Italian Serie A, Udinese) and Thomas Sorensen (Sunderland).
Ranking: 17
Achievements: Quarter-finalists 1998

ECUADOR

Ecuador's fortunes at football have been steadily improving since Montenegrin Dusan Draskovic took over as national coach in 1989 and proof of this is the team's first appearance at a World Cup final. In the qualifiers they won an impressive five straight wins (against Chile, Venezuela, Brazil, Paraguay and Peru). As a result they jumped 33 places in the FIFA world rankings, from 71st to 38th. Ranking: 38

ENGLAND

Most team members play with Manchester United and Liverpool, clubs that took all the country's domestic tropies in the 2000-2001 season. Sven-Goran Eriksson is the coach, and star players include David Beckham (captain), Robbie Fowler, Emile Heskey and Michael Owen (all Liverpool). Owen is one of the best strikers in the world; defence is provided by Sol Campbell, Ashley Cole and Rio Ferdinand.
Ranking: 10
Achievements: Winners 1966; 4th in 1990; quarter-finalists 1954, 1962

FRANCE

The defending champions will be looking for the tremendous teamwork that won them the cup in 1998. The team's coach is Roger Lemerre; a possible weakness is the team's central defence. Zinedine Zidane (from Real Madrid) will play midfield, Marcel Desailly (team captain) and Mickaël Silvestre in the centre, Bixente Lizarazu and Lilian Thuram at full-back and Fabien Barthez is goalkeeper.

Ranking: 1

Achievements: Winners 1998; 3rd 1958, 1986; 4th 1982

GERMANY

One of the countries with the most achievement in the history of the World Cup, the team has been going downhill in the last few years. Star players like Jürgen Klinsmann, Lothar Matthäus and Rudi Völler have gone and there are few other players in the team to match their standards. Exceptions are Oliver Kahn, considered one of the world's best goalkeepers, Michael Ballack, Jens Jeremies and Mehmet Scholl. Some hopes rest on the midfielder Sebastian Deisler, but he may be too inexperienced to prove himself at the 2002 World Cup.

Ranking: 12

Achievements as Germany: 3rd 1934; quarter-finalists 1998

Achievements as West Germany: winners 1954, 1974, 1990; runners-up 1966, 1982, 1986; 3rd 1970; 4th 1958; quarter-finalists 1962, 1994

ITALY

The Azzurri did not play strongly in the qualifying matches but hopes are high that they do well in the finals. Giovanni Trapattoni has many stars to choose from: Filippo Inzaghi, defender Paolo Maldini, Alessandro Del Piero, Francesco Totti and Christian Vieri.
Ranking: 6
Achievements: winners 1934, 1938, 1982; 2nd 1970, 1994, 3rd 1990; 4th 1978; quarter-finalists 1998

JAPAN

Japan has not been a strong team in the past, failing to qualify for the 1994 World Cup by letting in a last-minute goal in their match against Iraq. Since then there has been much improvement as the team has called on talented younger players. In 1998 the French-born Philippe Troussier took over as coach and he led the team to win the Asian Cup in Lebanon in 2000 and the final of the FIFA Confederations' Cup in 2001. Key players are Junichi Inamoto (Arsenal) and Hidetoshi Nakata (Parma).
Ranking: 35

KOREA REPUBLIC

This will be the sixth World Cup appearance for the Korean Republic, but they have never made the second round before. They are coached by the Dutch-born Guus Hiddink and one of the best players is the striker Seol Ki-Hyeon (now playing for Belgium); others include Hong Myung-bo, Yoo Sang-chul and Hwang Sun-hong.
Ranking: 42

MEXICO

This is the 13th time that Mexico has qualified for the World Cup, but they only just managed it, turning over three managers in the process. Javier Aguirre, a 1986 FIFA World Cup player, is now the current coach and he encourages a 4-4-2 formation. Defence is led by the long-standing star Claudio "El Emperador (The Emperor)" Suarez, and midfield by Alberto Garcia Aspe, brought back to the team by Aguirre.
Ranking: 9

NIGERIA

Nigeria has more than 200 professional footballers playing across the world and is now benefitting from its policy of encouraging its younger players to gain experience elsewhere. As a result players such as Finidi George, Victor Ikpeba, Sunday Oliseh and "Jay Jay" Okocha, and the proven Victor Agali, Celestine Babayaro and Nwankwo Kanu will form a strong team. In the past the hopes of the Super Eagles have been dashed in the first round of the Cup; this time no doubt they will be setting their ambitions higher. Shaibu Amodu has been acting as a caretaker coach: if his team does well in 2002 he should be given a permanent position.
Ranking: 39

PARAGUAY

The Paraguay coach is the Uruguayan Sergio Markarian. Unfortunately their goalkeeper, Jose Luis Chilavert, one of the best in the world, will not be playing with them for the first two matches of the World Cup as he was suspended for four games after spitting at Brazil's Roberto Carlos during a qualifier. It will be interesting to see how they manage without him.
Ranking: 13

POLAND

Poland is playing in the finals for the first time since 1986 - in their heyday they came third in 1974 and 1982. The key to their change in fortune has been the Nigerian-born player Emmanuel Olisadebe, who has taken Polish citizenship and turned the team's game around with his strong goal scoring.

Ranking: 31

Achievements: 3rd 1974, 1982

PORTUGAL

Portugal has some star players in Rui Costa (AC Milan) and Luis Figo (Real Madrid) and other players were part of teams that won FIFA World Youth Championships. Many hopes rest with Figo, considered by some to be the best player in the world. Coach Antonio Oliveria has said, "We have to be the first, instead of being the best."

Ranking: 4

Achievements: 3rd 1966

REPUBLIC OF IRELAND

Mick McCarthy is the coach of the team and the captain, Roy Keane, the most charismatic player. Others in the team are David Connolly (Wimbledon), Damien Duff (Blackburn Rovers), Matt Holland (Ipswich), Robbie Keane, Mark Kennedy (Wolves), Mark Kinsella (Charlton) and Clinton Morrison (Crystal Palace).

Ranking: 17

Achievements: Quarter-finalists 1990

RUSSIA

Russian football has created a new identity separate from the teams made up of players from several former Soviet Republics. The team qualified under coach Oleg Romantsev with a mix of newer and more experienced players. The team's star player is the striker Vladimir Beschastnykh; others include Dmitri Khoklov, Alexandre Mostovoi and goalkeeper Rouslan Nigmatoulline.

Ranking: 21

Achievements (as Soviet Union): 4th 1966; quarter-finalists 1958, 1962, 1970

SAUDI ARABIA

Saudi Arabia has performed to a consistently high standard in Asia in the last 20 years. This is surprising considering that they have had eight changes of coach since 1996. Expectations are high of the Asian Player of the Year, Nawaf Al Temyat, now playing for the team.
Ranking: 31

SENEGAL

This is the first time Senegal has played in the World Cup finals. Their coach is the French-born Bruno Metsu who has high hopes for his team.
Ranking: 68

SLOVENIA

Slovenia's has risen to prominence in the league tables under coach is Srecko Katanec, a national hero in Slovenia. He works his team hard and fosters strong team spirit. The team's most significant player is the temperamental Zlatko Zahovic.
Ranking: 25

SOUTH AFRICA

South Africa is one of the strongest African teams and the top-ranked African nation on the FIFA world rankings. In 2001 they lost to Germany in their bid to host the World Cup finals in 2006. Their coach is Carlos Queiroz and players include Shaun Bartlett (captain), Delron Buckley, Siyabonga Nomvete and Sibusiso Zumaand.
Ranking: 31

SPAIN

Despite their many talented players Spain has made no serious impact in the World Cup finals since their best finish, fourth place, in 1950. They have a new coach for the 2002 World Cup - Jose Camacho - who took over from Javier Clemente in 1998 and has a markedly more attacking style than his predecessor.
Ranking: 7
Achievements: 4th 1950; quarter-finals 1986, 1994

SWEDEN

Sweden qualified for the 2002 World Cup without losing a single game. Most members of the team play outside the country and the key players are the forward Henrik Larsson (Glasgow Celtic), who won the Golden Boot award in 2001, and the defender and captain Patrik Andersson (Barcelona). The team also includes the young player Zlatan Ibrahimovic who left Malmö FF in 2001 for Ajax Amsterdam, becoming the most expensive Swedish footballer in history. The team has twin coaches, Lars Lagerbäck and Tommy Söderberg. Goalkeeper Magnus Hedman leads a strong defence, and the team has shown itself difficult to beat.

Ranking: 16

Achievements: 2nd 1958, 3rd 1994, 4th 1938

TUNISIA

This is Tunisia's third World Cup final; in 1978 they had the distinction of being the first African country to win a game at the World Cup (by beating Mexico 3-1). In 1998 they had a difficult draw but played well and many of the players of those finals will be playing again in 2002. Old-stagers Chokri El Ouaer (captain and goalkeeper), Sirajeddine Chih and Adel Sellimii will be balanced by new stars Hassen Gabsi, Ziad Jaziri and Ali Zitouni. A leading force in African club football in recent years, Tunisia will be keen to establish a strong reputation internationally.

Ranking: 28

TURKEY

The Turkish team has done well recently, under coach Senol Gunes. The team includes Hakan Sukur, who took four goals in the qualifying rounds, Yildiray Basturk, Emre Belozoglu, Oktay Derelioglu, Arif Erdem, Tayfur Havutcu, Alpay Ozalan (Aston Villa), goalkeeper Rüstü Reçber and Hasan Sas.
Ranking: 23s

URUGUAY

Uruguay is a small country where football is very popular. The "Celeste" only reached two of the last six World Cup finals: in Mexico in 1986 and Italy in 1990.
Ranking: 22
Achievements: Winners 1930, 1950

USA

Since their poor showing in the 1998 World Cup, USA has been coached by Bruce Arena, who has led the team to many victories. The team now comprises players from all over the world. It is strong on defence (with goalkeepers Brad Friedel and Kasey Keller); the captain is Claudio Reyna (Glasgow Rangers) and talented winger Earnie Stewart (NAC Breda).
Ranking: 24
Achievements: Semi-finalists 1930